April 1999

Hostilities Only

Philip Cairns

Helmsman

A CIP catalogue for this book is available from the British Library.

Helmsman
20 Surrey Road
Dagenham
Essex
RM10 8ES

ISBN 0 9534706 0 1

Co-ordinated by Prospero Books, Chichester.

Acknowledgements

Rear Admiral E.N. Poland C.B. C.B.E.

Captain George Blundell D.S.O.

Lieutenant Commander D.V.Duff (May the wind blow)

Lieutant E. Willee (H.M.S.*Felixstowe*)

P/O. E.E. Harrow (H.M.S. *Stornaway*)

Ken Harrow (son of P/O. Harrow)

Richard Green (H.M.S. *Stag*)

Tim Riley (S.S.*Laconia* incident)

George Lestor (Dagenhan R.N.A.)

Horst Bredaw (German "U Boat" archives)

French Naval Archives

The Maritime Museum

Italian Naval Archives

City of Durban Municipal Museum

Kew Gardens Public Records Office

Foreword

It has always seemed to me that one of the most unfair anomalies in the conduct of war at sea between 1939 and 1945 was the lack of public recognition of the courage and heroism of the large mass of ordinary men and women who served afloat and in the shore based support establishments. Many books have been written about the technical, strategic and tactical aspects of the war. Individual examples of heroism and leadership have rightly and properly, been recognised, rewarded and chronicled but far too little attention has been paid to the vast mass of volunteers and conscripts who left their chosen careers to go to war and were thrown into a strange, new and seemingly barbaric world. One where the bonds which bound together the naval family must have seemed impenetrable. The shouted command, the unfamiliar language and the lack of creature comforts added to their discomfort. Many, who expected the navy to be a place of glamour and adventure, were sadly disillusioned. Philip Cairns, a son of the politically aware mining communities of Britain, brings home to us the feelings of a young man suddenly confronted by these harsh and unfriendly surroundings.

The reader is brought to grips with the meaning of belonging to the single entity, to the oneness of a ship's company. The contrast between the awe inspiring eight inch gun cruiser and Phil Cairns' next ship, the mine sweeper *Felixstowe*, could scarcely have been greater. In the *Kent* he experienced the horror of being torpedoed and took part in the team work which saved the ship. If that was not enough, he was to know what separation from family can mean, when his hopes for a return to home were dashed by his transfer to mine clearance duties in the Suez Canal and then to the *Felixstowe.* He saw acts of great courage in keeping the Canal open and in the *Felixstowe* he took part in the rescue of survivors of other ships before himself becoming a survivor and traffic victim. After four years separation his homecoming was accompanied by the weariness of the war veteran he had become and by being totally fed up with war and the navy. He was, after all, a Hostilities Only rating, he just wanted to collect his demob suit, but when he took off his uniform for the last time he acknowledged that he had worn it with pride and the memories of gallant comrades would be always with him. This is a story told from the perspective of the vast majority of men who served throughout the war, gallantly obeying orders in the good humoured and questioning manner of the British working man. Philip Cairns has made a useful contribution to our understanding of the "citizens" war.

E.N.Poland
Rear Admiral

Prologue

Why, the reader might ask with some justification, did the author leave it until he was in his seventies before embarking upon the onerous task of writing his first book? The answer which springs readily to mind is therapy, after a loss which ended forty two years of almost unbroken happiness, in truth that was the catalyst.

Ever since I completed my six years 'Hostilities Only' service in the Royal Navy a story has been knawing away inside me.

Some thirty years ago I contacted Keith Waterhouse with a view to him finding me a ghost writer to get my story into print. His answer was unequivocal:forget about ghost writers, and write it yourself. So now after three decades I have heeded his advice and produced Hostilities Only. It is the story of my war; from the viewpoint of a civilian on loan to the Admiralty.

No-one writing about events that took place over half a century ago could have hoped for my good fortune.

Hardly had I commenced writing, when there came into my possession two daily diaries, kept illegally. Both contained in remarkable detail accounts of events as they happened aboard two of the ships in which I served, HMSKent, a county class, eight inch gun and HMS Felixstowe, a Bangor class fleet mine sweeper of the thirteenth mine sweeper flotilla.

For the Kent diary I am grateful to Captain George Blundell DSO RN(Ret) who was then a Lieut Comm Torpedo Officer aboard Kent.

I am equally grateful to Ken Harrow the son of the Cox'n aboard one of our flotilla the Stornaway, one of the 13th M/S/F for the diary of his father.

In addition, I have received material and photographs from interested shipmates from across the UK and reaching out to Canada, Australia and South Africa. I have also had material from the German, French and Italian archives.

However, the most revealing information is contained in the book by American author Robert Whiting, Slaughter over Sicily, which mercilessly attacks the conduct in the Mediterranean arena by the American Air Force and ground troops, using such strong language as cowardice even against high ranking officers who are household names.

The title of my book, Hostilities Only, could conceivably convey little to present day readers but it is, I feel, an apt title for a chronicle of events that took place half a century ago. Two purposes are served by the title. It told the RN that we were only there for the duration of hostilities. By the same token it assured us conscripts that we were only on loan to the Admiralty. Finally, it throws a new light on all the events that occurred, all made possible by the diaries and the release of archive material.

Chapter 1

Rubbing the sleep from my eyes, I reached out to silence the alarm that had shattered the silence of my room. I lay back and vowed that tonight I would retire at a more respectable hour. I dressed and left the warmth of the house, then inwardly cursed as a blast of cold air met me as I opened the door. Reluctantly mounting my push bike I, for the umpteenth time, tormented myself with the thought that there must be a better way to earn my living. The time was 5am, an unearthly hour to be setting out on the depressing ride to my place of work, Henleys Cables, which lay on the banks of the River Thames at North Woolwich. It was a journey of some six or seven miles, often made in rain or fog and always, it seemed, against the wind.

I turned off the Barking bypass at the evil smelling mountain of chemical waste that rose up on the corner of the Becton Gas Works. Ahead I could already see the backcloth of the masts and funnels of the ships berthed in the Albert Docks. Passing the green painted frontage of the Ferndale Arms public house the waiting traffic told me that I had caught a 'bridger', which meant the road was closed to traffic to allow a ship on passage up the Thames to enter the lock, berth and be unloaded. The ship passing through was a Swede and it looked to be dangerously overloaded with timber. I watched as the Trinity House pilot steered the great ship through the lock with what looked like only inches to spare either side.

The scent of pine assailed my nostrils as I took in the scene in the basin. It was something to stir the imagination, for there was colour, movement and a cacophony of sounds. Ships from every nation in the world were berthed there, in a dazzling array of colours, their flags proudly astern. Tugs scurried across the water from every conceivable angle to manoeuvre into position, and from an impossible tangle of ropes and wires, much clanging of engine room telegraphs and frantic gyrations of the wheel, they emerged to pull away with a perfect line of barges. The whole scene was bathed in lights and looked like a picture postcard against the dark drabness of the surroundings.

The hoots of the tugs and the pilot's whistle told me that the bridge was about to swing back into position. I remounted my bike to continue my journey. My feet and hands were now numb with the cold but as I passed the red bricked frontage of the Harland and Woolf yard, I could already see the welcoming lights of the Royal Standard public house which, in spite of the early hour I knew would be open – a privilege shared with the great London markets of Billingsgate, Smithfield, Covent Garden and Spitalfields and much appreciated by the local workforces. The interior or the Royal Standard bore little resemblance to its regal sounding name, but inside glowed a warm coal fire. The air was filled with the aroma of coffee, and glasses lined the counter, each containing a tot of rum. Topped up with hot milky coffee, it made a blood warming drink and cost a mere sixpence.

Suitably warmed and refreshed, I made for Henleys to begin my 6am to 2pm shift. The long boring hours in front of the huge Callender machine that rolled out the sheets of vulcanised rubber, were often spent day dreaming of the great ships at berth in the dock and the sunny lands from which they came, and the end of the shift was always a welcome relief. I prepared for my journey home and reality swiftly returned as I mounted my bike; it was still quite cold, and fog was in the air.

The Woolwich Free Ferry was leaving to cross the Thames to South Woolwich, the tide was low and the great paddles stirred up the filthy sludge of the Thames as I pressed harder on my pedals to hasten my escape from the foul smell now emerging from the river.

My spirits rose when I remembered that I was to call at one of the typical dockside houses behind the Standard, for Con would be home on leave. A family friend, Cornelius Finbar Driscoll was, in spite of his name, a bona-fide cockney, born of immigrant Irish parents. He rose to greet me, tall and sunbronzed, immaculate in the CPO's uniform of the Royal Navy. It was he who first stirred my imagination with the stories of his travels, adventures and his many encounters with members of the fair sex. The visit was to be no exception, I left him with my thoughts in a whirl, as they were each time I met him. I'd had a couple of tots of rum with Con, I was warm inside and out and the wind was now on my back as I pedalled my bike on its homeward journey. I had time to reflect on my meeting with Con; was the grass really greener on the other side? I wondered. Were all young men like me, very impressionable, and seeking an escape from a humdrum existence? Time alone would tell.

Home was Dagenham, in Essex, a massive conurbation of public housing, built by the now defunct London County Council to house a huge slum clearance from the East End of London. It was an endless mass of red bricks and red tiles relieved only by its many grey intertwining streets. It became the butt of many jokes but, in spite of this, it was a brave and imaginative project. The houses boasted gardens front and back, inside toilets and a bath fed from a hand pumped coal boiler in the kitchen. Each of these items was an innovation at the time. The area boasted an unrivalled library service, two outdoor swimming pools, many beautiful parks and a large number of excellent schools.

I neared home and reflected that it was a good place to live and in sharp contrast to the squalor of the dockside I had just left behind. Perhaps I was wrong to be so disgruntled with life. I had a happy home, a job, and there were now over two and a half million unemployed in Great Britain.

Little did I then know that my dream of a life at sea was soon to be realised, but not quite in the way that I had envisaged. It was 1938 and war clouds were gathering over Europe. A dithering British government was now engaged in feverish diplomatic activity. Germany, Italy and Spain were firmly in the hands of fascist dictatorships under Hitler, Mussolini and Franco. The balance of power was threatened. Czechoslovakia had already been abandoned and 'sold down the river'.

Neville Chamberlain, the British Prime Minister, alighted from a plane from Germany and, holding a piece of paper aloft, announced to the world that there would be "Peace in our time". He must, however, have had doubts about the validity of his own statement, because he immediately ordered the re-armament of all three services. This re-armament programme, on its own, was to solve the unemployment problem in Great Britain. Having built all these new weapons of war, the government realised they would now need extra men to man them, and so it was that a Conscription Bill was introduced in Parliament. This, of course, was only a safeguard for had we not been assured that there would be peace in our time? Initially a quarter of a million twenty year olds were called up to do six months' training with one of the three services, followed by a period in Reserve. But events were to quickly overtake this scheme.

By an accident of birth I was in the first group to be called up and I registered in July 1939. So it was that my wish of a life at sea was realised, not by any specific action of mine, but courtesy of HMGovernment.

My call up papers arrived and I volunteered for service in the RN, knowing that my chances of selection were few as most of the men called up would be destined to join the Army. However, I passed my medical A1 and shortly afterwards learned I had been accepted for service in the RN. I admit that I was overjoyed. There were, however, to follow times when I would curse the name of my mentor, one Cornelius Finbar Driscoll.

The Nazi jackboot was stamping its authority all over Europe and the Luftwaffe had already decimated Poland. On a momentous Sunday 3rd September a solemn Neville Chamberlain announced to a stunned British nation that we were now in a state of war with Germany.

It was, I remember, a warm sunny day and everyone, it seemed, took to the streets to discuss the momentous events that were taking place.

We were a large family consisting of four boys and four girls, the three eldest, two boys and a girl, were married and I was already an uncle to five nephews and two nieces. My sister Nora had four children all under eight and one was a new born baby girl. Nora lived just four doors away and her husband was at sea in the Merchant Navy.

The first hour of war was both critical and tense. Everyone was afraid of the unknown, would we perhaps suffer the same fate as Poland? However, the fear uppermost in everyone's mind was gas - poison gas. We had been warned to be prepared for gas attacks and had been provided with gas masks to meet this eventuality. A type of oxygen tent had also been devised for infants, but they were still in short supply and my sister had no tent for their new born baby. I could feel the tension in my family circle and I could see the fear in their eyes, but everyone's thoughts were their own and thoughts were abstract.

Our mother, Mary Anne as everyone knew her, had seen and coped with a multitude of problems in the course of bringing up a family of eight in the direst of circumstances, but there was little she could do about the present danger to her flock. Her son in law was at sea in the dangerous waters of the Atlantic, her youngest son was about to join the RN, and three other sons would soon follow into one or another of the services and now her youngest granddaughter was without protection from the threatened evil of poison gas. Mary Anne walked towards us as we stood perplexed and helpless. She was a short, rounded figure beaming happiness and reassurance. She had almost reached us when, horror of horrors, the air raid sirens wailed out their first Red Warning of the war. There were to be thousands of such Red Alerts to shatter the quiet of the night and day, but never again would they have the impact of that very first one. Everyone's thoughts must have been running riot and conjuring up a series of wild scenarios. Everyone loved and trusted Mary Anne and now we were expecting a miracle of her, even that was not beyond the bounds of possibility.

Sister Nora then set everyone back on their heels by coolly and deliberately announcing to us that "If my baby has no protection, then I'm not going to wear mine"! The consequences of this statement were too horrendous to contemplate - remember everyone was expecting enemy planes to suddenly appear and drop the dreaded gas canisters out of the sky. It was our first taste of the horrors of war. Then Mary Anne spoke out: "We must all put our faith in the mercy of God," she said, and it was my guess that in that first five minutes, she had feverishly said a full deck of the rosary in her mind. And it worked, because shortly afterwards the All Clear sounded, everyone heaved a sigh of relief and there was much forced laughter. Our first alarm had a happy ending. Nora's baby eventually got her oxygen tent and, in spite of its wide use in the trenches of World War I, gas was never to be used against the population of Britain.

My summons to report for training arrived and I now had to go through the motions of severing my connections with civvy street and prepare myself for entry into the Senior Service, with all its accompanying feelings of excitement, curiosity and, not least, apprehension.

For the last time I made my way to my place of work, Henleys, to say farewell to my workmates. A journey now made even more horrendous, there were now no street lights, every house was blacked out, as was every building, train and bus. All transport had to progress through the grim, eerie blackness, with dim sidelights, hooded so they could not be seen by a possible enemy plane overhead.

Reaching North Woolwich, I said my farewells to my companions of *The Royal Standard*, they wished me well and we drank a toast to my safe return with the traditional rum and coffee. At Henleys they made quite a fuss of me; I suppose I was a bit of a celebrity, being one of the first conscripts to leave the company. After a small celebration and many farewells I left for home and a completely different lifestyle.

Passing Con's turning, I pondered on the thought that he would now already be serving in some theatre of the war. There was a startling change to the scene in the docks, it was now dull and sombre, all the animation appeared to have gone. The ships at berth there would soon be leaving to face an enemy bent on their destruction and, sadly, some of them would be destined for a watery grave. I now had plenty of food for thought as the blue seas I had dreamed of were transformed to hostile waters and many of the sunny beaches would be landmined and edged with barbed wire.

The very first day of the conflict saw the sinking of the liner Athenia with the loss of over one hundred lives, many of them Americans and America was still a neutral country. It caused outrage in government circles, something to do with a Geneva Convention. In reality it was just another piece of paper that was to prove no more effective than Neville Chamberlain's "Peace in our time". We had to learn the hard way that this was to be a no holds barred conflict, one that sadly the Senior Service was ill prepared for.

On 17th September *HMS Courageous* was sunk, an ageing aircraft carrier pushed into service, she went down with the loss of five hundred lives, many of them Pensioner Reservists and Hostilities Only ratings like myself, with no training, no uniforms and, more tragically, no personal life belts. They were an ill prepared crew hurriedly mustered to man an ill prepared ship. Even the statutory life saving equipment was inoperable, due to rust and lack of maintenance. Worse was soon to follow. HMS Royal Oak, a battleship and the pride of the Navy was sunk by a U Boat in the supposedly impregnable harbour at Scapa Flow in Scotland. The mighty thirty thousand ton ship went down with the loss of eight hundred lives.

These were mortal blows to the pride of the RN, who had failed to learn any lessons from World War I. It was a Navy far removed from the public's perception of our Senior Service, a Navy preoccupied with showing the flag, rather than keeping in step with the demands of a modern fleet.

Chapter 2

I left home on 24th October to join my first ship, *HMS Royal Arthur*, which was, in Naval parlance, a stone frigate, a term used by sea going 'matelots' to scoffingly denote Naval depots and training establishments and the crews manning these establishments were known as barrack stantions.

I alighted from the Hammersmith train at Liverpool Street Underground station and joined the stragglers making their way to the Great Eastern main line terminal. No-one seemed to be in any hurry and we closed in on each other as we reached the platform of our destination. It was now that you could see they were all young men of my own age group, each of whom would be carrying an envelope of instructions and a travel warrant. The branches of the London Underground system would today be carrying many such young men, each of them homing in on platform six to board a train taking them to the beginning of a journey that could bring possible glory, disability and even death. They had all made their choice and were now off to Skegness on the cold, bleak, East coast of England.

I boarded the train anxious to leave the smokey, steam-filled platform and the sub-zero temperature and seek the comforting warmth of the carriage. Placing my scant possessions on the corded luggage rack, I settled in my seat and took stock of my fellow travellers.

It was like the parrot house in London Zoo. Everyone was talking at once and questions and answers were coming out fifteen to the dozen. Mercifully some way down the line the din subsided and the conversation became more measured and took on a pattern. There was a reason behind these questions and answers; we were probing each other, seeking an affinity with someone, we wanted someone to relate to, someone to share our fears and doubts with. For we had fled the nest and were seeking new relationships to help us cope in a new and strange environment.

I alighted at Skegness Station with my companion of the journey George Seager. Holiday posters on the platform welcomed us to 'Holiday in bracing Skegness'. This holiday was at the invitation of HM Government and was to last not six days, but six years.

HMS Royal Arthur, it transpired, was the famous Billy Butlins holiday camp at Skegness. We left the station and boarded a coach to the camp, the front was laid out in neatly tended gardens. Behind the gaily painted main buildings there were rows of what looked like brightly coloured garden sheds. This proved to be our accommodation.

It was, to me, a thought provoking moment when I entered the gates. We were saying goodbye to our civilian status and entering a new world with a vastly different set of rules. From this moment, democracy went out of the window, now you would do what you were told, regardless. Yet democracy was the very thing we were fighting for. Eventually we would become an essential part of a fighting ship and we would have no more rights than the engines that propelled it, nor yet the guns that protected it.

Hammock instructions at H.M.S. 'Royal Arthur' *Butlins Skegness.*

The biting wind was piercing my painfully inadequate, flimsy garments, and striking the very marrow of my bones. I can never remember feeling so cold. I was standing on the threshold of Butlins Holiday Camp, Skegness. Some holiday, I reflected. The scene before me was an indictment on the Naval authorities, during my short stay at least one young man was to die, and rumour had it there were more. The camp which would be cold from the renowned East coast winds in a good summer, was now reminiscent of Scott's camp in the Antarctic, and there, all of the campers were to perish.

It was a great relief to enter the warmth of the dining room where we had a very welcome meal and thawed out, after which we fell in outside to meet our instructor, Petty Officer Wiggins, or Wiggy as he became known.

He was a kindly man, dragged from a well earned retirement and given the unenviable task of turning a bunch of wide eyed, greenhorn, twenty year olds into suitable Naval personnel.

Wiggy had completed twenty two years in the RN, signing first for twelve years and then an additional ten. He was a gunnery specialist but had also served in the submarine service. When in the classroom, the lads would quite easily lead him into telling stories of his exploits, mostly humourous, but some quite serious. Through him we were also learning a lot about Navy customs, terms and clichés, all of them an essential part of our education but not exactly part of the curriculum.

Our first day ended, we retired for the night to our sleeping quarters, the inside of which contained a wardrobe, a dresser and a double bed divided down the middle by a series of six inch by one inch planks, effectively turning it into two single beds. This caused us some amusement as were were then ignorant of some of the strange practices that prevailed in the RN. The chalet was, of course, unheated and felt desperately cold but, quite exhausted with my first exciting day with my companion of the train, George Seager, I retired for the night.

The tannoys that a few short weeks ago had woken the happy campers with a jingle and a breezy "Good morning campers," now sounded a Navy reveille on a slightly out of tune bugle and a cry of "Come along then my hearties, wakey, wakey, lash up and stow, rise and shine, the morning's fine." In fact it was freezing cold and snowing. "Lash up and stow" of course referred to the hammocks you slept in aboard ship. The lashing and stowing of hammocks was an art form than would be taught in the next part of our training. Stretching my limbs and rubbing the sleep out of my eyes I was amazed to see my Naval issue blanket covered in ice. It had been cold enough through the night to condense our warm breath and then freeze it.

The walk to the wash place proved fruitless as there was no running water, all the pipes were frozen and we shared buckets of water obtained from another source for our ablutions. It was quite beyond belief that the powers that be could not foresee that water pipes would freeze up in an unheated wash place built only for use in the summer. It also occurred to me that they did not give a damn anyway. On returning to the chalet my morale was at zero and I heartily cursed the name of Cornelius Finbar Driscoll.

Most of the lads like me had a very meagre wardrobe, usually consisting of one suit, probably purchased from the Fifty Shilling Tailors (now worth £2.50) and shoes in varying states of repair. Not to worry though, for would we not just go down to the kit store and there 'Jack Dusty' would issue us with our slops, or uniform? To our dismay there were hardly any slops available, just a few oddments that would do precious little to help us keep warm. This setback was received with surprising calm and resignation, if you consider the hardship we were suffering with the elements.

We must have looked a pretty pathetic sight as we went through the motions of drilling like servicemen, whilst being dressed like Fred Carnos' Army and, had the enemy seen us, I'm quite sure the order would have been given to invade at once.

The extreme conditions, coupled with the inoculations we were receiving combined to lower our resistance and there were quite a number of us adversely affected. It was commonplace to see someone in distress. The situation I believe was quite alarming, recruits were collapsing left, right and centre, there was much rumour about the cause of the problem, including the claim that at least one rating had died. No-one reassured us. Was it perhaps food poisoning? We were never to find out and once again it appeared to us that no-one cared.

Eventually we were all kitted out in our first uniform and it was quite a thrill when we were all mustered in full kit. Everything seemed to fall into place, we all felt much more confident and much more important. We were now warm and comfortable in our serge suits and woollen jumpers and our feet were now clad in wool socks, stout boots - our morale was sky high.

Returning to our accommodation with our brand new uniforms, the excitement was intense as we hurriedly tried them on for the first time. Some of the items were hopeless misfits and what followed was the most hilarious couple of hours. Caps were too big or too small, jumpers too wide or too tight, and likewise the trousers. All the natural comedians in the class had a field day as we donned our uniforms regardless, and some of us could not help but fall about laughing.

The commencement of our training at Skegness was a very harrowing experience and I felt the authorities had much to answer for. Unfortunately there were to be many instances of lack of sensitivity on the part of the Navy and I was to be at the sharp end of a number of them. However, Skegness was generally a learning experience for us all. Many firm friendships were established. Ginger Newall, Alex Alexander and, of course, George Seager, were to join me on my first seagoing ship. Our spell at Skeggie was nearing its end and we were eagerly looking forward to our first leave to see our loved ones again and, secretly I suspect, to show off in uniform in front of our friends and family.

We had a great farewell party where Wiggy was the honoured guest. We had clubbed round and bought him a pewter tankard suitably engraved. He most definitely had a tear in his eye when we made the presentation in our local. He may have received more tributes from future classes at Skeggie, but ours was the first - we would be the first on a number of occasions, but Skeggie was special.

We left Skeggie and made our way to the station and on our way to our much looked forward to leave. I ruefully glanced at the poster inviting us to 'Holiday in bracing Skegness' and reflected that 'bracing' was hardly the word to describe the hypothermia of Butlins.

Chapter 3

The journey to Liverpool Street station was pretty uneventful if you consider the train taking us home contained a bunch of lads who, for the first time in their lives, had been subject to a regime of Service discipline. Suddenly we were again free spirits but were aware of this fact and the horseplay that took place was about the equivalent of what you would expect of children on an outing. We pulled into Liverpool Street Station and our steam loco ground to a halt with billows of smoke and the hissing of steam, followed by the noisy opening and slamming of doors. Lots of hasty farewells followed and there was a lot more purpose and speed about our exit than there had been on our arrival some four weeks previously.

I caught the Metropolitan train on the underground, changed at Aldgate East and boarded a District Line train to my home in Dagenham. I settled down and vainly wondered what the other passengers thought of me in my uniform, secretly hoping they thought I was a hero returning from sinking U Boats in the Battle of the Atlantic

Isolated from the pack, I was once again thinking as an individual. My thoughts happily turned to the anticipated meeting with my friends, neighbours and family, who would for the first time see me resplendent in my uniform. It was a joyous meeting with my family. I had many stories to tell them and they briefed me about events at home. Sister Nora's husband Matt was home on leave from the MN.

Matt was to become a legend in our family and among our friends. He was a very streetwise East Ender and in the MN he was a 'Donkeyman' in charge of the engine room, 'Stokers' and 'Greasers'. His present boat was the *Highland Chieftain*, a meat boat on the South America run to BA. He had an arrangement with PLA Police and was one of the best organised smugglers in the London Docks. Our households were never short of meat and goodies. Black Markets, 'spivs' and smugglers were to become an integral part of life in wartime Britain.

My favourite story among the many he related, concerned a frozen pig. He had filled his taxi for the day with loot, when suddenly this frozen pig became on offer, just as he was about to board 'Smallie's' taxi. Quick as a flash he recruited a 'dockie' with a motorbike and sidecar. In a flash the pig was sat in the sidecar with a cap, coat, scarf and glasses, a knowing nod to the copper on the gate and away went the pig on its way to Dagenham. What a character he was.

The novelty of my uniform soon wore off, three days into my leave and everyone had seen me and even in my local, *The Eastbrook,* I had become just part of the fittings. I was now just another matelot on leave. My short leave was now over and I was about to join my second ship, HMS Pembroke, another stone frigate of course. Chatham was one of three famous Naval depots, the other being Portsmouth and Devonport. There was a strong sense of rivalry between them, accentuated by the fact that every ship in the fleet belonged to one or another of them. The barracks were situated on the River Medway in the county of Kent.

I entered the great crested wrought iron gates of Chatham and immediately felt the sense of history that prevailed. The entrance road on the left was lined with the imposing figureheads of great Naval heroes, their eyes staring down on you, imposed a feeling of awe, perhaps that was their intention. I took in my surroundings and saw that all was activity and I could now almost smell the salt in the air. I proceeded on my way. I took in the accommodation blocks on the right, one of them would be my home for the next few weeks. Before me stretched the huge parade ground and beyond that the drill shed that housed the office I was seeking.

I suddenly stopped and looked down below to the parade ground in front of me. A group of ratings were running up and down the access steps with rucksacks on their backs. Some of them appeared to be in difficulties and struggling to make the climb. I learned to my horror that the rucksacks were loaded with sand, both lots of men were under punishment. Punishments in the Navy varied in their degree of harshness according to crime. I then reasoned that the men doing the rucksack punishment must have at the very least murdered an Admiral or something as heinous. It was not so, this was the Navy's way of breaking stubborn non-conformers. I understand that it ceased when a visiting MP saw it in practice and made representations to get it stopped.

I had been watching, fascinated by what I was seeing, when suddenly a voice thundered in my ears.

"Come over here that rating."

I turned to see the red face and bulging eyes of a Petty Officer.

"Get your cap on straight," he yelled.

I was not aware that it wasn't on straight, but I made an adjustment.

"Who are you?" he bawled.

I explained that I was a new entry.

"Get down to the new entries office at once or you will be joining that shower down below."

My heart sank as I went on my way. What had I let myself in for? I mused. The Navy called this power of command and it was one of the many nonsenses that I could not come to terms with.

Thousands of conscripts like me were now being knocked into shape to take their place alongside the professionals aboard ship with, hopefully, a semblance of what it was all about. In spite of the urgent need for our services, our training was to take about ten weeks. It was intense and I found it extremely interesting. Every facet of life aboard ship was taught and enacted. It was a markedly more strict routine than the one we had all experienced at Billy Butlins.

The new entrants were fell in outside Nelson Block and my spirits were low after my altercation with the PO on my arrival. We were to meet our new instructor. I felt I might have to react to this bullying and hectoring which I thought would be my lot during my training at Chatham. I was wrong, for Chief Petty Officer Thompson was equally as pleasant as Wiggy of Skegness, but there was a difference. Thommo was 'pusser' right down the line. No-one was able to get Thommo 'swinging the lamp', a term for spinning Naval yarns. He stuck rigidly to his job of instructing us, but he did so with an acceptable discipline. After all, Chatham was a rife with senior officers and Vice and Rear Admirals; every officer was given an eyes right and a salute, an operation carried out dozens of times a day. I enjoyed my training at *Pembroke*.

When we first mustered to meet Thommo, he walked along the ranks and stopped by me, looked me up and down and told me to fall out in front. He then announced to the class that I was to be their class leader. I was stunned but I can assure you his choice had nothing to do with my IQ and everything to do with my six feet one inch, thirteen stone frame. He had not known me long enough to establish whether or not I was as thick as two short planks. The job carried with it a chain of office a bosun's whistle worn round the neck, and the privilege of night leave during the week. My selection put me on the spot for I was no more entitled to it than anyone else in the class. I was right up front and ready to be shot and I did not have to wait long for the first shot to be fired. My duties entailed me marching the class between places of instruction, maintaining discipline in the absence of our instructor and supervising mess meals and cleaning.

The living quarters were cramped, ill lit, dingy and depressing and at night we had to take to the labyrinth of underground shelters for our night's sleep. There were hundreds of bodies down there lying in rows and the stench of the sweat mingling with the smell of Jeyes Fluid was appalling and it seemed to linger in your nostrils. It was no wonder then that anyone within travelling distance went home at every opportunity. There was a direct line to London from Chatham, but my journey home entailed four changes of transport.

Finance dictated how often you could avail yourself of the opportunity. Our weekly pay was pathetic, a miserly fourteen shillings (seventy new pence) a week and - wait for it - half had to be allocated to your wife or next of kin. Money was a very sore point with us conscripts. There was now full employment and stacks of overtime money to be earned. Servicemen received a mere pittance for the dubious privilege of fighting for our country. Once again, no-one thought it of any consequence.

My journey home was about twenty miles but it was quite exacting and a typical night's leave went something like this. You fell in for inspection and then you started running, the object being to board the first coach at the gates to Gravesend, get your breath back, alight from the coach at Gravesend, run along the High Street, then down the hill to the ferry, which hopefully would be in. If it was just casting off, on went your gas mask and case, then you jumped. Yes, there were some who fell in the drink. Crossing the Thames to Tilbury, the flat topped guard rail would be lined with matelots ready to leap ashore before it berthed. A run to the platform to catch the train to Dagenham Dock, then it was over the crossing gates and another run to the Chequers to board the bus to the Civic Centre. Dignity then decreed that I walk, for I was in my home town. The sheer physical effort of this exercise bore testimony to our fitness and demonstrated the desire to get away from Chatham.

The comfort of my home was so welcome, now I could put my feet up and relax, but only for a while, for there was something about life at that time that made you savour every hour at home. A meal with the family, then it would be off to the local for a drink with my pals.

Whatever choice I made for my night's leave, it would be a late night. I remember once a really thick 'peasouper' had made visibility nil. It took me three hours to reach home and I had but two hours' sleep before the dreaded alarm rang for me to rise and return to Chatham. When the alarm rang to break my night's sleep, I would invariably question the wisdom of taking my night leave. However, once back in barracks, I knew I would repeat the punishing routine over again. I had to catch the 4am milk train from Dagenham Dock, but the rest of the journey back to Chatham was in sharp contrast to my journey home and I had until 7.30am to arrive and pick up my Station Card.

The NAAFI would be open and a fry up breakfast was on offer to those of us who were still solvent. Sitting back and listening to the exploits of the returning heroes was an education in itself. It has been said our Anglo Saxon swear words have their origins on the Naval messdecks. I was now listening to expert exponents of the art, every other word was an expletive and mixed with the smattering of the messdeck language they had acquired, the whole meaning of the message was lost. It was still always received with raucous laughter and it still tended to assault my ears, but gradually, of necessity, I became inured to it. I felt like a choir boy thrust into the company of a bunch of foul-mouthed, illiterate, alcoholic sex maniacs.

We were, I think, at that time a pretty moral people. There always has and always will be the womaniser and the lady free with her favours. The lady would be considered a slut, but the man would just move on to his next conquest.

Our training was going on apace and my Christmas and New Year were spent with my family. It was our last festive season together for six years, it was one to savour in the memory. They were always great occasions - as many as forty of the family and our relatives sat down for Christmas dinner, prepared, cooked and served by the incomparable Mary Anne, who was completely unflappable. She had an endless itinerary of songs, which she sang from morning 'til night. The festive meal would span all of three hours and the afternoon would be given up to resting, while all the goodies digested, a little imbibing and much reminiscence. The parties of Number Two were renowned for their liveliness and duration. The music was mostly provided by 'the old Joanna' and piano accordion and the singing and dancing was continued with little respite for two days. They were wonderfully happy occasions and I felt that this time, even more so, I believed perhaps it was because the baby of the family was leaving the fold. We were not, of course, aware that my next 'hooley' would have to wait three years.

I returned to Chatham a little heavy of heart. I had a great time on my leave and this time, for the first time, I felt a bit of a wrench when I said my goodbyes. However, once back aboard amongst my 'oppos' I quickly settled back into the routine of classes and drilling. This I knew would be the final stint in Chatham and then it would be off to the unknown territory.

The squeak had now gone out of our boots and our collars were shaded down to the desired Cambridge Blue. We were thinking, acting and even looking a little more like the real thing. The discipline in barracks was harsh but I suppose 'Chiefy' was right when he told us the bullying and doing things at the double were an essential ingredient to getting you to react to orders without question. For the safe running and efficiency of the world within the confines of a fighting ship meant that, at all times, our lives would be in each other's hands.

On completion of our training we marched in our passing out parade, where the CO took the salute and now, as far as Chatham was concerned, we were the first conscripts ready to take their place alongside the real sailors. There were many of us not too sure about this, but time alone would tell.

Chapter 4

Now we were sent home to what would be our embarkation leave. It was to be a good leave and during it I celebrated my twenty first birthday, a celebration held three months early, for who knew where I would be on the actual day? I was given a great party to which I invited my friend George. He was able to meet and eat with the family. It occurred to me that I had probably bored him to tears with my stories about them. When I spoke of them in future he would find it easier to relate to them.

The news of the war at sea was pretty grim, but my family put on a very brave face when it was time to say my goodbyes. I now know that the parting of a son from the fold in times of war bears much more heavily on the family than it does on the soldier or sailor going to war.

We were young, brash, insensitive perhaps, we believed we were off on an adventure. Our parents would naturally think we were possibly going to our demise. This was something young men then could not, or did not want to, contemplate.

Among my twenty first birthday gifts was a prayer book, a rosary and a St Christopher on a chain which would be linked to my identity disc. P. CAIRNS RC. C3JX 167723. If the St Christopher worked, and I fervently hoped that it would, it was a chilling thought, but it meant that no-one would have to read my identity disc. I knew that there would be many prayers said for me in the Holy Family Church where as a lad I served at Mass.

My Catholic education, however, was practically nil. I was educated in my local Protestant Elementary school. At Assembly each morning the order was given for Jews and Roman Catholics to fall out. Religion had therefore been at the bottom of my curriculum. It is, however, an established fact that to millions of Servicemen, friend or foe, in times of peril, it would come rushing back to take prime place in our thoughts.

The return journey to Chatham was time for quiet contemplation, the excitement and high spirits of my leave were already behind me and I was now about to sail into the sunset. Would I encounter a fair wind and calm seas, or troubled, stormy waters?

Once inside barracks there was a flurry of activity. A final medical and a series of inoculations swiftly followed. Then it was off to slops to acquire our tropical gear, comprising a full rig outfit in white drill material plus white top and shorts and a white hat, all of which would provide stacks of work for 'Mo' Slutsky and his sewing machine en route to our destination, as he set about making all our gear look 'tiddly' for the journey ahead.

We left the gates of Chatham in trucks to begin our journey at Chatham Station. Boarding the train we then, by a miracle of shunts and turning of railway points, arrived at Folkestone on the South coast, without changing trains.

The war on land was in limbo and the Great British and German fleets were playing war games. These 'big ships' of the RN as they were known on the messdecks were the glamour boys of the fleet. The massive convoys crossing the Atlantic with the vital supplies of arms and food were fussed over and protected by the 'little boats' - destroyers, frigates, corvettes and minesweepers. The waters they operated in were deadly dangerous and hostile. The Atlantic was infested with U Boats and surface raiders of the German fleet from the coast of Europe, right across the Atlantic to America.

It was for this reason that the Admiralty in its wisdom considered it too dangerous to risk troopships through the Bay of Biscay for entry into the Mediterranean. Consequently, we crossed the then relatively safe English Channel from Folkestone to Le Havre in France, then of course unoccupied. Our journey continued by train from Le Havre in the North right through France to the South coast Mediterranean port of Marseilles. I remember two things about the train ride: one French food, even on a dilapidated station platform, was excellent; and two, French trains have no sprung suspension and they ran on square wheels. All our backsides and spines bore testimony to this fact.

We alighted from the train inside Marseilles docks. We must have been a sight to see as we all went through the contortions of reshaping our limbs to give us a slight resemblance to Homo Sapiens once again. Eventually we mustered to march along the dockside and be brought to a halt alongside this magnificent gleaming white, luxury liner. To our amazement we were marched aboard. Imagine our delight when we were informed that this was a troopship. We could hardly believe our ears. The ship was the brand new cruiser line *Ande*s, the most recent addition to the Royal Mail Lines fleet and yet to do her maiden voyage, a voyage halted by the advent of war. To the eternal credit of the shipping line, they gave us the full benefit of the cruise, as laid on for their wealthy patrons. We were to enjoy the luxurious comfort and unbelievable menus just as they had been provided. It was like a dream and something probably never again equalled in the transport of troops in wartime.

Leaving the harbour at Marseilles, the troops lined the guard rails of the Andes, which was literally starting out on its maiden cruise. The only things missing were the lovely ladies and the garlands and streamers that I had seen many times on the newsreels at the local cinema.

During the next few days, whilst enjoying the warm sun, blue skies and flat calm of the Mediterranean, I would quietly give three cheers for one Cornelius Finbar Driscoll, for had not everything he had promised come absolutely true?

Our first port of call was Port Said, that bustling, noisy, colourful den of iniquity at the entrance to that great Egyptian marvel, the Suez Canal. *Andes* nosed in to berth. I watched the bowman on the Fo'castle of the Andes skillfully throw his landline almost the length of a cricket pitch. It was equally adeptly caught by one of the shore gang and so all the ropes and wires of *Andes* were passed ashore to be secured around the bollards on the jetty. I watched with interest as it was one of the skills I would have to learn. The scene ashore then caught my eye and I felt the thrill of the occasion. My first trip ashore in a foreign land. Everything was strange, the warm, dry, still atmosphere, the musty, spicy smell, the people, the language. All this I was about to confront for the first time. There was a mixture of Arab and Western dress, some of the ladies were garbed completely in black with a nun-like headdress and facial yashmak. This contrived to show only their dark mysterious eyes to the viewing public. Some would be attired in typical Western fashion. Likewise the men, long white gowns and sandals for some but many would be sporting quite immaculate Western suits and collar and tie. All, however, had one item of dress in common - the traditional world-renowned red fez.

The whole population of Port Said, it seemed, was on the streets, trying to sell you either goods or services. The more mundane service perhaps was offered by the young and persistent shoeshine boys, they were everywhere.

Much more catching were the little lads of six or seven on every street corner crying "Ghilly, Ghilly Mister Ghilly, Ghilly." This I found out had to do with magic. Three tin cups were on the pavement in front of the boy, then from inside his gown he would produce a half dead, day old chick, this he would place under one of the cups, then challenge you to pick which one the chick was under, after he had dexterously moved the three of them about. They were quite brilliant and I never saw one of them beaten.

The open fronted shops were vibrant with activity; no-one passed without being exhorted to buy. The Simon Artx Bazaar was famous on the waterfront and Simon was a well known character who sold everything from suitcases to dirty postcards. Pavement cafes were once again Arab mixed with Western culture. The communal Hookah or bubble bubble pipe sat happily beside the suited client drinking the local Stella beer.

We were all walking around wide eyed with curiosity and wonder, instinctively we broke into small groups. The den of iniquity tag given to such foreign ports was no misnomer for we were offered a wide variety of salacious services. "You like small boy mister?" "I get you very pretty girl, very cheap." See exibish mister, plenty naughty girls, I take you." My group chose the 'exibish' as the relatively save haven to begin our shoreside education. We had drifted into the seedy back streets, following our tout and entered a dimly lit dive where, to the accompaniment of reedy Egyptian music, a succession of scantily dressed girls performed obscene acts with a variety of objects. I admit it made my eyes pop out, but on leaving I felt sheepish and a little shamefaced. I satisfied myself it was only a curiosity. The battle with my conscience was short before I followed them in. In reality I was afraid not to conform. I could have said I wanted no part of it and there were those that had the courage to do just that.

I found it quite refreshing to return to the less degrading street scene. Returning aboard the Andes offered no escape from the local entrepreneurs, there were bum boats alongside offering for sale a wide variety of wares. Business was transacted by lines hanging from the decks down into the boats. The traders tied objects on the lines and if something caught your eye, you were trusted to pass back the agreed amount of Piastres.

The *Andes* was of course berthed almost in the High Street and the whole panorama of a bustling town was laid out before your eyes. The scene on the street was bedlam as buses, open flat backed lorries and an assortment of clapped out bangers, each one grossly overloaded with humanity, rushed by at breakneck speed. The clack, clack, clack of the Arabic voices strove to rise above the din of the rattling, protesting engines. To add to the symphony, every driver's horn or klaxon appeared to be permanently on. No-one, it seemed, used their brakes and minor collisions were accepted as the means of stopping or slowing down. As for pedestrians, there appeared to by two types, the quick and the dead.

The horse drawing the countless Gharries were as immune to the tumult around them as the famous Metropolitan Police horses in the 'Smoke'.

I joined my oppos for my evening's delicacies from the superb Andes kitchens. Then it was a shower, a change of gear, before my run ashore with George, Ginger, Furness and Alex Alexander.

Alex was a sight to behold, basically he was the shape of an Easter egg or perhaps Humpty Dumpty describes his form better. As with Ginger I would guarantee that within minutes of his arrival on the messdeck, he would be known as Fenders, which is the shortened version of Fender Belly, a common nickname for fatsos, which is derived from the big round rope fenders used to protect all boats coming alongside. Alex had knock knees and size eleven shoes. His teeth were discoloured with two gaps, his mouth was permanently open and above it a turned up nose exposed his two nostrils. Imagine this lot screwed into a permanent grin, plus a voice sounding like a corncrake and you would be entitled to question why I should join Alex in a run ashore. A market stall holder in the Chrisp Street Market in Poplar, he had long since lost his voice chords, which is where I came in because I was to write his letters for him and eventually read his incoming mail. I can assure you it is not as easy as you may think to take on this onerous duty. Fortunately they concerned his mother and family, there was no female involved and, in truth, I don't know how I would have handled it if there had been.

We left the *Andes* gangway and picked up the first two Gharries lined up and awaiting clients. Gharries were a part of the street scene and reminiscent of the Victorian horse drawn transport of London. We made a deal with the drivers to transport us to the best bar in town.

The beer was dreadful and tasted of onions but we were later introduced to Stella, a beer that was to become synonymous with all the Allied Forces in Egypt and to be quaffed by the millions of bottles. I was quite taken with the quality of the bar and the service that was provided. The preconceived picture in my mind of Egypt and Arabs were, of course, implanted by the cinema. It was of camel trains, sand storms, searches for hidden oasis, near empty water bottles, hallucinations and, of course, all Arabs had to be both mysterious and sinister. Nothing could be further from the truth. The bar was immaculate and every round of drinks brought with it a plate of hors d'oevres. I found the Egyptians happy, easy to get on with people. They appeared to understand our ways and possessed, to a man, a very comprehensive knowledge of English.

There was a mixture of robed and suited locals in the bar. We were soon in the company of some R. N. Signalman and a party atmosphere was under way. We began swapping yarns and they were very interested in the luxurious *Andes.* "Make the most of it lads," we were advised, "whatever you land up with the other end won't be anything like that." Six bottles of Stella later and we knew about 'bag shanties' (brothels), 'bints' (Arabic for girls; a further four bottles and we were trying out our newly taught Arabic on four of the locals who were sharing a communal Hookar. "Sahida affendi," we ventured. "Sahida," they returned and clapped their hands saying "quois, quois kateer" (good, very good). By now our new found oppos were treating us to their whole repertoire of yarns, lamp swinging and naval ditties. In addition, we were still continuing our language class, but the killick in our company had introduced us to Zibib, an aniseed-based alcohol like Pernod. We were now having some difficulty talking English, never mind Egyptian.

Throughout the evening George had made do with two John Collins and an orange juice, but he joined in everything and in spite of his nervous eyes appeared to be enjoying it. Furness was as drunk as a 'fiddler's bitch', Alex seemed about the same as when he arrived and wanted to move on with the 'bunting tossers'. I managed to convince him that we only had leave until 10pm. In the process of our farewells to all our new found friends, Alex managed to swap places with the hubbly bubbly men. We three then had to join him. They put on our caps, we put on their fezes and took over the Hookar. It was all quite hilarious and George and I managed to pass on the Hookar. We were later to learn that the smoke of the pipe contained Hashish, which was legal and widely smoked throughout most Arabic nations.

We made quite a noisy exit from the bar and were warned of the Naval Patrol on the street nightly to endeavour to keep a little decorum. We all piled into the first Gharry and it was no surprise when Alex dumped a surprised Abdul into the back with us and took over the reins. Abdul had no need to worry because many East Enders were familiar with horses, they abounded right across London. Those street side railway arches now inhabited by car mechanics, spray booths and instant MOTs, were nearly all horse stables plus the odd farrier. Nevertheless, Abdul was still pleased to take over the reins when we arrived at the Andes gangway. His reward was five Akkers, about a shilling, and he seemed well pleased.

We mounted the gangway, Alex was still grinning inanely, George as usual looked worried, Ginger was as 'pissed as a newt' and didn't give a monkey's. I was just happy. We successfully made it to our accommodation and Ginger decided to give all and sundry a rendering of the latest addition to his repertoire of ditties learned from our oppos of the evening.

"I don't give a f___ for the Captain of the top
or the killick of the working party.
He can chew my knob
for a couple of bob
Cos I am Jack me hearty."

There were a few threats of violence to his person before George took off his shoes and lowered him onto his bunk.

I lay back on my pillow and George sat at the foot of my bunk, while we went over and over the amazing time we had enjoyed on our very first run ashore in a foreign land. We said our goodnights, I was once more alone with my thoughts. The rightful occupants of an *Andes* cruise, I reasoned, would have an entirely different itinerary to the one I had just completed. What we had just been through was a typical matelots' run ashore. This would be the size of it wherever my port of call might be. This is because it's almost protocol to do as your peers do. It is quite possible the crew of Nelson's Victory followed the same predictable course as in the 'Andrew'. It appeared nothing must ever change.

I was beginning to understand what a complicated, batty, outrageously humourous world I was now about to encompass. A world where it appears you are under scrutiny, not prying, intrusive scrutiny, but on the messdeck it seems it is necessary to put everyone into a category. Perhaps it's because it helps the harmony of the close knit mess to know how far you can go with each other.

That was enough philosophising, the Stella beer and the local Zabib were taking charge of my senses. I lost the battle with my eyelids and slid into a troubled, dream filled sleep.

Chapter 5

My reverie was brought to an end by the gravel voice of Alex. "You coming on top" he growled, "she's just about to cast off." The shore party was standing by to let go, a succession of orders from the Bridge of the *Andes* and one by one the wires and hawsers were let go. Only the bow hawser was still secured to the bollard ashore as the Captain skillfully swung the stern of the great liner away from the berth - just imagine the strength of that taut bow-line.

"Let go fo'ard," he yelled. The Andes capstan payed out enough slack rope for the shore party to release the bow rope from the bollard. *Andes* continued astern for a while then it was hard-a-port.

We were on our way to the entrance of the Suez Canal.

The Andes nosed its way into the Canal and appeared to dwarf her surroundings, as it eased its way down its length. To starboard the desert stretched into infinity.

There was much to catch the eye, a road ran parallel and at intervals there were service stations down its length. Its unerring straightness was broken in the middle by the Great and Little Bitter Lakes on one of which stood the town of Ismailia. Once through the Lakes we again entered the cut channel and eventually left the canal at Port Suez.

The sunny Mediterranean and Suez Canal and the town of Ismalia were now left behind in the wake of the *Andes*. I was destined to return to all three venues under much less amenable conditions, conditions in which the enemy was doing its best to bring my participation in events to a speedy end.

Leaning on the guard rail, looking at the schools of porpoise who were our only company, other than the odd Arab Dhow, I reflected that the term 'going to war' was at the moment a contradiction in terms. In reality we were going away from war and into comparatively safe waters. As the warm breeze fanned my cheeks and the Andes ticked off the tranquil nautical miles, my thoughts turned to my oppos from Skeggie and Chatham, who would now be fighting the relentless Battle of the Atlantic.

We were aware that we were receiving a very poor apprenticeship for what lay ahead and that this was a honeymoon period, but our turn would surely come. However, the thought of being tossed about like a cork in little boats and being so seasick that you just wanted to die, swiftly turned my thoughts back to the tranquillity of my present war, where the seas were too calm, the ship was too comfortable, my companions were too amiable, the food was too good and there wasn't an enemy in sight.

The passage through the Red Sea continued without any incidents to relieve the monotony and we had to content ourselves with Tombola, messdeck games and quizzes to while away the tedious hours.

The object of my seven thousand mile journey would soon heave into sight and there was a ripple of excitement as *Andes* majestically entered Columbo Harbour. Everyone was on deck to take stock of their new surroundings as Andes dropped anchor and swung into the stream.

The first thing that hit you was the stifling heat. While we were under way a welcome breeze gave you relief. We were now in equatorial waters and one hundred degrees-plus temperature would be the norm.

A quick glance round the harbour showed me little of the promised island paradise. The tall tower of the International or Grand Oriental Hotel dominated one end of the harbour. At the other end there was all the dockside paraphernalia of Walker's Yard. The centre was taken up with the unprepossessing sight of Cory's coaling berth with the factor's name emblazoned down its length. Everything appeared to be quite British and did something to make me feel at home in this distant land.

Then I saw her for the first time, a long, sleek, elegant looking lady, whose looks had earned her the title of 'The White Lady of the East'. I was looking at what would be my home for the next year or so. The pride of Chatham, she was of course the eight inch gun cruiser, *HMS Kent*, a ten thousand ton county class cruiser.

Our transfer from the Andes was accomplished by the *Kent's* liberty boat. It approached the Andes like a homing torpedo, to swiftly slow down, swing round in an arc, and with faultless control on the throttle, pull alongside, without so much as a bump. A feat in which all Naval ships take great pride and something I was never to excel at.

A man in the uniform of a PO alighted and sprinted up the gangway. We were lined up ready for his perusal, he greeted us quite pleasantly and then proceeded to issue a few words of wisdom, intermingled with a number of dos and don'ts. I was pleased to note that he spoke in measured tones and Chatham's power of command was not in evidence. He passed along the ranks and looked up at me - and I mean looked up for he was not a centimetre above five feet in height. Here we go again, I thought, once again my six feet frame was about to mark my card.

"You," he said, "are going to be No five on P Gun."

What's No five, what's P Gun? I wondered.

He told me P Gun "is the crack gun and you're going to see it remains the best my son".

Later, as he had predicted, I became his No five and once again it had to do with brawn not brain. There were some quite emotional farewells and if any of us were to meet again it would only be by chance, because at that moment we were the only twenty ratings with an address, *HMS Kent*. A last wave and we were off to meet our Naval destiny.

Half the Kent's ship's company appeared to be lining the guard rails as we pulled alongside the after gangway. We were all pleased that 'Shorty' Munsen, our PO, had briefed us of the necessity to salute the quarterdeck. This of course was the homage always paid to the crucifix that hung on the quarterdeck in the days of sail.

H.M.S. 'Kent' *Crest*

Boarding the *Kent* was quite a culture shock, after the beautiful panelling and luxurious furnishings and drapes of the Andes. It contrasted sharply with the *Kent's* purely functional interior of angle iron, rivet heads and nuts and bolts. This was a fighting ship and all things fancy and combustible had to be kept to a minimum. The passage on the Andes was soon to become a distant, indulgent memory.

The warmth of our reception quite surprised us and it was a relief to us all. Remember, everywhere we went we would be first, the first civvy conscripts to be cast into the strange, complex world of HM Navy.

The crew of *Kent* we learned had already been on foreign service for two years and had completed a commission on the China Station when war broke out. They were preparing for their return to Chatham to be paid off and join their families in a well earned leave. The fortune of war decreed that they would have to forego this privilege; they were professional fighting men, training to a peak of perfection after two years together, and fully trained ships and crews were now at a premium. To their eternal credit I was never to hear them complain or whinge.

Showing the flag days were now over and it meant even more intense practice and training. The HOs had to be welded into the unit. It was really hard but we got there with the unstinting help and support of the professionals. Now it was for real and our survival would depend on being more alert, more efficient and faster on the draw than the enemy.

I was now an integral part of the Kent's ship's company. I had been allocated a mess and told which Watch I was in. There were two Watches traditionally termed Port and Starboard. A killick, or leading hand, was in charge of the mess and he was responsible for allocating jobs and duty rotas aboard ship. How strange that he should be an Irishman rejoicing in the name of Timothy O'Gara and what a splendid fellow and fine leader he proved to be.

There appeared to me to be much showing off for our benefit in the mess. These men had been closeted together in the confines of a messdeck for over two years, they all knew each other's strengths and weaknesses and each other's jokes and party pieces. We were therefore like a blood transfusion to them, a completely new audience to indulge themselves in and to me it was hugely entertaining.

The complement on *Kent* numbered about eight hundred and many of them would single you out eagerly seeking information about home. Once your home town became identified all your 'townies' aboard would seek you out and eagerly ply you with questions. The conversation swiftly became animated as places and points of interest were identified. At times the talk would become wistful and sad, as in turn they spoke of wives they were longing to see, of children who many of them had yet to see for the first time, of aging parents, and young men talking of brides they had married on the last week of their leave, a distant two years ago.

I was very grateful for these messdeck and guard rail chats, it was an opportunity to reassure yourself about the amazing complexity of the routine aboard ship. We HOs really were wet behind the ears and for a time we showed up poorly, alongside the sixteen year old Boy Seamen.

H.M.S. 'Kent'

Chapter 6

My first day on Kent was spent making myself familiar with my surroundings and for this reason I was pleased we were still in harbour.

I found that the ship was divided into territories, it was a jungle, it was just like the animal kingdom. My first journey into this jungle took me unwittingly into the territory of another species. I was immediately attacked not by the king of the jungle but most certainly the by king of the messdecks.

Master at Arms John Underwood was the 'Jaunty', a man known and feared throughout the messdecks of all Chatham ships. The Master at Arms, or Jaunty, was the senior rank on the lower messdecks and was responsible for the punishment, policing and discipline aboard ship.

I set out on my voyage of discovery and, mounting the ladder between decks, my eyes reached deck level to behold a long stretch of immaculately scrubbed timbers. I cleared the opening, straightened and took stock of my surroundings. Then my thoughts rushed back to my first brush with authority upon my entry into Chatham as, once again, my ears were assaulted by a deafening cascade of words. Not again, I thought. I froze in my tracks. Perhaps it wasn't me that was being attacked, but turning to focus in the direction of the sound, my first fears were realised. There were only the two of us, the hunter and the prey. He was massive, over six feet tall and as wide as a barn door. His face was contorted in rage and he looked extremely aggressive. What could I possibly have done wrong?

"Over here," he commanded.

I submitted to his request.

"What is a snivelling sprog OD doing in my Rec space?" he demanded.

He looked down at the white plimsolls on my feet and looked even more enraged.

"Haven't you heard of Chinese Foot Rot?" he bawled.

I said something like "No Chief".

I now thought that he must go into cardiac arrest.

"Chief" he ranted. "You dare call me 'chief', I'm the Master, Master at Arms Underwood. Everybody knows MAA Underwood," he raged.

He then did the most astonishing thing, reaching out and grasping a one inch diameter awning post he let out a roar and bent the steel rod at almost right angles. He then turned to me and said: "If you cross my path again in the next twenty four hours that is exactly what will happen to you."

In my very first excursion aboard *Kent* I had committed three offences and learned three lessons. First, that every branch has its own recreation space; two, although plimsolls were part of your kit the wearing of them was banned; three, to the uninitiated, the Chief's uniform was the same as the MAA. Wrong. He had a round MAA badge on his lapel.

His behaviour left me totally dumbfounded and I could not reach the safe haven of my messdeck quickly enough. Excitedly relating my experience to the lads on the messdeck I was quite disconcerted to find myself looking at a sea of faces, all grinning like Cheshire cats. One of them disappeared to return with a photograph of the Jaunty lying on his back with a piano on his chest and four ratings sitting on the piano. So that was it, he was an exhibitionist and the show had been put on for my benefit, knowing I would return to the mess to duly impress the new entries with his masterful feat of strength. He was only one of a host of outrageous characters who were to lighten the often long monotonous days at sea in wartime. I was tired out and was now about to retire to my sleeping quarters for the night.

It is worth my while making the comparison between the sleeping quarters on the Andes and the Kent. Two stout rods ran then length of the messdeck, supported at intervals from the deck head (ceiling); every four feet there was a notch in the tube; between the two notches was your bedroom. Between the two parallel bars you suspended your hammock, a rectangle of very coarse canvas containing a course horsehair mattress. A wooden stretcher kept the ends open and gave you reasonable access. You then performed a feat of acrobatics by grasping the rail with both hands and swinging your feet off the deck, aiming your body at the opening in your hammock. No mean feat at any time but after a run ashore, this sometimes turned into a pantomime. When a matelot tells you they are comfortable, don't believe him, they are just an expediency to save space. They were guaranteed to give you curvature of the spine, but I will concede they kept you reasonably stable in a rolling sea.

It was a safe bet to say that 90% of matelots partook of the weed, ranging from 'tailor mades', 'ticklers' (tinned cigarette tobacco) and finally the obnoxious tobacco leaf, rolled and bound expertly and often rum-soaked into a tight long roll, hence the name 'prick of tobacco'. Six old stripeys smoking this foul substance could put up a sizeable smoke screen for the ship. Now try to imaging the messdeck just before 'out pipes'. Dozens of bodies hanging in the air like fruit bats, noses about three feet or so from the deck head, portholes all closed and battened down for sea, dense tobacco smoke swirling round your head like a cloud, making you both a primary and a secondary smoker. You will now understand what a miracle it was that every matelot on the messdeck didn't suffer from collapsed lungs. There's a thought for Cancer researchers. Perhaps the ozone and briny was an antidote, who knows?

I was just seeking a position of comfort in my canvas banana skin when I got a most pleasant surprise over the intercom. I was introduced to my very first DJ who played a variety of pleasing records just before an order given each night to 'pipe down'.

It was the bugle first sounding off "wakey, wakey", then the Bosun's mate on his whistle, followed by a wide variety of exhortations from the Bosun's mate. Each one would have their favourite cry and this one was:

"Come along my hearties,
let go your cocks and grab your socks,
lash up and stow,
come along, rise and shine, the morning's fine."

This was the start of my first day as a hand, part of ship.

It would have been great just to drop out of your 'flea pit' (hammock) and sit down in the mess to bacon, egg and tomatoes, but in the 'peas and gravy' you had to earn your breakfast. It was out of your hammock, into the shower, back to the mess to lash up and stow your hammock, and then it was off to your part of the ship for your early morning stint of duty. It was 6am and for my first three mornings I was to do what 'Jack' had been doing for centuries, scrubbing decks, decks that were already immaculate were scrubbed and scrubbed again. We weren't making the decks any cleaner, we were filling in a part of the day that began at a totally unnecessarily early hour. What was being achieved by this died in the wool piece of nonsense? Every task performed daily could have been accomplished with less than half the ratings employed. However, that was the way of it and, of course, when she was at sea, all the personnel would be required to fill the twenty four hours of Watches.

In spite of the early hour it was already impressively hot. The sweat fell off me in buckets and it seemed an eternity before I was dismissed to join my messmates for breakfast. In spite of the heat I ate heartily and thoroughly enjoyed the banter of the mess.

At breakfast I was introduced to what was a messdeck preoccupation, finding out what was the 'latest buzz', which was guessing when we were leaving harbour and where we were off to. No-one was more anxious to know than yours truly. I just could not wait to sail into the blue as part the *Kent*'s ship's company and to see why a set of customs and practices, little altered since the days of sail, should make her the highly trained efficient fighting force she undoubtedly was.

To my immense relieve the buzz had been correct, and we were sailing at 0400 hours. I had also found that the German pocket battleship *Admiral Von Scheer* was back again, operating in the Indian Ocean; one of the reasons Kent had been moved to the East Indies Station in Columbo.

"D'ye hear there," the voice followed the shrill call of the Bosun's whistle.

"Prepare for sea."

"Cable party muster on the Fo'castle."

"In all boats."

"In all wind scoops."

"Down all dead lights."

"Close all watertight doors."

"Secure for sea."

The orders followed in quick succession. You didn't hang about, everyone had specific jobs. Gangways and all boats had to be raised and secured. Every exercise was accomplished by a time tested routine. Communication was by voice pipe, an amazingly simple network of tubes with mouthpieces placed in strategic positions.

"Fo'castle to Bridge."

"Bridge," came the reply.

"All boats secured Sir."

"Thank you Jackson," and so it would continue until Nunber One on the Bridge was satisfied *Kent* was ready to get under way. The last order was "Raise anchor". This exercise was under the control of the engine room branch and as soon as the anchor cleared the sea bed where it was holding ten thousand tons of steel in a firm fixed position, the eighty thousand BHP of the Kent's mighty boilers took over control. Then with the anchor securely housed the Bosun would call: "Hands fall in for leaving harbour".

*Ken*t was under way. This is what I had dreamed of in what now seems the distant past, in fact it was a short sixteen weeks ago. In truth it was a let down, I had no sense of being an essential part of a great fighting ship, apart from the dummy exercises in Shorty Munsen's gun crew as No five on P Gun. All I had been was a skivvy scrubbing the decks, washing the paintwork, sweeping out the mess and flats, drawing the food from the Galley, washing up all the pots, pans and dishes, emptying the rubbish down the 'gash chute'. Our gaols were full of men doing this every day, they were paying a debt to society. What had I done wrong? In the words of the 'eternal sailor', "You shouldn't have joined 'opps'." Cornelius Finbar Driscoll, you have a lot to answer for.

Chapter 7

We were leaving behind the safety of the harbour and were steaming out of Columbo on my first mission. In harbour it had just been our home, now it was a ship prepared for combat and it would be manned in Watches right through every twenty four hours. The safety catch was still on and only when you hears the 'klaxons' and the call of "Hands to actions stations," would Kent be ready to meet whatever was in store for us in the vast expanse of the Indian Ocean. I had watched in admiration the skill with which the expertly trained crew had gone about the quite complicated routine of preparing for sea and leaving harbour.

With one of my oppos, Ginger Newall, I had been posted to port mid ships lookout position. This again was a boring duty but at least I knew how vitally important a job it was. I have previously mentioned that the *Kent* was a strictly pusser ship and we had already been schooled rigorously in the importance of the job. It was essential to spot the enemy surface craft or aircraft as quickly as possible, your very survival depended on it. You were the eyes protecting the hundreds of men down below in the bowels of the ship. There were at all times a minimum of sixteen pairs of eyes continually scanning the sea and sky every second of the day and night at sea, including a man in the crow's nest high on the mast of the ship.

The giveaway was usually a thin wisp of smoke on the horizon from a funnel. Each lookout position scanned the sixty degrees of ocean and sky immediately in front of them. There was a voice pipe from each position to the Bridge. Upon seeing anything suspicious, speed was of the essence in reporting. It went like this, in a loud clear voice, "Bridge red ninety degrees, smoke on the horizon."

This way, before you had finished your message, the officer of the Watch had his glasses focused on the position; that split second could be vital. The Bridge would now be a hive of activity, this could be a friendly vessel on a known course, it could likewise be an uncharted friendly vessel. Out there were surface raiders, enemy supply ships and the main reason for our presence, the Admiral *Von Scheer* returned to once again stalk the shipping lanes.

The *Von Scheer* could conceivably be the next wisp of smoke seen on the horizon by a lookout. That was surely enough to keep everyone on their toes. Kent steamed thousands of miles in search of the enemy but in the vast wilderness of the Indian Ocean, it was like looking for a needle in a haystack. It was compensation to know that the enemy intelligence would be aware of our presence and that would probably restrict the enemy's movements at least.

Our travels took us from Ceylon to the Laccadives Islands off the West coast of India to the Seychelles, Maldives, Diego Garcia, the Chagos Archipeligo and back across the Equator to the Nicobar Islands.

It was lonely and boring work. The *Kent's* turbines carried us over endless miles of this hot, blue liquid desert. Only the Kent's graceful bows disturbed the flawless surface and the wake astern was but a memory of our having passed this way. The rhythm of the engines pulsated through the decks like the sound of a manic drummer and with the swish, swish, swish of the bow wave, contrived to make a two note symphony.

There were reliefs. We anchored off some of these remote islands, most of which were British possessions. It was wonderful to get relief from the dull monotony of the previous days. A stillness descended as the great turbines were rested. We stood down from semi-action stations and the laughter and banter returned to the messdecks. Then I was to hear the following pipe for the first time. "Close the port heads. Hands to swim the port side."

The 'heads' (lavatories) were closed for obvious reasons. The gangway would be down, the boat boom would be lowered with its trailing lines for securing the boats and a duty lifeguard would be patrolling in a dingy (small boat). Now countless Johnny Weismullers would start performing, diving thirty feet from the deck, the more decorous ones from the lower stern and the less adventurous from the bottom of the gangway. It was as hard to describe the joy of this exercise as it is to describe the relentless, humid oppressive heat of all the steel messdecks in these Equatorial waters. It was always with reluctance that we returned aboard the sauna of the messdecks.

"You won't get nothing, Stripey."

"What d'ya mean? I've got 'up homers' here."

"Plenty of jungle juice here, Bunts," someone called to the 'bunting tosser' (signalman). Bunts was a well known piss artist (heavy drinker).

"They'll have you in the pot you 'doggo' looking bastard," they yelled to Alex.

"Yeah," responded Alex, "and I bet I taste better than that 'diesel duff' (meat pudding) that Lucrecia Borgia (the chef) served up today."

It was very, very rare that anyone took exception to this repartee and, in any case, if anyone called you a bastard, it was a term of affection in the Andrew.

Many of these island paradises are now the haunts of wealthy holiday makers; this one was totally primitive. There were no roads, just paths through the jungle, no substantial building of any kind and no currency. There was just nothing to buy or sell and they conducted their living by barter. The natives were completely shy of the visitors, it was an education. We walked down a dirt track with the occasional face peeping at you through the undergrowth. It was exactly like a scene from *Tarzan and the Apes*, or Robinson Crusoe, Treasure Island, Swiss Family Robinson, any of these classics could have been born here. I marvelled at the fact that a few short weeks ago I was with my family in the trappings of civilisation and now, here I was experiencing at first hand the sounds and smells of an island completely isolated from the world, a pinhead in the middle of a vast ocean, yet the people were living, breeding and surviving here, just as in our world. Nature provided for their every need, the trees and shrubs were a source of food, medicine and building material. The surrounding ocean was their fish market. Inevitably civilisation and the name of progress would arrive to spoil it all and undoubtedly there would be commodities and produce ready to be exploited.

We topped a rise on our track and there in the distance could be seen the telltale radio mast. We came to a clearing and here there was some semblance of order. It passed, I suppose, for a village. Here there were what appeared to be Elders who at least stood their ground. They made gestures and grinned at us through stained and gapped teeth. Only their essential private parts were covered and there were many ribald comments from the 'fanny rats' (womanisers) amongst us as their eyes fell upon the nubile figures of the young females. Here I witnessed something that no doubt stemmed back to the days of discovery and missionaries. Many of the lads had come bearing gifts and proffered the natives 'nutty' (chocolate), sweets and tobacco. I found this to be common practice and much to be applauded. The cynical ones assured me it was to beg their favours.

We had stretched our legs, filled our lungs with fresh air and for me it had been quite an enthralling day, a realisation of one of my daydreams back home in North Woolwich making cables at Henleys.

Chapter 8

Twenty four hours after entering Walker's Yard in Columbo for necessary repairs, The White Lady of the East looked as though the *Admiral Von Scheer* had got at her. Everything was in disarray but, in fact, it was organised chaos. One thing I was pleased about was the relaxing of the scrub deck routine. Now we spent many hours rigging awnings ashore; this had me mystified. Tim O'Gara solved the mystery for me and it was to show one more quite interesting and humourous aspect of life aboard Kent.

"This is for Wednesday's 'sod's opera'. Lofty, got any talent among your HOs?" he asked.

I pondered a while and said: "You can try Scouse Walker, he used to give a song and fancied himself as a comedian on the *Andes*."

Twenty four hours later a quite impressive temporary theatre had been erected in a quite lovely setting at the corner of the harbour alongside Walker's Yard. The picture was completed by a couple of large ban yan trees which provided some welcome shade.

'Sod's opera' was just one more sample of the Andrews' ability to find a telling pseudonym for anything it set its mind to. Sod's opera for ship's concert was typically clever.

The Marines Band were the backbone to it, providing instrumental solos and singers. Scouse sang his songs but his stand up comedian routine came in for some stick. It was a super show, I thought. The whole ship's company were present from the Captain down. Many of the officers took part. the best items were the sketches put on by the crew, who mercilessly panned their superiors. One of the highlights was to me quite startling, after much prompting and popular demand, up onto the stage jumped the Padre, dressed as a matelot and he proceeded to perform the time honoured strip show of the Navy.

"This old hat of mine,
The inside is quite new,
But the outside had seen some stormy weather..
I cast this had aside,
I mean to travel wide,
Far across the sea I long to roam."

At the line "cast this hat aside" each item of clothing is discarded until the performer is down to his underpants. A great cheer would ring out and the whole ship's company chanted:

"Sing, sing, sing,

Or show your great big ring."

'Ring' was Navy parlance for backside. The performer then made his choice. He declined to sing, instead he turned his backside to the audience and pulled his pants down.

I couldn't perceive a man of the cloth performing this act. I had already seen it performed by the crew. I admit to being taken aback by this performance but the whole day and the atmosphere of the occasion told me much about the officers and men who made a career out of life in the strange but surprisingly close and caring world aboard ship in HM Navy.

H.M.S. 'Kent' *Officers and men with Sports Trophies (1939)*

Superficially the China Station was a quiet number (easy job), there was no shortage of volunteers for the posting and if you had signed on for ten years there was no better place to earn your living. This applied to both single and married ratings. What was on offer was a rent free home with three excellent meals a day. Cigarettes, tobacco, chocolate, sweets and general sundries were on sale in the NAAFI aboard, for what amounted to 'peanuts'. A free tot of rum or three pence a day if you were teetotal. For a small fee you could get all your washing done by the 'Dhobey Firm', likewise tailoring or repairs. All the board games were available, including a complicated Chinese game known as Marjon. The favourite games by far were Tombola (Bingo) and Ludo (Ukkers). The name Ukkers was an obvious target for the messdeck 'poets' and if a game was in the offing the cry would go up "Ukkers you F______s." An excellent library was available and widely used. There were cricket and football matches, rowing, sailing and swimming regattas and, as previously recounted, ship's concerts and sod's operas. All the exotic places in the Near and Far East were visited in the ceremonial showing of the flag too numerous to mention.

On return to base it would not be the usual matelots' run ashore, they were really well organised. A substantial number of the crew would be shacked up ashore with a Chinese wife who attended to their every need. Jack would go ashore with his oppos, have his night out and return to his 'wife' for the night. In the morning he would be woken for his breakfast and a complete washed and ironed kit would be ready for him. I was assured that these concubines were almost without exception faithful to one man.

What a life, and they got paid for it. To many it was the life of Reilly and they would sign on for a further ten years. You would, however, often hear a messmate who was 'chokka' (fed up) cry out in anguish "Roll on my F______g twelve".

Just a little insight into a lifestyle that no longer exists in the RN. Now they were performing the job for which they had trained, the prosecution of a war. I was among the few to enjoy the privilege of serving alongside a crew with two full years together and trained to the peak of perfection.

The 'tiffies' (engineers) and 'dockyard mateys' had returned the Kent back to the crew. That, of course, meant the skivvys had to get to work to bring the *Kent* back to the condition that had earned her the title of White Lady of the East. Paintwork had to be cleansed of the dockyard mateys' grime and the decks, the bain of my life, had to be brought back to their pristine condition. Jimmy the One (First Lieutenant) would tell you a "clean ship is a happy and efficient ship". If this was so, I was serving on a world beater.

Everything ship shape and Bristol fashion, *Kent* once again left harbour to go on patrol. This time we sailed East from Ceylon into the Adaman Sea. The voyage was again without incident, that is until we reached the Nicobar Islands where I was to witness the most bizarre ceremony.

The usual routine was followed; we anchored ship, "Hands to bathe" was piped and the *Kent's* water babies had their mad hour or so. "Up spirits" was piped at Noon when the crew received their tot of 'Nelson's Blood' (rum). We took dinner, then "Hands to muster on the quarterdeck" was piped, "dress of the day number sixes". The full Royal Marines Band was mustered there. We were fell in, then marched off single file to ring the complete upper deck with ratings, all facing outboard, an impressive sight.

A boat pulled away from the landing stage ashore, to call it a boat did it an injustice. It was a beautiful, ornate, viking type craft with a fabulous bow tapering up some ten or twelve feet and exquisitely carved and painted. The *Kent* fired off a twenty one gun salute and, as it neared, I saw its full splendour elaborately furnished, it was drawn by twenty four gleaming warriors, twelve each side, all rowing in perfect unison.

In the middle on something like a throne, sat the Sultan of the islands. The craft drew alongside in a perfectly executed drill that the *Kent's* boat's crews would have been proud of. Then off stepped this magnificent but bizarre figure. He was black, over six feet tall and he was dressed in a flowing white gown, his Sultan's sash, all bejewelled, with various orders and medals across his chest. On his feet were spats but no footwear. On his head was a tall top hat and in his hands a pair of white gloves. He was ceremoniously piped aboard and the marines struck up with some suitably marshal music. He then inspected the guard of honour. This was followed by the National Anthem. Some talking and gesticulating took place and the party moved off to the ship's side looking down upon another craft tied up to the boom. The ships' derrick lowered its hook into the boat with a net on the end and to my utter astonishment the hook was raised and inside the net was the most enormous giant turtle which was deposited in the ship's portable swimming pool, then down went the hook once more to return with a second giant turtle. Whatever, I wondered, was the object of this exercise? I mean, they could hardly be kept as pets could they? I was to find they were a very privileged gift to the whole ship's company. The Sultan and his retinue retired to the wardroom for their 'big eats' where nothing would be spared in its lavishness. The whole ship's company were to enjoy the luxury of turtle soup.

We raised anchor and set off on patrol. Once again each surface craft encountered had to be challenged and return the necessary code number, a boring procedure. I had just come off morning Watch and was blissfully sinking into the land of nod when "Hands to action stations" was piped over the intercom. The adrenalin began pumping, in seconds it seemed, from the chaos of everyone rushing to close up. I was on the four inch gun deck and the Kent was ready to face whatever it was that was out there. I saw a large merchantman, there was an immediate sense of relief that it was not the Von Scheer. At the most it could be a Q ship, a disguised Merchant ship, some of which were capable of inflicting severe damage. After much signalling and calling on loud hailers, some positions were closed down from action stations and a boarding party was organised, of which I was part. We were issued with gaitors, belts, rifles and live ammunition. A boat was lowered and we pulled across to the merchantman. I really felt important and was delighted to be chosen. We boarded her by her own scrambling nets placed over the side. A thorough search was made and it was soon established as an enemy supply ship. Sadly it was identified as being Vichy French, the part of the great nation divided down the middle, and we were aboard that half that had thrown in its lot with the Germans. She was impounded and the boarding party escorted her into Columbo Harbour. Mind you, we did have the Kent's eight inch guns on our side as well, however, I'm never very clear about what would have happened had she had call to use them.

Chapter 9

The Ganges boys were a very special breed, trained at the notorious, or even infamous, *HMS Ganges* in Norfolk. These may sound like strong words to describe a Naval depot for the training of young lads, but I was told some horror stories about the regime entrusted with this task. Among their numbers were many orphans, lads from other institutions, boys anxious to get away from broken homes, many of them abused both physically and sexually.

The training was so tough and arduous that when it was suggested for young offenders it was considered too arduous. The public, mediums of the press or the cinema showed them as a finished product, usually covering the high yardarm at Shotley with button boy standing precariously at the top of the mast.

Before reaching that stage they had been subjected to being screamed at continually, harassed and beaten by the obscene 'Stonarky', a length of rubber hose used quite indiscriminately. They had no redress and even release from it all was made very difficult as many had nowhere to escape to.

When they eventually left to join a ship it was often only a marginal improvement. They rose half an hour before the rest of the crew and began scrubbing and 'holystoning' decks in coarse duck suits, with bare feet, often in freezing conditions. The 'holystone' was an abrasive block operated from a kneeling position which made the boys' knees red raw. The officers thought this of no consequence and it was condoned.

These boys on *Kent* were tough, fit and all were first class seamen, steeped in Naval tradition and pusser to the core. Mixed with the undoubted admiration for their skills was a profound sense of shock that they were the target for lecherous male predators aboard ship. The boys had their own messdeck, separated and even protected from their peers. Many of them had been prey to the predators before they joined a ship and were worldly and streetwise. The harsh regime of their lifestyle was coupled with very poor pay, and poverty often would lower their resistance to the advances of the lechers.

Boys were invariably drafted to the big ships, that is cruisers and above, and did have a choice of ship, which meant they could volunteer for ships serving in exotic parts of the world. The boys' shore leave was very limited and restricted to a few hours. The run ashore was again a temptation to acquire some easy cash.

There was a strange acceptance of this tawdry trade in flesh. The penalties for being caught were severe, but as with all things in life, where there's a will there's a way. Just one more facet of life in the confines of a Naval messdeck which, once again, most certainly had its origins way back in the days of Nelson.

I was learning a little more of the men around me, both the boys and the men recruits had been through the Navy 'mill'. In consequence the end result was the Navy ended up with the recruits they wanted. Men who had signed up regardless. They would suffer the monotonous routine, the harsh discipline and total lack of democracy that existed on HM ships, for the fruits of the lifestyle offered. We were an island race and for centuries men had fallen for the lure of the sea. We had always depended on men with salt in their veins for our very survival and I would either be absorbed into the system or suffer the consequences.

This voyage was notable in my mind for two events, the less serious of the two concerned my first day's instruction on the wheel. I was being introduced for the first time to the arts of steering a ship on a given course. An art nowhere as easy as it seems. There were just four of us in the wheelhouse. The Coxswain who was instructing us, myself and two other HOs, on each side on the rev counters. I began by making a real pig's ear of it. Within five minutes the voice pipe sounded in the wheelhouse.

"Bridge to wheelhouse, Captain speaking."

"Coxswain speaking, Sir."

"Have you some inside information about submarine activity in this area that I am unaware of?"

"Er, no Sir."

"Then perhaps you can explain to me why we are steering a zig zag course, Cox'ain?"

"Yes Sir, it's HOs under instruction."

"It's a good job we are in the Indian Ocean, it looks to me as though the man on the wheel needs all of it. Get him on course."

"Aye, aye, Sir."

By the time the Coxswain came to my rescue, I had done everything bar loop the loop. Calm as a cucumber the Coxswain picked up the course and said: "Now let's start again. Keep calm and remember when I give the order five degrees to port, as soon as she answers, your Gyro repeater will relate to starboard, but keep your eye on the centre marking, then reverse your wheel to starboard rapidly and as soon as you feel the ship move back to starboard, meet her and you will then gradually centre on course, all right?"

All right I thought, how can this be right, it defies all the laws of common sense? Of course, right it was, and ten minutes later I knew what to do but I was still a learner driver for some time. As with driving a car you do most things, eventually, in your subconscious. Once I had thrown off the tension and relaxed I was as proud as a dog with two tails and a street full of lamp posts. What would Cornelius Finbar Driscoll think of me now? I thought. It was a thrilling sight and a thrilling feeling to look out across the twin turrets of A and B guns onto the immaculate Fo'castle and feel the graceful bow of *Kent* slicing through the ocean. The whole ten thousand tons of Kent and all who sailed in her were in my hands at this moment. Within a week I was a fully fledged Able Seaman in HM Royal Navy.

We were two days out and the buzzes were still abounding but the only certainty was that we were already further South than we had every been and that meant nothing at all.

Kent was my first and last big ship. Were they all like this? I often wondered. Minutes after tot time the noise level on the messdeck must have risen about ten decibels. I never ceased to marvel at the crew's endless capacity to amaze me with their behaviour.

The pipe simply said "Train all windscoops fo'ard." Windscoops are shaped like coal scuttles and are inserted in each open porthole whilst the ship is in harbour, particularly in the Tropics. The object is to direct any welcome breeze into the messdeck. In the event of a change of direction of the wind, it would be desirable to reverse the windscoops and face them the other way. A simple exercise you might think, but not on the Kent. A rating would stand in the gangway of the mess and the following drill would take place. Each porthole would be manned by a rating, then the man in the gangway would shout:

"Windscoops, wait for it."

"Windscoops, a - bout turn."

At which order all the windscoops would be reversed in unison.

Mad as March hares I used to think. Somewhere there was a reason for this behaviour, perhaps just below the surface we are all a bit loopy in one way or another. When a group of men are thrown together in the small confines of a messdeck in times of war, it quickly becomes apparent to you that you can't put on a front. The messdeck is your home, your dining room, your bedroom and very often your coffin. Your messmates become your family, you find apparently good men with bad faults, bad men with good qualities and this is what makes you tolerant of each other. The loopy, lovable, humourous aspect of this lifestyle is a substitute for the face of your identity that you have abandoned. Paradoxically, it may have been that this semi-madness was the only thing that kept you sane.

A summons appeared on the messdeck requesting that I present myself to the 'court of Neptune' at 1400 hours the following day. It meant of course that *Kent* would be approaching the Equator which is the domain of King Neptune and it was necessary to attend his court to get passage across the line. This particular investiture concerned only the newly joined HOs. The centrepiece of this ceremony was the swimming pool, the incumbent turtles had long ago been reduced to turtle soup and their huge shell backs were trophies badged away somewhere aboard ship. Nothing was spared in the pageant, the costumes and the regalia were very impressive. We were given bloodcurdling accounts of the fate that awaited us in the Kent's version of this historic occasion.

In the event it transpired to be a rumbustious couple of hours, as everyone joined in the fun. First of all our names were read out, two of Neptune's courtiers were dispatched to apprehend us. We were led to the court, sat in some sort of a chair at the edge of the pool, where we were lathered with a king size shaving brush, shaved with a king size open razor, then jettisoned into the pool where we were set upon by mermaids, dolphins, pollywogs, sea serpents and various other inmates of the deep. If you survived their pretty genuine efforts to drown you, you were granted a certificate which protected you from all these creatures of the deep if at any time in the future you should be unfortunate enough to be plunged into their domain. The certificate is a treasured memory.

We continued South to the Chagos Peninsula where the statutory intelligence call was made. It wasn't much in the way of excitement of a run ashore; there was no leave but at least it was land, something other than the relentless monotony of the endless tract of the Indian Ocean.

It was the crow's nest lookout that this time sent the crew to action stations. I was working part of the ship when the klaxon sounded and "Hands to action stations" was piped. I speedily made my way to the four inch gun platform. Tim O'Gara the gunlayer on P1 had already trained his binoculars in the direction of the report.

"Looks like a couple of ships under gunfire," he ventured. "There's another straddle directly over them," he continued.

"This is what we joined for lads," said Tim.

I could already detect the excitement in his voice. There was an air of anticipation, of expectancy around me. I remember clearly my feelings at the time, watch the others and behave just like them, I told myself. They're professionals, I mustn't on any account let myself down. Subsequent events, however, led me to believe that fear was the overriding factor in everyone's behaviour and not necessarily the enemy. I believe the scorn of your fellow shipmates was feared the most, in consequence your face and your reactions became those of a poker player.

Everyone on the Bridge would be giving orders, making decisions, which course to take, what speed. The Director in the gun central tower would be making calculations. The *Kent* in fact was steaming full speed ahead in the direction of the targets. The Yeoman of the Signals made the challenge to the ships under fire. It was the reply to challenge that caused all the red faces on Kent, for the 'victims' were in fact two innocent whalers and the 'salvoes' were the blowing of Sperm Whales. I saw the salvoes and I can vouch for the fact that things looked just as they had been reported.

The aftermath was a mixture of relief and disappointment. I firmly believed that these men who had been together for over two years, fully convinced of their own ability, had a desire to prove themselves. The exploits of Commodore Harwood's squadron of *Archilles*, *Ajax* and *Exeter* in disposing of the Graf Spee, was still fresh in the memory. The spouts of the Sperm Whales could well have been salvoes from the *Spee's* sister ship the Von Scheer and that probability had most likely been uppermost in many people's minds. It was therefore an anti-climax, the scent of battle had permeated the air and the adrenalin had been flowing. Now it was the harsh reality of more miles of boredom. Everything had suddenly gone flat and you could sense the frustration. The crew were getting a bit chokka. The dull routine, coupled with the debilitating heat of the messdecks in these one hundred degrees-plus temperatures, appeared to be taking their toll.

It may have been the sobering thought once the adrenalin had ceased to flow, that if the Sperm Whales had indeed been the *Admiral Von Scheer,* some of us may have now been dispatched to Davy Jones' locker. We returned to base in Columbo and proceeded to water, fuel and store ship. On completion, we immediately 'slipped' and left harbour.

Chapter 10

We headed South for Chagos Archipelego and Diego Garcia but were suddenly ordered to alter course and head North. The intention was to find and shadow a possible contraband ship. The mission was made almost impossible, the weather closed in on us and we endured two days of very rough seas and bad visibility. Consequently the Walrus was unable to take off and our quarry escaped our attention.

This was turning into a most interesting trip. In the forenoon we arrived off the Solomon Islands, there was much excitement as we stood off and prepared to lower the 'pinnace', which was manned by the Torpedo Officer, Lt Comm Blundell, a Midshipman, a PO Telegraphist, a Leading Seaman and five crewmen. It was an armed landing party. The islands were supplied and maintained by a boat from Mauritious which called just three times a year. It appears that radio contact had been lost and it was feared the occupants had been overthrown, hence the landing party. The pinnace made its way through a pass and down a lagoon. When the main pier was sighted a look through the binoculars established that the British flag was still flying. The natives there were friendly and the problem of the loss of radio contact was simply because the batteries had gone flat and could not be recharged. It was just another incident in one of the tiny islands that was still, however, an active part of the British Empire. But there is another reason for relating this story. It concerns the Midshipman, or snotty, who took part in the armed landing party.

Midshipmen, according to the immortal Captain Bligh in his now famous eulogy at the time of the mutiny, "are the lowest form of life in the RN". Entering the RN as a potential Midshipman was the equivalent of being sentenced to a stretch of hard labour. From the minute of their entry they are subject to a regime of bullying by 'psycho' PTIs and PO GIs. Only the reasonably strong survive. Even when they are drafted to a ship their denigration doesn't cease; they are the equivalent of 'fags' in a public school. Then just to further demean them they are known throughout the Service by the revolting name of 'snotty'. This particular snotty who took part in the armed landing party and could quite conceivably have been killed, had, according to Lt Comm Blundell, the distinction of making "the best cup of 'pusser's kye' (ship's cocoa) in the Watch. He was, in fact, the spouse of Queen Elizabeth, Prince Philip of Greece.

At that time the fact that he was a Prince of Greece was of absolutely no consequence whatever. He was just another snotty. Princes and princesses were ten a penny and, in many cases, existing in straitened circumstances as many monarchies were, even then, doomed to be vanquished.

This incident was just one more headache for the Naval authorities, brought about by the fall of France. History twenty years forward was repeating itself. Every single unit of the French Navy and Merchant fleet was having to make decisions, whether to fight with Britain or the Germans. It was the cause of endless conflict even aboard individual units which were in themselves divided.

To me the scenic beauty of Columbo was nothing short of magnificent. A walk to the Victoria Park opened up a vista of colour and beauty that transfixed me. A panorama of trees, shrubs and plants fell away below you. Alamandas, Periwinkle, Rhododendrum, Poinsettas, Acacias and Convulvelous, household names, growing in wild profusion in enormous patches of colour. In the background the hills were also a blend of blues, lavenders and greys, shimmering in the equatorial haze. At the time of sunset, this magical scenario was even more enhanced as its rays picked out the cloud formation floating overhead.

There was of course a price to pay for this vista of beauty. The climatic condition that brought it about was the sole reason for the sometimes suffocating, oppressive heat that turned the messdecks into saunas.

We stored and fuelled ship, then left harbour during the forenoon Watch. *Suffren* and *Gloucester* followed. We were now F/Ship fourth CS and the Bridge was packed to overflowing as we engaged in exercises all day. An eight inch sub calibre shoot was followed by night exercises when we did a shoot with the Widnes target ship. Everyone appeared happy with the results but there were still mumblings about when it would be the real thing.

The course was due North so we knew we were heading for a new venue and it was soon confirmed that we were heading for Bombay, that great city of India's Western seaboard. It was raining and the sea was quite choppy, we anchored offshore and I watched a snotty struggle to take the motorboat alongside the jetty. Eventually we went in and berthed. What a contrast to Columbo. Here was a lively, thrusting city, vibrant with activity. Here was a scene slightly reminiscent of the Albert Docks back home, where my dreams had started. Here was a typical matelot's run ashore. Bombay had been host to men of the sea for generations.

The wealth of the Indian continent had been copiously extracted and then shipped out through this port of Bombay which was both commercially and strategically one of the most precious jewels in the crown of Empire. Bombay, like many other great cities, was a port of two worlds. The unashamedly rich, alongside the hordes of the underprivileged poor. Emaciated and ill clad bodies abounded around the dock area, crippled beggars accosted you every yard of the way, some of them pathetically young.

Trinkets, baubles, bangles and beads were proffered for sale, a veritable feast for the ladies, but of course of little interest to Jack ashore, who had seen it all. However, a bejewelled casket caught my eye and that was all it needed for one of these indefatigable salesmen to cling onto me like a leech.

Once you had broken through the appalling crust of deprivation around the docks, a gentle climb led you gradually into the area of affluence. The statutory symbols of the Raj were everywhere to be seen. The Yacht Club, the Army and Navy Store, the Taj Mahal Hotel and all the other trappings of the good life.

The intrepid salesman was still dogging my heels and when we eventually stopped for a beer he only had the one trinket and I had to admire him for his persistence. Sat down with my beer I at last agreed to examine it. It was excellently made and after a bit of haggling, he accepted my offer of only a few Rupees, which probably was a good day's work for him. My oppo George was busily examining my purchase when we were joined at the table by a couple who asked us to join them in a drink. This we readily agreed to. Mr and Mrs Elliott were, of course, British and he was a Government officer of sorts. They had both witnessed the arrival of the *Kent* and we were invited back to their residence which was in the exclusive British Quarter.

To me and George it was just like a film set. We drove up to the entrance of this home between the trees, ornamental shrubs and flowers, to enter what was to us a palace. Polished wood floors were covered in elegant, colourful, Indian carpets, giant pots of greenery were everywhere, spacious cream walled rooms were entered through round archways. We followed them to the patio, furnished in soft and colourful upholstered cane furniture. We sat down and took in the view over the green lawns, down to the sandy beach and the sea through a vista of Acacias, Laburnums and Rhododendrums. It was a magical sight, soft-footed servants attended to our needs and we eventually relaxed somewhat after a couple of Mr Elliott's best malt whiskies. They asked endless questions about home in Britain and just like many others we had spoken to, they could hardly comprehend how the folk at home were coping with the rationing. It was our stories of the intensity of the blackout and the removal of all road signs in Britain that really gripped their imagination, however.

The Elliotts, it transpired had a son in the Navy still doing his training in England. Perhaps that is what induced them to offer us their quite fantastic hospitality. We left still feeling out of place in the splendour of our surroundings which belonged to the beautifully gowned ladies and splendid uniforms of the officer class.

"Before I drop you off back aboard ship, I'm going to drive you the Malabar Hill to see the Towers of Silence that I have been telling you about," Mr Elliott said. Mrs Elliott suggested it was perhaps too macabre, but George and I were only too anxious to make the visit in spite of the bizarreness of his story.

The Towers of Silence were the burial grounds of the Parsees, a Persian sect living in Bombay. The Towers of Silence consisted of a number of circular buildings enclosed by a twelve foot wall. Inside there were three layers of shallow grave pits, outer for men, inner for women and centre for children. They all sloped towards the centre pit. The funeral procession climbed the patch to the entrance and only the bearers were allowed inside. The body wrapped in linen or rice paper, was unclothed and placed in one of the shallow graves, complete silence was observed. Above on the walls and in the surrounding trees sat many vultures. Immediately the bearers withdrew, the vultures pounced on the body and quite incredibly the body was completely stripped of flesh in about fifteen minutes. The vultures' feast included aerial battles for the flesh, this in full view of the mourners outside. The bones then dried and bleached in the sun and air and in a few days they were removed to the centre pit, in two or three months they were reduced to powder and the rain water washed them through a filter bed of shells, sand and charcoal. A grotesque story and as far as we could establish, none of the crew we spoke to had visited the sight. "Now there's something to tell the folks at home," said Mr Elliott as he drove us back to Kent.

What an enthralling day we had and it was certainly one for the scrapbook. The day with the Elliotts had done something to change my views about the Raj and it also made me reflect even harder on the behaviour and attitude of the officers towards the ratings. Remember I was a civvy matelot and hopefully still not, for want of a better word, institutionalised, like the case-hardened time serving matelot.

Whilst on Watch on the Bridge I began to detect chinks in the officers' armour and it was already obvious to me that there was a certain amount of friction between them. It was also apparent to me from the ship's company that our present Skipper was not as well thought of as the sick Captain Ashmore who they had left in Hong Kong. There were exceptions. The Torpedo Officer Lt Comm Blundell was a very amiable and approachable man, as was my Divisional Officer Lt Comm Sitwell, one of the famous literary and artistic family of Sitwells. We have found 'the up homers' of all 'up homers', but would we ever return to this great country that boasted an emperor and empress? Opulent palaces, princes, princesses, maharajahs and maharees, an illustrious, almost make-believe world that was now engaged once again in a world war. A war perhaps fought to preserve this status quo. Now the rich and powerful would join with the poor and deprived and, as a nation, make one of the greatest of all contributions to eventual victory against the Nazi aggressors. The bravery and heroism of the Indian troops was once again to become a legend.

Chapter 11

Twenty four hours out of Bombay and we had all swapped experiences and analysed our runs ashore. Some had visited the infamous Caves district, the notorious Red Light district of Bombay. Some out of curiosity, others no doubt to participate in the very doubtful delights of the services offered. Once again the men who had indulged themselves would be very anxiously monitoring their 'manhood' daily for any telltale sign of a 'doze' which would confine them to rueful admission to the VD mess and ostracise them from their messmates, but more of that later.

Rocket launch of 'Walrus aircraft from a County Class Cruiser.

The orders went out to launch *Marina,* our Walrus reconnaissance aircraft. This seaplane gave a new dimension to the county class cruisers, and it was an invaluable asset in the hunting down of the enemy. The launch of the Walrus was a complicated, highly skillful operation and fairly hazardous. It was a tribute to Mitchell the famous designer of the Spitfire that as early as 1926 a rocket propelled plane would be in service in the RN. The launcher ran almost at right angles from port to starboard and it meant if possible manoeuvring the ship so the launch was into the wind. The intrepid pilot would warm the engine and gradually raise maximum revs. The seaboat's crew would be lowered as an emergency.

At maximum revs the pilot would raise his arm and he would be launched by rocket propulsion. The initial impulse was a strong G force on the pilot but once clear of the ship's side, the engine took over and then screaming and protesting, tantalisingly slowly became airborne.

The weather was far from good and this added flavour to the buzzes of why it had been launched in the present inclement conditions.

"Bet there's bleeding bovver out there," said Ginger Newall.

"Calm down lads," said Tim O'Gara in his rich Irish brogue, "it's probably only a routine flight."

"What, in this bleeding wevver, 'ooh are you trying to kid?" replied Ginger.

The weather had certainly closed in and there was some worry about the Walrus. Low cloud, rain and poor visibility was now the order of the day. There was immense relief when a throaty roar of the Walrus was heard. There followed a further quite extraordinary exercise. I was aware of the saying "oil on troubled water", well I was about to see it in operation.

The *Kent* manoeuvred into a position so that the starboard side took the full force of the elements and into the water on the lea side oil was poured, which immediately appeared to calm the water. At a signal, the Walrus circled and made a near perfect landing. It still needed a pretty good feat of seamanship from both the Walrus and the seaboat's crew to fix the hook from the ship crane and hoist it inboard. Cool heads and steady hands were the requirement of the day.

The convoy made its *rendez vous* outside Bombay. It consisted of six ships all of about ten thousand tons. They were carrying about six thousand trained troops from famous regiments, Royal Scots, Norfolks, Ox and Bucks, East Lancs and they were off to reinforce the Desert Army.

We learned the joyous news that we were headed for Durban: the messdeck was jubilant.

Four days out we learned that Italy had joined the fray and this put an entirely different aspect on this convoy. It would not be long before her subs were operating in these waters. Our trip would take fourteen days.

I had another great thrill while on Watch - saw the arrival around the ship of a number of albertrosses. One squatted on the yardarm. They looked enormous, a wing span of about eight feet, they were both beautiful and graceful with a snowy white undercarriage, a black upper body, with black bars on their wings. They took off from the water like a flying boat with frenzied paddling of their great webbed feet, creating a bow wave with their chest.

I loved these Watches in the small hours of the night. You were alone, away from the madding crowd, there was peace, quiet, you could think, ponder, reminisce; all these things were virtually impossible in the mad mad world of the messdecks. The only sounds other than the rhythmical throb of the Kent's turbines and the swish, swish, swish of the bow waves, were all soft indeterminate noises that accompany objects in motion. The small talk in the wheelhouse had been expended and the usual cups of pussers' kye had been downed. A great favourite at sea, pussers' came in big thick slabs. They were basically slabs of chocolate, or cocoa, jammed full of vitamins and always looked like oily sludge. It was particularly welcome on cold and wet nights but was still a popular evening drink in the Tropics. It was very probably introduced into the messdecks, like most other things, by one Horatio Nelson.

The lull in the back chat was broken by the Quartermaster at the wheel, 'Speakie' Lowe: "There's land ahead, Mr Christian," he intoned, giving a perfect impression of Charles Laughton in the *Bounty*.

I raised my powerful night binoculars and focused intently ahead.

"Land, I can't see no land ahead," I replied. Keeping up the act Speakie replied "An officer's an officer and a Midshipman's a Midshipman but a 'Spro' AB still wet behind the ears, is the lowest form of life in the Royal Navy."

There was laughter all round at this brilliant bit of mimicry. Returning to his normal voice with its faint Wiltshire burr he said: "See that very faint glow right down on the horizon Lofts? Well that's Durban."

I raised my glasses again and sure enough there ahead was a very small area of light. Speakie, a three badger (ten years' service), had been entering harbours for a very long time.

The arc of light gradually grew, like a giant mushroom and little individual balls of bright lights appeared one after another on the horizon. They slowly grew until they stretched out like an enormous string of fairy lights. The Navigator of the Charthouse had by the magic of a pencil, a ruler, Greenwich Mean Time and a Chart, drawn centuries ago by an ancient chartologits, pointed the bows of Kent straight in the direction of the entrance to the port of Durban.

Chapter 12

The beautiful, always mysterious dawn had long since broken when *Kent* nosed its way into harbour. The almost eternal blue sky and the golden sun shone down with an English degree of comfort. The entire guard rails of the Kent were lined with the ship's company whose very tropical rig looked even whiter than usual. The shoes had a fresh shine and every back appeared to be that bit straighter. The crew knew that this was a special visit to a special place and, to a man, they were proud of the spectacle they knew they provided.

We were tying up to a jetty which was always preferable to anchoring in the harbour, particularly when there was a good run ashore in prospect. No-one was prepared for the scene that greeted us. Held back behind barriers, controlled by the local police were hoards of cheering people, many waving Union Jacks. We were completely taken aback by the fervour of our welcome and a bit mystified as to its reason. It was as though we had just returned from a famous victory at sea.

The men off Watch were busily climbing into their tiddly suits, ready when "liberty men" was piped to dash ashore and savour the delights of Durban. Duly inspected they strolled down the gangway, prepared to follow the usual practice of piling into taxis and ordering the driver to take them to the "best boozer in town". What happened next was beyond belief. As we watched, the waiting, welcoming throng literally fought each other to grab the lads as they approached the barrier and whisked them into waiting cars and away.

I was Watch aboard and I had to be content with viewing Durban from the deck of *Kent*. It was an impressive harbour, surprisingly modern, with industrious tugs busily scurrying across the water plying between a wide variety of shipping and many corners of the globe. I remembered how impressed I was with the Durban skyline, as we approached the harbour entrance, like a miniature New York I thought. It all tended to whet my appetite for my run ashore the following day. The returning liberty men only added to my anticipation with their stories of the quite unbelievable hospitality offered ashore.

The main bulk of the Watch ashore liberty men had long left and just a few stragglers strolled leisurely through the dockside gates. I suppose on that particular run ashore I needed to be alone. I sometimes needed to be by myself and do my own thing. Heading for town I reflected that it was the first dockside area I had ever passed through that wasn't seedy, run down and generally tawdry. I was soon to find the reason for this, a state of affairs that exists to this day and is still only being addressed at the periphery. Apartheid, the separation of a nation into have and have nots, solely because of the colour of their skin. The taxi driver pulled up, opened the door for me to board and drove me to the City Square. I had obtained a small amount of Rand from an oppo aboard and reached into my belt pouch for the money to pay him.

"Ev thees royd on me meesta," he intoned in that awful sort of gutteral English spoken in South Africa. I remonstrated but he waved his arm, put the cab into gear and drove off.

I knew I would bump into some of the lads and made my way into a bar and ordered my first drink. The barman placed it before me and I reached for the money to pay.

There was the noise of a coin being banged on the counter and a voice at the end of the bar called "Over here barman", and so this generosity continued. Crossing the square in front of the Civic Hall I saw for the first time the Zulus and their rickshaws. First impressions took in their magnificent headdress of multicoloured feathers, they looked a fine sight. I accepted the offer of a sightseeing ride around town. He took me the length of the very impressive West Street, not unlike London's Regent Street, I thought. I took in the fine shops and the fashionable ladies, there were calls and hand-waves from oppos enjoying the sights. We turned off and travelled the lovely seafront with its luxury hotels and stylish high rise accommodation. I alighted on the seafront and paid off my Zulu warrior. That's how I know the Zulus from films, depicting them as braves. As he trotted away, I reflected that it was very undignified to see any man pulling a carriage along with another human as a passenger and immediately changed my opinion about them looking a fine site and concluded that it demeaned them.

It was a lovely seafront and as I strolled along at peace with the world, I reflected upon how long it was since I had been completely alone and isolated from the pack. I felt good. I had known from the very beginning that, if I was truthful, I was a round peg in a square hole and although I could never be completely immersed and part and parcel of this mad Naval world I was now in, I was completely intrigued and fascinated by it. I loved the outrageous characters, their attitude to life and would not have missed it all for the world. Always at the back of my mind was the knowledge that I would soon be back in civvy street. How wrong I was.

My isolation and train of thought was broken by the screech of brakes as a taxi pulled up and leaning out of the window I beheld the grinning face of Alex, alias Fender Belly, Alexander. The two other occupants were both fellow HOs, Bill Abbey and a future bain of my life, an Aberdonian 'Jock' Keith. I remembered earlier at tot time giving Bill Abbey 'sippers' and upon seeing him remembered it was his birthday. "Bin looking for you Lofts," Abbey said to me. "Wot's all the Greta Garbo stuff about? Come on, we're going to the Regal for big eats and it's on Abbey." Bill had attended my birthday party in Blighty. "Won't be as good as yours Phil," he said, "but come on, let's celebrate."

"*Regal*," Alex told the taxi driver and we were on our way to a venue that would normally be beyond our finances, but the endless days at sea and the lack of shoreside facilities at our Columbo base meant we were fairly flush. We entered the Regal and I reflected such venues would be the province of officers only in most ports of call.

Jock Keith was a smooth talking Scot who was capable of talking himself out of or into anything. He was short with a pock marked face. He had a quite irritating perpetual tight-mouthed smile and he certainly fancied himself with the ladies.

We were attracting a little attention all of it I must say good humoured, when Haggis left the table, made his way to the vacant stage and took the mike in his hand. Among other pronouncements, he made one telling all the clientele how lucky they were to have among them a well known pianist who, he was sure, with a little encouragement, would entertain them with a few numbers. He was, of course, referring to me. I was completely embarrassed. This was typical of his attitude, he was absolutely full of flannel. Most people I found grossly exaggerated my prowess on the keyboard and because I could play most popular music fairly well in three or four different keys, their untrained ears thought I was Fats Waller. However, once I had put the exaggeration of this introduction behind me, I got into my routine. It worked. It always did. I never ceased to be amazed at the popularity of a piano, playing the right tunes in the right atmosphere. By the same token I was quite well aware that if I had played completely out of tune, I knew that on that night any matelot off the *Kent* would have given me an ovation, such was their unbelievable fervour.

I returned to my table to join my oppos where we finished off our drinks. Bill Abbey called our waiter to get the bill for our food and drinks, the waiter held out his hands and said there was nothing to pay, someone had met our bill and left without a word. It was all unbelievable to every one of us. It was a birthday Bill Abbey would be unlikely to forget.

At breakfast the messdeck was buzzing with excitement as one after another we related our experiences of the previous day. There were already stories of romances and three ratings had gone Awol.

Today *HMS Kent* would be performing a normally peace time duty, we would be showing the flag.

Aboard Kent rifles were issued to be cleaned and polished, white belts, gaitors and hats had to be blanco'd to a brilliant white. The full ceremonial Royal Marines Band had probably been without sleep as the tiddlied up their uniforms and instruments. Around eight hundred officers and men would take over the centre of Durban. After what seemed an eternity we all mustered on the jetty. There were a few moments of chaos and we all shuffled about and spaced ourselves out. At first individual orders to different units echoed along the jetty. Then the Company Sergeant Major took charge of the whole assembly and in Naval tradition three abreast, we were ready for the off. "Forward March," he bellowed in a voice that probably reached the Town Hall.

There is, I am sure, no sight to compare with that of the RN on the march. The majestic six foot-plus Mace Bearer leading the RM full ceremonial band, the red, blue and gold of their uniforms, the white pith helmets which made them look that much taller, the shine and glitter of their instruments and Jack in his Navy blue set off with a Cambridge blue, white lined 'dickie' and white hat, belt and gaitors. The colourful scene was something that the Army's khaki or the RAF's greyish blue just could not match. There is something different, something perhaps romantic about seeing men of the sea marching with military precision on dry land. Then there is the very nature and timbre of their music found in the Naval marching songs.

The band had entered West Street just tapping out the marching rhythm on the side of drums. Now the whole column was in line they struck up with the *Kent's* own marching song, The White Horse Inn, chosen because the ship's crest was Pegasus the flying white horse. Then followed *Hearts of Oak*, *Anchors Aweigh*, *Sons of the Sea*, all guaranteed to raise the emotions. We were halted in the square in front of the City Hall. The square was a sea of faces. It was strong, stirring, emotional stuff, this was wartime, patriotism was flowing through everyone's veins, no-one could stand outside it, it gripped you and that is exactly what it was supposed to do. This was blatant propaganda, a very necessary propaganda at that time, people needed this to spur them on to greater effort to overcome the horror and the sacrifice that came with total war. My guess is that every man on that march was walking tall and even an old sceptic of the system like me would just at that time probably have signed on for twelve years.

Chapter 13

That evening we were entertained in the magnificent City Hall. It seemed, looking round the huge hall, every eligible lady in Durban was present and I guess some ineligible ones as well. This reads like a dream but this was not dream, this really was Durban in the very early days of the war.

There was no need to sort out your ladies for they all came looking for you, and so it was that I met Mary. Mary the anonymous face in the crowd who, it transpired, had, unbeknown to me, been dining with her parents on the night I played the piano at Bill Abbey's birthday celebrations. It was her parents that had paid for our celebrations as they left.

There were two orchestras providing the music and the first waltz of the evening set this momentous of all evenings on its way. What followed reminded me of a film I had recently seen set in the campus of an American university. It was the evening of the Campus Ball and the girls were making bee lines for the beau of their choice; so it was this evening. I was blissfully unaware that a fair haired, blue eyed, tall and slender beauty was homing in on me. In a preconceived plan she had strategically placed herself in my vicinity to make sure that the first waltz was going to be ours. This was like all your birthdays and Christmasses rolled into one unforgettable day.

I was swept off my feet, it's no use my denying it. I was flattered, my ego was boosted sky high. From the first dance we only had eyes for each other and by the end of that dance I had learned that Mary had first seen me as I mounted the stage in the Regal to play the piano.

I had met a fair haired blue eyed beauty. I was flattered by her attention but I knew that the chances were that I would never pass this way again. We were on the floor together dancing at every opportunity, but always in the back of my mind was the thought that I would have to be back aboard by midnight. The only connection between the Ball we were at and Cinderella's Ball was that if I was not back aboard by midnight, the only thing I would turn into was a man under punishment.

The last waltz was drawing near, all the ingredients of love at first sight were there. I had been through the whole gamut of emotions. During our first dance you could have driven a taxi between us and we walked back separately to her parents' table. Now we were holding each other so close that there was hardly room to place a cigarette paper between us and our arms were round each other as we returned to the table. The contact continued as we held hands. I had brushed her cheek with a kiss, softly kissed her lips and now, a short six or seven hours after meeting, we were oblivious to everyone and tasting each other's emotions in the long drawn out kisses of a couple in love. I knew the futility of it all, I doubt then if Mary did.

To a woman who thinks she's in love, princes and fairy tales do really exist, but sorrowfully, I knew that she was going to get hurt. Although I cursed the common sense, practicality of my reasoning, I also knew that I was right. A further eight of the crew had been through the same traumatic experience and deserted, including a Leading Hand who was already married. The Kent was to sail from Durban less eleven of her crew.

How strange that Jack virtually shunned by settlers in times of peace should be feted to the heights of heroes in SA, a country where Apartheid laws made it as obnoxious as the very enemy we were at war with. For the Nazis had been attempting to breed a pure Aryan white race by the process of death camps for some time.

"D'ye hear there, hands to muster, prepare for sea." We cast off in the heat of the midday sun, there were hundreds of people at all the vantage points to wave us farewell. There would be many sad faces among them as there would in the spick and span crew who were once again lining the upper deck in the traditional leaving and entering harbour routine. Mary, I knew, would be there, anonymous in the crowd as she was when she first saw me and I sincerely hoped she was not too unhappy.

We cleared the harbour entrance and said farewell to a great city where we had been given a great time by a great set of people.

It was desperately hard to get the visit to Durban out of your system, even for those who were not starry eyed with romance. We cast off from Mayden Wharf just before noon and once again were given a tremendous farewell. These fantastic people were waving from every vantage point as we left harbour.

The fate of the deserters crossed my mind as I recalled that the last act before leaving Mayden Wharf was to throw the kit of the four deserters who had failed to return to ship, on the jetty. It was going to be tough out there now and I fleetingly wished that I was one of their number. It would be very difficult for them. They would be relentlessly pursued and they would be living a clandestine existence and always looking over their shoulders.

The next port of call would be in sharp contrast to the city of Durban. We made a *rendez vous* with our convoy which contained some famous liners, Devonshire, Lancashire, Delwara, Talaba, Rajula and Rhona. We were Northward bound to the port of Mombasa, the main seaport of Kenya.

Italy's entry into the war put us within easy range of air attack as we neared our destination. Intelligence said that Italy had eight subs operating in these waters. Quite unbelievably they were to lose four in quick succession. The trawler *Moonstone* and destroyer Kandahar got one each, one ran aground on a reef and the fourth was rammed and sunk by *Falmouth.* This was great news and cheered everyone immensely, but I was still hearing both Officers and men hoping for action on the four inch gun AA platform. To everyone's surprise, we completed the journey without incident. Mombasa was instantly forgettable.

Kent was now aware that there was a war on, we were still on the periphery of the real action but one sub is all that is needed to despatch you to the depths. There were at least two that had looked at us with that object in mind and there may have been others that we knew nothing about. One thing was sure, the war was hotting up. It was making the return to civvy street seem further and further away.

Today there is a burial party, one of our oppos had died aboard. The circumstances of his death were horrendous. I have spoken of the men aboard who, regardless of the dangers and the consequences, are prepared to frequent the dens of iniquity that abound in all sea ports. It could be argued that they are catering for the needs of certain people in society and the fact that they are frequented justifies that claim. Their existence could also possibly be excused by the colloquialism I first heard aboard ship and that is that "an erect penis has no conscience".

Even amongst time serving matelots there was a surprisingly high percentage of celibacy, especially with the married or engaged men. How do I know? The messdeck I soon found is an open sort of confessional for all subjects and facets of life. Everyone knew who were the fanny rats amongst us, everyone knew if married or engaged men were 'having a dabble' and no-one cared two hoots, that was not your business.

Aboard many ships of the Navy were what were known as 'prophylactic chambers'. These were compartments where if you were seeking company of the opposite sex for the night not necessarily in a brothel but any female ashore, you could acquire condoms. They were issued free. On returning to ship after an encounter you were advised to visit the 'bougey' chamber, the matelots' name for it. Here you first of all washed the relevant parts in Condy's crystals solution, a disinfectant, and also squirted the same solution down the eye of your penis with a bougey pump, hence the name.

An indelicate story perhaps, but it emphasises the importance the authorities placed on the prevention of VD. There were then, I understand, five different diseases on offer, each one more horrendous than the rest. Obviously they were notifiably listed diseases and infections, but no-one who had participated knew if they had a dose until the incubation period had ended. The unlucky ones were confined to a special isolated mess known romantically as Rose Cottage throughout the Navy. Apart from being isolated from your oppos, you suffered severe loss of privileges. You remained in that mess until pronounced clean or in many cases until you reached port and were dispatched to hospital. Oh, mother, is it worth it? Some could be treated but they knew it could recur at any time, and that included when they were at home on leave, if you were serving in home waters.

The young man being buried today had died in the isolation ward of Cerebral Syphilis. His family would get a letter that he had died from an accident or perhaps 'in action'. The latter perhaps was ironic. That burial was, perhaps, a salutary lesson to some aboard and to many more it would make the course of their celibacy that much easier to confront. It was some couple of days before the ship got back to its usual state of potty normality.

There were five ships in the convoy. Italy's entry into the war had further stretched our naval resources and the area of safe waters was gradually diminishing. Our last excursion to the Gulf of Aden had passed without incident and some surprise had been expressed as to the failure of the Italians to use their available air power.

The messdeck was at breakfast and the explosion was clearly felt. The call to action stations followed almost immediately. I reached the four inch gun platform and looked across to port and saw the stricken ship. I was witnessing my very first act of war and my first reaction was one of apprehension. My thoughts then turned to the crew who would now be fighting for their survival. *Suffren*, our French oppos, was already standing by to pick up survivors.

The convoy continued on its way, that was always the order, no matter what the situation. The danger of our situation was now becoming much clearer to me. We had no Ascic (submarine detector equipment), the subs consequently held all the aces. The attack was somewhat mystifying to our Command. Why had they only attacked one ship? Why hadn't they gone for the bigger prize of the escorting cruisers? I must confess, I was grateful. It brought into focus something we all, of necessity, put to the back of our minds.

What would it be like when, and if, it happened? We were all at some time below decks to eat, to sleep, to work part of the ship. Always when these thoughts appeared in my mind, I was selfishly grateful that at least my action station was on the upper deck where you had a better chance against underwater attack. Deep in the bowels of the ship the stokers and engineer room crew, magazine, ammunition lockers and repair parties were behind locked, watertight doors. I must emphasise that these morbid thoughts would only manifest themselves at such times as this. Aden had suffered a very heavy air attack but when we entered harbour there was little evidence of any serious damage and we were raid free during our stay. I heard Guns prophesy that this time our four inch AA platform would swing into action, he was desperate to see it in action.

To my relief we left harbour to shadow the French armed Merchantman *Captain Caraibe.* This event took place at the same time as the three French fleets in Alex, Oman and Dakar were giving us so much trouble with their divided allegiances. We never knew at this stage who was friend and who was foe.

We shadowed the Captain Caraibe at about four miles astern. At dawn actions stations we got orders to make her return to Mombasa and, if she did not comply, sink her. We ordered her to stop engines and silence her W/T. During the interchange she received a message which we could not decipher, so we jammed her transmission. She then complied without orders and returned to Mombasa. What followed was a complete diplomatic and Naval cock-up. She had time to dismantle her gun breeches and throw all her depth charges and pistols overboard, rendering her useless as a possible addition to our fighting strength. Some of the officers aboard were furious and openly said we should have sunk her.

Chapter 14

The next thing I heard had nothing to do with shells and bombs. Quite the contrary. It was the wonderful news that we were heading South for Durban. There was quite audible cheering on the messdeck when the news became known. The journey South was completed in quite surprisingly rough weather, when we were tossed about like a cork. It was therefore fitting that as we neared Durban, the weather abated and we arrived off Durban in one of the most spectacular sunrises I had ever seen.

We had done a lot of sea time lately and that made Durban a particularly welcome sight. We entered harbour at about 10.30am through the surprisingly narrow piers. It was belting with rain and we headed for the extreme end of the harbour.

These Durban people really were quite amazing, here they were once again, waiting with their cars to whisk us away and entertain us with their own brand of quite remarkable hospitality. I was Watch ashore and this time I got into my best tiddly suit, an extra comb of the hair, perhaps a more vigorous rub of the toothbrush, a final brush of my shoes on the back of my trousers and I was over the gangway with the first of them.

Mary's address and phone number were in my pocket. I headed for the nearest phone, politely refusing at least two offers of a car. I reflected afterwards that they must have viewed my refusals as strange. Preoccupied with finding a phone I was startled to hear my name called. I looked up and to my utmost delight and total surprise, the lovely figure of Mary was running towards me. We fell into each other's arms and kissed unashamedly, oblivious to everything around us. It was a wonderful moment. Nothing remotely like it had ever happened to me before. In truth it is likely that only in wartime Durban could such things happen anyway. Everywhere else that *Kent* had taken me such lovelies as Mary were the province of officers only, never did the lower deck get within speaking distance of someone like Mary. Female company was always almost exclusively from shoreside brothels. As high as a kite. I hailed a taxi, sat in the back and caught up with events.

"How did you know about Kent?" I asked.

"Easy," she said, "there's another ship like yours already in harbour." It was the *Cumberland*. "When you had entered the harbour, it only needed a judicious phone call from Daddy, and I was off in a taxi. I just knew you would be back," she said. On such long shots, perhaps the dreams of women are often hinged.

We alighted from the taxi at the beautiful Marine Beach. I was surrounded by opulence and affluence. Everything about it exuded class. We took two chairs on the beach and, holding her hand, I closed my eyes and let my mind go back to Dagenham, the squalid London Docks, the hot stinking cable factory, and then I thought of my hero, one Cornelius Finbar Driscoll, and I smiled, I loved him. "What are you smiling at?" Mary asked me. It would have been difficult to explain so I merely said: "An Irish Leprechaun."

Mary said: "Let's go home and see Mum and Dad and tonight we will all go to the Blue Lagoon."

"What's the *Blue Lagoon*?" I asked, "a swimming pool?"

"No," she replied, "it's a smashing outdoor gardens where we can dance in the moonlight to a great band, in the most romantic of settings."

Mary wasn't exaggerating. Her father parked the car and a short walk took us to our venue. It was quite magnificent. The first thing that caught my eye was the dance floor, which appeared to be marbled. It was probably the marvellous lighting effects. It was in effect an amphitheatre with seating and tables rising in layers from the floor. The lighting, the trees and shrubs made it like a scene from a film, and we two were romantic leads.

The last waltz was ours and as far as we were concerned we were the only couple on the floor. Our goodnight kiss at the dockside was just a lingering au revoir, because we both knew that unless something unforeseen happened, we would be together again for at least one more night.

What a wonderful night the city of Durban had given us once again but when we went down onto the messdeck, our high spirits were quickly dampened when Furness and Abbey drew us aside and quietly told us that Scouse Walker was doing a runner that night. Hopelessly in love he was deserting ship to run away with his lady love. He left a letter for his family and a couple of personal items with Bill Abbey for him to deliver in the UK. If apprehended he faced one of the most serious charges in the Navy, desertion, second only to "in face of the enemy".

My thoughts rushed straight away to Mary. We would both appreciate the dilemma of Scouse. Had he perhaps made the right decision? Scouse, like me had been forced to join up by the Conscription Act and now he could survive to marry and live happily ever after in the safety and sunshine of South Africa. How long would I be remembered should I get blown sky high when next the *Kent* left harbour? By my family yes, but to the authorities I would be just one more expendable statistic. Likewise my enemies in the Germany and Italian Navies; we were trying to blow each other out of existence at the bidding of our masters. It didn't matter who was right and who was wrong. Jack was in endless supply to all three Navies, young, fit men willing to do their bidding.

It is dangerous to philosophise in times like these. A necessary armour in your fight to justify what you are suffering, is the justness of the cause you are fighting for. Therefore, it's got to be out with the philosophy and in with total blind allegiance, so it's "Rule Britannia ...". I was having a real tough battle trying to restore the equilibrium of my thoughts. When I eventually went to the land of nod it was to dream, not of Mary, Durban and war, but of the simple, uncomplicated peaceful Saturday and Sunday nights dancing at the 'tanner hops' at our local Church Halls. Now that really would be heaven.

"Wakey, wakey, lash up and stow away. Wakey, wakey, lash up and stow," etc.

I now found myself clockwatching, doing things twice and just generally getting through the day with a complete lack of concentration. Willing the clock hands round to 1300 hours and the first liberty boat. I was experiencing the classic symptoms of a first love, but this was something quite different. My scenario wasn't the tanner hop or the local boating lake. It was set in wartime in a distant land, a sailor returning from the battle to a city of beauty and affluence, far above my station in life. A beautiful girl, but a romance that was perhaps doomed to failure right from the moment it began, across a crowded room.

I dressed at least one hour too early and the liberty boat sped me across the harbour in a mood of elation, mixed with despair. We arrived at the end of Mayden Wharf together. It was no use, as soon as I saw her, all my resolution evaporated. We held each other closely, quietly and when we boarded the taxi I could just then have said to the driver "take the road North out of Durban and keep driving," but common sense then took over and I settled for the WVS Restaurant in West Street. It was essential to keep with the crowd and be occupied.

The afternoon took care of itself as Mary wanted to see the film on show. We walked to the Metro cinema, the film was followed by the Pathe News and I was completely unprepared for what followed. There was a news item (propaganda really) showing a convoy under attack and as soon as a destroyer crossed the screen, they were all standing up and cheering. It was quite unbelievable behaviour and was apparently only reserved for the RN.

They were a people small in number, isolated from their homeland and surrounded by the indigenous population of the vast African continent. They looked to us to protect them and keep the sea lanes open for their essential supplies to be maintained. Mary squeezed my hand and gently kissed my cheek. Again, the next move was easy, we walked to the Regal where I knew most of the lads were having their farewell party. By the sound of it the wine must have flowed freely and I can tell you that our entrance was anything but anonymous.

I admit I didn't mind the publicity, it was a privilege to have someone like Mary on your arm and the very lively atmosphere was just what we needed tonight.

When I mounted the stage to the piano, I looked across at Mary and I think she knew what was in my mind, for it was fitting that it should end where it had begun. It was a happy, noisy, if sometimes off key, sing-song and the locals just loved it. It ended with the rather touching Maori Farewell, "Now is the hour when we must say goodbye."

The crunch was about to come and I was fighting to keep my cool, my heart was racing as we alighted from the taxi to say our goodbyes. I had carefully rehearsed it a dozen times in my mind. We held each other and I kissed her tenderly, it was when I gently kissed her cheek that it all fell to pieces, for a tear was falling down her face. I instinctively held her close once again and she was sobbing when she whispered "Please come back to me." I lamely replied "Yes, of course I will." We parted and I made for the ladder down to the liberty boat, her hand was raised in farewell, as my head sank below the level of the jetty to board the liberty boat.

The lads in the boat were all tanked up to the eyebrows, perhaps they were the wise ones, to them it was just a matelots' run ashore. Roll on next port was their philosophy, they were right of course. Don't get yourself involved, there's a girl in every port.

I knew that I had just been suffering the pangs of a first love, a genuine first love, in a hopeless set of circumstances. It was a tough world.

We left Durban and as the gangway was raised once again, the very last act was to throw the hammocks and belongings of the deserters into a tender alongside. It seemed to heighten the drama of their actions and I thought in particular of Scouse Walker who was a fellow HO and had trained with me at Chatham.

Chapter 15

Heading South at what appeared to be full speed, the clatter of our Aldis lamp shutters told us we were in communication with three distant ships. It would prove to be one of the most memorable convoys of the war. Heading South to where we now knew was Australia, we were accompanying three of the world's greatest liners, *The Queen Mary*, *Aquitania* and *The Mauritania*. It was an awesome sight. Unlike most wartime convoys there was to be no zig zagging, this time it was full speed ahead as the four of us made a beeline for the port of Freemantle in Western Australia.

We arrived without incident to embark thousands of Aussie troops for duty in the Western Desert of Africa.

The high spirited Aussies were to give us a few headaches on the long journey to Columbo. Three times we had problems with 'man overboard' and we only rescued one. Our biggest headache on this trip was, however, the weather. It was horrendous, the seas were mountainous and sweeping over our Bridge structure. Everything had to be lashed and secured and life lines were run the length of the deck for the safety of men who had to traverse the upper deck to get to their place on Watch. It lasted nearly three days and the mighty liners did not escape its anger either. The anchor worked loose and had been making an awful noise, clanging in the hawse pipe.

We were glad to make Columbo and we went straight into dock for repairs, we had severe damage. The harbour was chokka with ships and the Queen Mary had to go round to Trinco to berth. All the ships suffered some damage and they discharged a number of casualties to hospital. The *Kent* was encrusted with salt and no-one was looking forward to the pipe "Hands to clean ship", but that was for tomorrow. Mercifully we were granted a 'make and mend' that afternoon.

My hammock had never been so welcome, particularly after our Durban excursion, which had the effect of putting our spartan life aboard ship into sharp perspective. Everyone aboard was suffering from the hangover of Durban. We had, though, just had a real battering and everyone was played out. When I climbed into my hammock I had a good chuckle when I remembered Shorty Munsen's crack. We were in the teeth of the gale, desperately trying to keep our feet as we went about our duties, when he said "You don't call this rough do you? This is a cruise liner. The last boat I was on had nets on the top of the funnels to keep the stokers in, when the weather was like this."

When next we left Columbo it was for the purpose of a practice shoot. This one involved the whole of Kent's armaments. I had been through many dry runs, both at sea and in harbour. It was going to be an attack, simulating an actual engagement with the enemy. The cruiser *HMS Gloucester* was to be the enemy, it also involved the target ship Widnes. The order to fire was given in succession to A and B guns, then to X and Y. The impact of the detonation seemed to press the starboard side of *Kent* into the water, for it sprang back like a cork. There then followed a broadside from all eight guns, which seemed to suck the very air from around you, the impact was enormous.

I was at my action station of No five P1 gun, a twin four inch AA gun. A plane overhead was towing a wind sock or droque, this brought the order "load, load, load" from the Gun Captain. The all enveloping crump, crump of the eight inch was now joined by the ear splitting crack of the four inch. At first I was petrified, the noise was horrendous. I had to co-ordinate with the rest of the Guns Crew.

So this was what it was going to be like if and when we faced the enemy. I can tell you I didn't like it very much. Is this really what the ship's company was itching to get into? All these thoughts were racing through my mind. I concentrated my mind once more, the crew would be watching me and that was enough. I had wondered why orders were always screamed, the noise of the firing was awesome. The dummy action continued. I had got into the swing of it but I was glad when it ended. The order "cease fire" was given and the quiet was a relief to my ears. My nostrils were filled with the acrid, pungent smell of cordite. My head and ears were still ringing from the assault of the four inch guns' earsplitting crack.

Everyone was apparently delighted with the success of the shoot, from the Gunnery Officer down to Tim O'Gara, who gave me a friendly pat on the back and said "Well done Lofts." I just about heard him, my head still felt as if it had been inside a bell, while someone struck it with a fourteen pound hammer.

I marvelled at the discipline of these men and their intense desire to be the best. I assumed that they had been no less affected than myself. I was to find out later to my cost that it was not so.

We were heading for Trincomalee, which you could be forgiven for thinking was a town in the Emerald Isle, but was an exotic haven of peace that would delight any shipwrecked mariner. Azure sea, long sandy beach with waving palms and a gradual rise to the summit to light your rescue beacon. The island in the bay was known as Sober Island, for some reason or another, and here for more than a century any RN ship right back to the days of sail could anchor and relax. It was owned and maintained by the Navy and a working party was being organised to effect some repairs. I was delighted to find myself a member of the mixed party of Doc, Engines and Torps, all officers and about twelve seamen and a Leading Hand.

We left in the pinnace and stopped some way out and dropped a small explosive charge overboard. The plume rose and with it came an assortment of exotic coloured fish. Doc quickly identified the edible ones we would take ashore on our desert island. We landed and proceeded with an assortment of paint, tools and rope and timber to begin our chores. As we crossed the silver sand and climbed the patch to the 'lodge', it was easy to let your imagination run riot. Pigtailed seamen with headbands and knives between their teeth and eye patches, carrying barrels of salt port and rum. We reached the lodge and, would you believe it, the first thing we did was to renew the flag on the mast. It was a Jolly Roger. It was a tradition for every party using the lodge to hoist it, ever since the days of sail.

The view was breathtaking, you just run out of suitable adjectives to describe it adequately. It was one of the happiest days for me. The officers and men completely relaxed in each other's company. How different it was aboard ship with its status barriers. We repaired paintwork, awnings and the diving board and pontoon. It may seem incongruous that HM Navy should be more or less holiday making on this very beautiful island as if it was a peacetime romp. The lodge of course was only for the use of officers. The custodian was known as Parangu and he provided us with beer and sandwiches. It was a day to remember and everyone was reluctant to return to the heat and sweat of the messdecks and the tedious routine.

How lucky I had been in my travels aboard Kent. I had seen and experienced events, exciting, bizarre and beautiful. There was danger around, but so far we had traversed thousands of miles of ocean in comparative safety.

Where the luck of your draft chit led you was a lottery in the fortunes of war. I could have been directed to a destroyer that was 'shipping them green', right over the Fo'castle and Bridge in the cold, inhospitable grey and dangerous waters of the Atlantic, or running the gauntlet of the

Russian convoys. I wondered if perhaps I would swap my lot for the chance to get home amongst all the familiar things I love? A 'boiler clean' and a few days' leave, perhaps only a weekend or even a night's leave. Right now the joy of being able to see my home, my family and my friends, completely overrode any thought of the danger.

Mail from home was virtually non-existent. Mail was, like everything else in transit, subject to mine, torpedo and air attack. In addition, *Kent* was moving not only from country to country, but also from continent to continent, so the delivery of your mail became a paper chase. Eventually the absence of mail was stoically accepted as a casualty of war. Didn't someone say that "no news is good news"? We were getting plenty of good news if that was so.

Then again, another burden we had to endure was the messdeck temperatures of nearly one hundred degrees. Everything below deck was saturated with condensation, this brought on assorted heat rashes, 'Dhobey itch' and Chinese foot rot. Your body was still sweating in the course of taking a shower, this was all very debilitating. However, I will concede that just at this time, my oppos at home were getting the worst of it.

Chapter 16

We were off again, this time to screen the flank of a convoy which was skirting the Maldives en route for Columbo. It comprised of Dunera, Ettrick and Strathaird, plus two smaller vessels *Ramilles* and *Suffren* were the escorts.

Alone in the middle of the ocean you are given a clear indication of a man's insignificance in relation to the universe around him. We had been under way for three days, alone apart from our constant travelling companions the dolphins and the acrobatic flying fish. It occurred to me in the quiet of the Middle Watch, that Kent was like a single chocolate in the centre of a giant Easter Egg and the brilliant starlit sky was a silver wrapping covering it from horizon to horizon.

We had now closed in on the convoy and approached it bows on. I was looking forward to seeing my very first battleship. *Ramilles* was twenty four thousand tons with eight fifteen inch, twelve six inch and eight four inch guns. She looked unbelievably wide and she appeared to be a huge triangle. I was to get a further treat when she carried out a fifteen inch gun shoot, it was tremendous to witness for the first time and the Officer On Watch said it was about three thousand yards spread, the biggest he had ever seen.

Approaching Columbo we experienced wind, rain and seas of horrendous proportions. The monsoons had arrived, we moored with seas sweeping over the harbour walls. There was huge loss of life ashore and there were areas where the water was forty feet deep. This, of course, is a natural phenomenon in this part of the world, but it was said to be the worst in living memory.

It was now nearly six months since I had left the shores of England, which was exactly the length of time I was called up to serve in the Navy. The outbreak of war put paid to that. How much longer would my services be required? I then wondered. It was something that was often on my mind.

We were all excited to find that mail had at last arrived aboard Kent. I still only had received about seven or eight letters and four of them were from home. It may have been because of meeting Mary, but I opened the letters from home first. There was little in them to suggest that things were in any way difficult, which was rather surprising. They told me that everyone was working flat out; provided you could get to the workplace, you were employable. My simple mind had not then worked out why we could afford to make weapons of destruction, yet in time of peace we were unable to find work for millions of our people.

We were once again under way, now knowing our destination but a tantalising hint was safe enough. We were at sea again and I was happy. I hated the torrid, energy-sapping heat of the messdeck, at times the mere action of lifting your arm made the sweat pour from your body. There were those who suffered it in preference to the endless hours of Watchkeeping at sea. Many suffered Dhobey rash, Chinese toe rot and a variety of skin rashes. In spite of being free of these maladies, I was always happy to hear the pipe "prepare for sea".

I was due for promotion to Able Seaman and the event gave me food for thought. It was a natural progression from Ordinary Seaman and with most time serving men it was the limit of their ambition. To reach my next step of Leading Seaman meant exams which meant study and this was not on the itinerary of your average matelot. I already knew that I would be joining your average matelot in not wanting to know. I, however, had consciously made the decision for I had never taken kindly to the many mindless things about this lifestyle. In spite of this I had schooled myself right from my days at Skeggie to behave myself. I have said before, there is no democracy aboard and if you revolted against the system, there was only one winner and it was never you. I did everything to the best of my ability. In spite of this I had been reported for truculence on an occasion when I found it impossible not to at least show resentment, if only in my face. The disparity between the officers' lifestyle and the ratings' was in my humble opinion bordering on the obscene.

We had got the word, we were on our way, we were going to war. This time it would be the real thing and it is what all the officers and, I think, most of the crew wanted. When we left Columbo we didn't know it would be for the last time. We left with the *Orantes*, but parted company after twenty four hours and proceeded towards Aden. We were in fact on our way to the Mediterranean and things were hotting up. The Italians were stepping up their air attacks in Berbera and Aden.

It was goodbye to the beautiful and exotic island of Ceylon; it was a short six months since I had sailed into Columbo and disembarked from the liner Andes. I had already realised nearly every one of the daydreams that had excited my imagination back in my days working in North Woolwich at Henleys Cables. I had found romance, beauty, virgin desert islands, colourful tropical birds, brilliant flowers and plant life, the wonderful magic of dawns and sunsets that were indescribable and, not forgetting my friends of the lonely seascape, the whales, flying fish and, of course, the graceful, playful dolphins. All this had happened to me in a situation of war when I was aboard a ship that was relentlessly trying to hunt down an enemy that was wreaking havoc on the sea lanes that we were patrolling. In fact, the things of beauty I had seen were a bonus in the pursuit of something that was ugly, violent and obscene, the persecution of an all-out war.

The one thing that eased the pain of leaving this scenario was the dreadful strength-sapping, relentless heat. I never came to terms with it.

Chapter 17

I can't honestly say I was over the moon about our coming Med cruise either. We were going to the Med regardless, but I couldn't honestly subscribe to the attitude of the officers and men who showed annoyance at not being attacked by the Italian Air Force on our previous convoy. This smacked of Jingoism in my book.

The weather became atrocious and after dusk action station visibility was almost reduced to nil.

"Alarm port," came from the Bridge.

According to one of the lads in the mess who was on Bridge duty, *Kent* had been on collision course with one of the new K class destroyers, bows on to each other. He then said that according to the OOW, the Duty Officer ignored the rule of the road and altered course to send us passing each other dangerously close. I reserve my judgement on his claim that he could "smell what meal they were cooking on the K as they passed".

Dawn brought another incident, while at dawn action stations the alarm was sounded and we closed up at first degree.

"Alarm starboard, wheel hard a starboard." We turned swiftly and soon we were running in parallel with two torpedo tracks. We were now steering directly down the centre of them. We had escaped once again and the talk was of the very poor tactics of the Italian subs. We had to rely completely on the keen eyes of the lookouts and, so far, coupled with the inefficiency of the Italians, we were still safe.

Subsequent to the first alarm and the near collision, two seamen were charged with sleeping on duty in face of the enemy. They would now be confined to cells whilst awaiting charges. It was a very serious charge and a blow to the ship's security at sea. I have said before, the lives of everyone below decks was entirely in our hands. Sometimes sleeping was understandable, always, however it was unforgivable.

Aden was just a black, sizzling hot, barren rock and we left without regret to head for the Red Sea and Suez. We proceeded through the dull and hot Red Sea and entered the Sinai Straits where the barren mountains of rock towered up to about six thousand feet.

The moment Kent nosed its way into the canal at Suez you could sense the change in the atmosphere aboard. I again got the feeling that the whole ship's company were welcoming the prospect of some action. They were like the boxer trained to a peak, just waiting for the bell to sound to come out fighting and attempt to prove they were the best. As a crew of around eight hundred they were in the unique position of serving together for two years. Most of the Navy ships were now a hastily mustered mixture of time serving men, Reservists, RNVRs and HOs, which had to be moulded into a trained fighting unit.

It was common knowledge that our resources were stretched to the limit but no-one was prepared for what we were to see next on the banks of the canal. The aircraft housed in the three sided blast shelters were, in fact, wooden dummies, as were the anti aircraft guns. The deception was pretty pointless because the whole area was full of Nazi sympathisers. It did elicit a bit of humour though, Ginger Newall, always ready with a wisecrack, said, "I suppose they man them wiv bleeding wooden men." To which someone promptly replied "Away you go then, they're looking for volunteers." Ginger asked for that one.

We passed through the Bitter Lakes and the long Northern stretch of the canal, which was unerring in its straightness. It was a cue for Torps to give us another one of his pearls of wisdom.

"This is the only place in the world where you get the perfect proof of the curvature of the Earth and you can clearly see it bending over." Many of us observed it from the Fo'castle and it was quite uncanny what a fund of wisdom and knowledge that man possessed.

We cleared the canal and entered Mussolini's Mare Nostrum, his pet name for the Mediterranean Sea. The run to Alexandria was completed without incident. It was inevitable that comparisons would be made in my mind between now and my exit from the Mediterranean in *Andes*. Somehow neither the sea nor the sky seemed quite so blue and romantic now. There were submarines and mines lurking below the surface and enemy aircraft would be clouding the skies, ready to pounce and wreak their havoc.

We entered the boom in Alex and slowly proceeded to our berth. I had never before seen a fleet in harbour. Battleships, aircraft carriers, cruisers, many destroyers, minesweepers and support ships. Each of them was camouflaged in crazy patterns of varying shades of grey. There were many more units at sea, each of them an integral part of a great armada. There were to be a few famous battles fought out between surface ships of the British and Italian Navies. However, most of the ships lost and damaged and men lost and wounded, would be at the hands of subs, mines, torpedo bombers and the fearful JU87 dive bombers. Sadly our defences against air attack had not been given any priority. Admirals were still living in the time of Jutland. The short range weapons to combat the torpedo and dive bomber were woefully inadequate and consisted of 0.5 Vickers machine guns, as used in the first world war trenches, and twenty millimetre pom pom cannons that had a propensity to jam. We had been given options on the Oerlikon gun and failed to take it up until late in the war. Had all our ships been equipped from the onset of war, there would be many more ships and men still afloat and many more enemy planes would have been taken out of action.

If there were few major surface conflicts fought out the capital ships were essential to keep our convoys moving. The Italian fleet was more modern and mostly faster than the British, but they never had the same heart for the fight and seldom ventured out. It was just as well, because the enemy held all the aces.

The long leg of Italy dominated the centre of the Med and the islands of Sardinia and the Dodeconese and the coastline of Libya provided them with bases from which to operate air, sub and torpedo boat attacks. We had only three bases, a thousand miles apart, but they held the key to the front door of the Med in Gibraltar and to the back door at Suez with the brave island of Malta in the centre. Malta, unfortunately, was subject to constant attack from Sicily on the toe of Italy.

The Med would offer no hiding places for the fleet and it was to become even more hazardous with the imminent fall of France and the subsequent loss of land bases including the whole North African coast from Libya to Morocco. This created an impossible situation for the fleets of Gibraltar and Alexandria and the task of keeping the sea lanes open.

The fall of France brought about one more major problem for the RN. France was now a divided nation, one part Vichy, collaborated with the enemy, and the other under De Gaul became freedom fighters and fought the war alongside Britain. The French had major Naval forces in Alexandria and at Bizerta and Oran. They had, therefore, to join with us or be rendered inoperable by consent or force.

Admiral Cunningham was to achieve this end peacefully but Admiral Somerville had to resort to force and this was to further exacerbate the relationship between the former allies.

Our arrival in Alex signalled a period of feverish activity aboard. We immediately took the flag of Rear Admiral Renouf and became Flag Ship of the third cruiser squadron, comprising Kent, Liverpool and Gloucester. Neither officers nor men were particularly overjoyed at this turn of events. *Kent* would now become even more pusser if that were at all possible. We then proceeded to desecrate the immaculate decks of Kent by painting them blue, likewise the tops of the gun turrets and everything exposed to the sky. Apparently the white scrubbed deck helped the bomb aimer when he was endeavouring to drop a couple down your funnels. When I think of the mindless hours we had spent in this useless operation of keeping them white, I could spit, secretly of course I was chuffed.

The macho men who could not wait for bangs, booms and bombs didn't have long to wait. We had no need to look for the enemy, he came looking for us. "Action stations," sounded. "Enemy aircraft approaching."

I proceeded to my gun platform, the searchlights were already scanning the moonlit sky, long fierce blades of light, criss-crossing the sky. They locked on an aircraft almost at once, it was a moth, hopelessly drawn to the light. We fired our first shots in anger, the total barrage was awesome, in the harbour alone there were about forty ships hurling steel into the night. At eye level it was like an immense continuous fire cracker, a stick of bombs fell between us and Warspite. The plumes were enormous. "My God!" I thought. "Is this really what these dumbells aboard had been craving for?" A slight adjustment on his bomb sight and either us or the Warspite would have been searching the twisted metal of our ships for the survivors. This was at nightime we were in harbour, we were at rest. That is the meaning of harbour - a safe haven. The raid didn't last long, or so we thought, the 'candles' went out and as suddenly as the barrage started, it ceased. I stepped back and took a deep breath to clear the pungent smell of cordite from my lungs. Suddenly there was the roar of aircraft engines. It was not the slow monotonous drone of the planes in the sky ten thousand feet above. There were four of them, hedge hopping over the harbour wall. It was incredible, the deafening noise of their engines made it difficult for you to think. We didn't open fire with our short range weapons. *Warspite* had no such inhibitions, however, and we watched in astonishment as the red tracers of the *Warspite*'s pom poms were passing between our funnels at almost, it seemed, eye level. The attack at low level was the very first one attempted on Alex. Had they waited for Kent to berth in the harbour? What were they up to? No-one aboard the ships apparently had seen them release anything in the harbour and it was assumed to have been an abortive aerial torpedo attack. One thing we had learned from the night was who needs enemies when your friends are prepared to open fire on you?

The events of the night brought about the use of the famous London barrage balloon. They were flown all along the harbour wall and off the upper deck of many of the ships at berth.

I was anxious to get the reactions of the crew to our first taste of action. I never saw anyone jumping up and down saying how much they had enjoyed it all. There was one exception, Lt Comm Blundell (Torps), who said it was the most exciting night of his Commission.

The atmosphere on the messdeck was now infectious, as the Watch ashore prepared for "liberty men". Some of the old hands were obviously well acquainted with Alex and they were readily imparting their knowledge to anyone prepared to listen to them 'swinging the lamp'. If it turned out to be half as good as the picture they had painted, then it must be some place.

After the strength sapping torpor of the East Indies heat, Alex was literally like a breath of fresh air and, apart from the occasion when the Sirocco lifted the fine sand of the Sahara in its wake, I found it very agreeable, especially the bonus of the cool evenings.

The liberty boat sped across the harbour towards gate twenty seven in the company of a wide array of small boats, from the Admiral's ornate barge, Captain's motor boats, 'skimming dishes' and at least two crews enjoying a sail in Naval Cutters.

Like most things Naval, the run ashore was to be a set pattern, unless you were in the minority among this strange, mostly predictable band of men, who may opt for a culture run.

The well known fanny rats would head post haste for Mother Mary's brothels in the infamous Sisters Street. In many cases they would end up in Rose Cottage, the outrageous name for the VD mess aboard Kent, cursing their luck for months or even years ahead. A price most sensible men were not prepared to pay.

Once aboard the Gharry you had no need to tell Akmed your destination and Akmed had no need to tell Dobbin, just a flick of the reins and Dobbin was off to the Fleet Club, just as if he had been programmed.

We clip-clopped on our way, through a vibrant, noisy, colourful street scene. As in Port Said the noise level was in mega-decibels. Drivers of the grossly overloaded vehicles were just as demented and the continuous sounding of their horns and hooters suggested that they were operated from the accelerator. Added to this cacophony of sounds were the clanging, rattling noises of the Alex trams, just one more advanced innovation for which Egypt had to thank the French, who had indelibly left their mark throughout Egypt.

The Ghilly, Ghilly and Shoe Shine boys were once again much in evidence but my initial impression was that Alex was a much superior place to Port Said. The buildings were more elegant in places, the variety of shops more evident.

We alighted outside the Fleet Club, an impressive building right in the heart of town. It was everything we had been promised, the Beer Garden was in a landscaped setting, overhung by shady palm trees. Here you could enjoy big eats and quaff your Stella beer. Those entitled to a night's leave could book a room with the luxury of isolation and a bed with clean white crisp sheets to lie between. I will always remember the first night away from the claustrophobic, smoke-filled messdeck where, suspended in space your night's sleep would be shared with a mess mate grunting and snorting in each ear.

At the club there was a games room, a lounge, a quiet room and library. However, the piece de resistance to most matelots was the games of Tombola, now known as Bingo. The winning of just one line could set you up financially for the remainder of your stay in harbour. The Fleet Club was much loved by all matelots on night leave, it was a peace haven away from the harbinger of death which was your home at sea or in harbour.

Already, so early in the conflict, the Requiem of many men and their ships had been intoned around its tables, losses which were to reach horrendous proportions in a short passage of time. The evening of my first visit to the Fleet Club I was to hear about the run through 'bomb alley' which went from Alex to the beleaguered ports of Bardia, Sollum and Tobruk, so essential to the support of our troops in the desert.

No wonder then that men returning from these suicide runs let their hair down when ashore on leave. It was hazardous, unglamorous work, sometimes escorting and supporting the snail-paced gun boats, Aphis and Ladybird and the lumbering fifteen inch gun monitor Terror, as these brave men and ships pounded the enemy in the desert in support of our own Desert Rats.

I liked Alex and found it much more than a good run ashore for the matelots. It took me some time to realise I was enjoying first class food, entertainment and facilities and was able to afford them on my pittance of a matelot's pay. It says much for the cost of living prevailing ashore. At that moment I was enjoying a delicious coffee and French style pastries at one of the very delightful cafes on a pavement table, just watching the world go by. In the evening I could afford to dine in the swank Kalitychos

Greek restaurant and enjoy a three course meal and drinks served by bow tied waiters. Next move, into one of the local bars for a few bevvies and finally, end up in one of the night clubs in town. Here the hostesses would dance with you for drinks and you would not be ripped off. It was a great town.

I had just left the late performance at the cinema when the air raid sirens sounded. I noticed that there was no panic among the locals. Before I reached the Fleet Club I heard the drone of the enemy planes. All hell had been let loose in the harbour as one of the greatest concentration of AA fire opened up from the fleet. This was joined by the distinctive 'woof, woof' of the Army's Bofors ringed around the outskirts of Alex. The sky was criss-crossed by dozens of searchlights, it was one of the most spectacular sights I would ever see but, hang on a moment, I suddenly realised every light in the town was still blazing. I made it to the Fleet Club and was astounded to see half the matelots in town sitting at their tables in the Beer Garden drinking their Stellas and enjoying the fireworks. The reason for this bizarre situation was explained to me.

Ideally the Navy would have liked a total blackout of the town but had no jurisdiction over the matter. However, throughout the period when only the Italians were fighting us in the Med they never hit the town with bombs, this was partly believed to be humanitarian and partly due to the excellence of their high level bomb sights. This resulted in the locals having complete confidence in them. Not the least worrying aspect of this extraordinary scenario was the fact that shrapnel was falling out of the sky like rain.

There were a number of drunks roaming the streets and some still downing Stellas in the Fleet Club, in spite of the fact that Naval Patrols were around ready to pick them up at the first sign of trouble. Those picked up would spend the night in chokey to face charges the following day. They would each have their own reasons for going on a bender and not the least among them was the fact that it could quite conceivably be their last.

Aboard ship everyone was discussing the previous night's raid with talk concentrated on the fearsome Alex AA barrage and the bizarre situation of the fully illuminated town while it progressed. Fortunately none of the ships were hit but there was some damage to the harbour installations. The boom seemed to be going up and down like a yoyo as ships returned and left harbour. The enemy agents ashore, reputed to be numerous, must have had wrist ache tapping out the movements to their master. On deck that night I had no trouble in counting forty ships around me in the harbour and there were, of course, many more out on operations.

The blackout in the harbour seemed to intensify the brightness of the moon, shining down from the clear starlit sky and the ripple on the water threw off a million reflections. It was an eerie sight looking out over the sleeping fleet in the quiet of this moonlit night. In the sombre, peculiar light the psychedelic camouflage of the ships' sides gave the impression of a futuristic painting. The masts and yardarms formed crosses, turning the canvas into the apparition of a Marine graveyard.

A picture in sharp conflict with the events of last night, was this the same harbour that had provided us just twenty four hours ago with that spectacular display of lights and pyrotechnics?

What of the men at rest below decks in these slumbering arsenals of destruction? They were all a part of a lottery, in which the very next time they left harbour they would either be a winner or a loser. The Admiralty regrets etc. Our job was to make sure that it was the enemy that got the short straw. Such are the vagaries of war. The home they were now sleeping in would, at the sound of a bugle, be turned into a fighting ship. That's what made matelots special. You ate, slept and possibly died in a mutual environment, and out there you were all equal in the survivor's stakes from the Boy Seaman up to the Admiral. There was no place to hide, you were all in it together, win or lose in the lottery.

Chapter 18

We had only been in Alex two days and twice the Italians had paid us a visit, albeit not friendly ones.

Now were were gong to return the compliment. We slipped our mooring at 1000 hours, the boom was lifted and Kent began its entry into the gladiatorial arena. We were off to make a pre-emptive strike against the enemy. We made our exit line ahead, a slow single file. There were twelve destroyers, like greyhounds straining at the leash, impatient to send their bows scything through the flat calm of the Med, the battleships *Warspite, Malaya* and *Ramilles* followed by *Kent*. We all took up station and immediately took up the zig zag routine. This procedure, a constant alteration of course, was designed to make it difficult for the enemy sub to get a sighting and fire its message of death. It was a stirring sight to see the might of three of our great battlers ploughing through the sea together on their way to a mission, one broadside of eight fifteen inch shells from each ship would send twenty four tons of destruction towards the enemy. The destroyers were a joy to watch as they fussed around us, like Collies shepherding sheep.

We closed up at full night action stations and steamed into Sullum Bay, the Libyan coast was clearly visible. At dawn *Malaya* and *Ramilles* left us with escorts. We passed *Bardia*, *Warspite* and *Kent* launched their Walrus as spotter planes and we all opened fire. We were bombarding the enemies' workshops, stores and equipment and troop deployments. It must have been hell at the receiving end of this tremendous barrage as the spotter planes directed our fire on target. The spread of the salvoes from the twenty four fifteen inch and eight eight inch guns must have been enormous.

Kent alone fired off nearly one hundred rounds. The fleet then joined up to steam homeward, hugging the coast in a preconceived plan to tempt out the enemy's bombers. Our aircraft was ready at a signal to come out in waves. The action began almost immediately, "Action stations" and "repel aircraft" were sounded off. It was thrilling stuff, the "ack, ack" from four capital ships and twelve destroyers, bombers coming out of the clouds and the thrill of seeing for the first time dog fights overhead. The salvoes of bombs made a tremendous curtain of splashes, some four hundred yards long. Four Italians came screaming along our port side, the close range weapons opened fire and rapidly ceased as our fighters dived out of the blue right on the enemy's tails. The rattle of their cannons could be clearly heard and almost immediately three Italians plunged crazily into the sea like great flaming rockets. One plane came down quite sedately and we saw the pilot bale out in his parachute - at least one poor soul had survived. The action finished as quickly as it had begun. One of our escorts picked up the pilot. The operation was a great success, the enemy's positions in and around Bardia and Marsa al Ramla were devastated. The fleet was still intact and the fighters had shot down eleven planes and the shadow plane without loss. We were not attacked again, it had been a long and exciting day and the crew, if we could believe them, had seen and enjoyed taking part in a successful mission. I could well imagine how the action, being described in the Fleet Club and bars of Alex, would become the equal of the Battle of Trafalgar by the time some of the lads had consumed a few Stellas. This time in the lottery we were winners.

The destroyers in this action were *Hyperion, Hostile, Hereward, Nubian, Juno, Nero, Vendetta, Stuart, Diamond, Ilex, Mohawk* and *Waterhen*. Wonderful names that were to make their mark in future actions. They were always held in very high esteem by the whole fleet, they were our guardians, our protectors. What a sight it was to see them at high speed manoeuvres, their bows slicing through the water in seemingly impossible curves. It was the 'boats' that invariably stayed behind to pick up survivors of other actions, often in highly dangerous situations. Their losses were horrendous and in the first three years of the conflict they were to lose eighty nine ships. In addition, there were many severely damaged which made it back to harbour, there to be repaired, recommission and sail out again to do battle once again.

It suddenly occurred to me that we had been on the bomb alley run that always seemed to be under discussion in the bars and Fleet Club. I now knew what it was all about and I could now understand their fears. Perhaps it was the air cover that had made the difference, this time it was land-based aircraft that had protected us as we neared our own bases. Mostly the fleet had to rely on cover from our aircraft carriers which needed good weather for taking off and landing. Possibly the land-based air cover was to be a permanent feature for the future.

We returned to Alex and most of my thoughts concerned a game of Tombola, a few Stella beers and the delight of those crisp white sheets and a bed in a room on my own. Something I had always taken for granted was now a dreamed about luxury - perhaps we would have a raid free night.

Neither of my dreams were to be granted. We were guard ship for two consecutive nights and no leave was granted. The air raids were now a nightly feature, there were as many as six alerts per night, so far with only minor damage to out buildings. Our escape from damage owed much to the intensity of the combined Naval and shore-based AA. The balloons and kites flying from the fleet and about the harbour seemed to have put paid to the Italian hedgehoppers, for now at least. There were also luckless fleet tankers and target screens placed strategically around, protecting the capital ships.

Kent was credited with shooting down a bomber in the previous day's action, the crew of which were captured by the Army in the desert. The BBC News reported the action as a "call to arms". Their correspondents and photographers had embarked on *Kent* and reported "severe damage to enemy installations on the road to Alex" and "heavy loss of troops and equipment".

The atmosphere on the messdeck was now much more restrained, the reality of war was now implanted in people's minds. The consequences of twisted metal and twisted bodies was now ever present. Even the harbour was now just a place to tie up in, there was no guarantee of your night's rest, nor yet of your safety. Continually broken sleep patterns, and the heavy adrenelin flowing during air attacks, made sleep sometimes difficult even when you were stood down and off Watch.

The rum issue that was the lifeblood of all Naval messdecks, was always the saviour of any messdeck suffering the chokka and cheesed off syndrome. The drawing and issuing of rum was, as I have already described, sheer pantomime. It was undeniably strong stuff but I always felt the build up and the anticipation of the pipe of "up spirits" probably doubled its strength once again. A messdeck before and after tot time were two entirely different worlds. It was the habit of some crew members to 'bottle' and 'badge' their tots. There were some in the mess who would use their tot as currency and forfeit it to the Dhoby firms, money firms, loan barons or Jewing firms, such as my oppo Mo Stutsky. All of this was highly illegal of course and it has been known for "clear lower deck" to be piped whilst the Crusher and RPOs searched the messes for contraband.

Chapter 19

"Hands to stations for leaving harbour" was piped at 1400 hours, so we were not to get a full night's sleep. We left with the cruiser *Gloucester* and escorts *Janus, Defender, Hereward* and *Hyperion*.

We swept through the Kithera Straits with the intention of intercepting Italian troop ships reported to be in the region, with no success. We then proceeded West of Crete to pick up a convoy out of Piraeus. Our inevitable shadow plane turned up and reported us as a battle cruiser. The convoy had been bombed prior to our rendez vous and, in the late afternoon, a plane came out of the sun. It was spotted late and heading straight for us. She released a torpedo and we turned away like mad. It passed safely astern. There was hell to pay on the Bridge, the plane was a 'sitter' for our guns. The TS omitted to give the "commence fire" to the four inch platform and the port pom pom was just changing over and no-one had headphones on. We did get some rounds off but she escaped. It was a black mark and the Rear Admiral was furious.

To make matters worse the acute angle of the four inch gun fire had damaged our own aircraft with blast and it was inoperable until repairs had been effected. When we berthed in Alex everyone was whacked out and there was a despondency aboard. *Kent*'s pride had been very badly dented on this occasion.

There was an international incident caused by the bombers on the inevitable night raid, a stick of bombs wrote off the Italian, the French and the British Yacht Clubs at the end of the harbour. A peacetime luxury for the idle rich would now need extensive repairs when peace was declared.

There was now no respite, we were off again, it was the ungodly hour of 0345. This was done to outfox the enemy agents ashore. If we wanted them to know our movements then we would leave in daylight. This must be a big one - we had on board an American Fox News camera and correspondent. We led *Liverpool* and *Gloucester* out with three destroyers and to port was the battle fleet *Warspite, Malaya, Eagle*, the Aussie *Sydney* and the *Orion*. There must have been every destroyer in Alex out there, at a guess eighteen. We, the third cruiser squadron, were all warming up our guns with 'throw off' shoots.

We were all agog with excitement, there were always little titbits of the truth let out by the Bunts and Sparks who were privy to the signals being passed. The buzzes were so numerous they must have caused atmospheric interference with the real thing. The third cruiser squadron left the battle fleet to sail West North of Crete, everything at this stage was to a preconceived plan. The battle fleet made its rendez vous with us again South West of Crete. The intention was to draw out their bombers against an apparently sitting target, then off would go the *Eagle's* aircraft and hopefully pick them off. They were having none of it but *Eagle* did shoot down our shadow. The management was completely mystified by Italy's lack of resolve. They did attack the convoy we were covering and HMS*Cornwall* received a direct hit which destroyed her steering gear, so the ship had to be steered by her engines.

The sight at dawn was magnificent. Two battleships, one aircraft carrier, six cruisers and around eighteen destroyers. They were a fine sight in V formation, the destroyers were cutting up the calm, blue Med into an impressive aqua display. The Med could, however, turn quite hostile, and this it did today. It was quite remarkable, wind, cloud, rain, poor visibility could make sub and aircraft that day quite ineffective. It calmed down just as suddenly as it had begun.

There was no break, we seemed to be continually at second or first degree of readiness. It was all very tiring, yet so far nothing of note had happened. Perhaps we were too impatient. The destroyers had to leave to refuel, that is when we learned we were Malta bound. It was an enormous sea operation. We now learned that the Gibraltar fleet under Sir James Somerfield were on a diverging course for Malta from the Western Med. The Gibraltar force consisted of *Renown, Resolution*, the carrier *Ark Royal* and *Enterprise*, *Sheffield* and about fourteen destroyers. Both forces were feigning a major onslaught on Italian bases when, in fact, the convoy and some of the fleet were carrying vital supplies to Malta. The main reason for the armada was to gain safe passage through the Med to Alex to get urgent Naval reinforcements to the East Med fleet. These units consisted of the carrier *Illustrious*, battleship *Valiant*, plus *Calcutta* and *Coventry*, two AAcruisers. All four ships had been extensively modernised and carried aboard precious radar and other sophisticated devices.

The fourth day out was full of incidents, reconnaissance reported the Italian fleet out in large numbers. The scene was set for a major Naval sea battle. Surely this time it must come. *Kent* was now unescorted, as our destroyers were refuelling in Malta. "Alarm starboard" went out, a sub periscope was reported. It escaped. What a pity our destroyers were not with us. Our shadow plane was shot down. The 'Ities' in the Cant 501s have no life expectancy at all, but the brave men could always be picked up accurately reporting our position to Italian headquarters and in that they had bravely done their duty. For a period of time today, the whole might of the combined fleets plus the new additions, were massed together in a majestic display of sea power, something which conceivably may never happen again. The picture was completed by a large number of the fleet carrier planes flying overhead.

It was all frustration on the Bridge of *Kent.* Latest recce information told us that all the Italian units were legging it for their home parts. There was further grief when a formation of about fifty planes reported heading for the fleet, turned tail and ran. They must, however, have broken up into smaller formations, a string of bombs fell ahead of us. This was followed by a piece of Naval history. We witnessed the very first attack by JU87, the much feared Stuka divebomber. The *Eagle* was right on our beam and the attack was mainly directed against her. They all, mercifully, missed - just, for she was enveloped in the plumes of the explosions. We had a clear view of the bomb release and the pilots' bodies straining backwards as they pulled out of their screaming, quite terrifying dive. Another small diversion was the appearance of a single floating mine, it was dispatched without exploding.

The air attacks followed one after the other. We seemed to be banging away with our four inch continually and on two of the waves of attacks, we actually opened up with our eight inch at high angle, it was like bedlam. They were now dropping too close for comfort and, at one time, *Eagle* was enveloped in a long string of bombs and for a moment she looked as though she was hanging on the side of the Niagara Falls. The sound of the falling bombs was similar to the approach of an express train. Another string fell perilously close and resulted in fountains of water drenching our port side. The *Eagle* flew off her fighters to join in the mayhem. The men down below said later they thought we had been hit. Illustrious had her Fairey Fulmas in the air and at one time they were confused with the Italians and the *Eagle* opened fire on them, fortunately unsuccessfully.

The air attacks continued, it was bewildering to the management, they were coming at us in small formation and flying at around fourteen thousand feet. The fact that not one single unit had been hit or even damaged, was the Italians' bad luck. The gods were shining on us. One more string fell across our bows and another down the starboard side, once again the plumes of the explosions were rising higher than our masts. The *Kent* shuddered with the impact and this time there was shrapnel flying around. One of the air defence platforms was showered and a large piece dented the tin hat of a lookout. What a lucky fellow. The Bridge considered that if they had attacked in large formations, they could have caused immense damage. It was a technique they had yet to learn. The AA barrage from the fleet was tremendous but the enemy were flying at about the extremity of our range.

The essential reinforcements to the Eastern Med were safely through, the vital supplies had reached Malta. We had brought another convoy through from Piraeus and the only casualty was the bomb that had hit the *Cornwall*. We had no knowledge yet of the damage to other vessels, aircraft, or the number of casualties. We had given the enemy every opportunity to do battle with us, this they had steadfastly refused. Now with the addition of *Valiant, Illustrious* and two refurbished specialist AAships, *Calcutta* and *Coventry*, we were capable of inflicting immeasurably greater damage on them, if ever they did get the urge to do battle with us.

We were heading for Port Said with the convoy of eight ships, the sporadic high level of attacks continued and, once again, we were subject to an aerial torpedo attack by a single plane. Were the Ities just plain useless, were we just 'shit lucky', perhaps this luck of ours was making us feel blasé or even bomb proof? Time alone would tell.

The third cruiser squadron of *Kent, Liverpool* and *Gloucester* were still intact and we were back in Alex to catch our breath. We had been in at the beginning of the war at sea in the Med, but there had still only been the one surface confrontation, at Calabria. The Bridge had again been awaiting with apparently keen anticipation, a meeting with Italian surface forces. The operation we had just completed had been successful, with only the damage to HMS*Norfolk* as a deficit. It occurred to me that a confrontation could possibly have cocked up the whole exercise. I was completely mystified by this desire to try our luck but then I was merely a civvy on loan for the duration.

What was my own reaction to being under fire from a foe whose only objective was to end your participation in events? Guns and the GI were generous in their praise of our conduct, so far we were shaping up to our responsibilities quite well and we were giving the professionals no cause for concern. Analysing my feelings of events, I was secretly quite pleased with my reactions.

My action station on the four inch gun platform was a position of almost complete isolation from the reality of what was going on around me. The intense noise put a curtain of sound around the whole platform, obliterating all else and needed intense concentration because everything had to happen in strict sequence. The horrendous "craaack" of the four inch guns, reputedly the harshest of all guns on the ear, never failed to start the bells ringing in my head. The crash of the returning shell cases, the slamming of the breaches, the pungent acrid smell of the cordite, fear and the adrenalin it started flowing, were great motivators. Somewhere in my mind was the thought that the quicker the guns fired the better was my chance for survival. I was quite oblivious to the string of bombs that had apparently scraped our paintwork or the resultant shrapnel that had embedded itself in various parts in close proximity to our position. I was aware that the whole ship had shuddered, I was physically and emotionally drained and my head now had a close affinity with Quasi Modo. I thought again of my officers and shipmates who were apparently burning for a piece of the action.

Chapter 20

There were already bad omens about this trip. As we prepared to get under way nothing was going right. It started with a fire in the Torpedo Office, ropes and wires were getting snarled up and kinked. We had trouble streaming our mine protecting PVs and Jimmy the One injured his foot. *Kent*, *Liverpool* and *Gloucester* left with four attendant destroyers.

It's a complicated operation leaving harbour in daylight; at 0200 hours in the morning it is downright hazardous. Who wants to start work at 0200, you are neither asleep or awake? Sleep was at a premium and now for the first time we were going into two Watches, which meant four hours on four hours off, right through the day and night. If you were closed up at action stations during your Watch off, "hard luck, you shouldn't have joined".

Almost immediately *Jervis* and *Hereward* got a ping and dropped depth charges. Oil and bubbles were reported on the surface and although no further contacts were made, no positive kill could be claimed. It almost seemed to require a note from the sub's Captain before a kill was positive. The Italians had a known strength of ninety five subs in the Med and they were faster, smaller and more manoeuvrable than ours. In spite of this our gallant destroyers were to inflict grevious losses on them.

Hero and *Hasty* left us to return to Alex, no-one knows why. We proceeded through the Kathira Straits and into the Aegean and passing Gavdo Island we presented a perfect target for attack from nearby bases. Nothing came. We then met our convoy in the Kaso Straits, eight ships en route to Pireaus from Port Said, in company with *Calcutta* and escorts. We were closed up nearly all day, fending off high level air attacks, which were all abortive, then once again Kent was attacked by a single torpedo bomber, again we had to take evasive action. There was no damage to friend or foe. Off the island of Skyros we hove to while *Jervis* took oil from us.

We headed North in the Aegean after safely delivering our convoy to Pireaus. It became a scene of breathtaking beauty as we sailed through islands of beautiful colours. On a flat, calm Med it was too idyllic to fight a war in and everyone was affected by its tranquility. We sailed right up to the Dardenelles and it was a thrill to see Gallipoli Peninsula with its impressive memorial to the events that took place there in the First World War.

Heading South we met up with a force consisting of the battleship *Valiant*, fleet carrier *Illustrious,* plus the cruiser *Orion* and seven destroyers. Something was obviously afoot.

The Monitor *Terror* and the gun boats *Aphis* and *Ladybird* had already made their way through bomb alley and the *Terror* had fired off two hundred and twenty shells, each weighing one ton, on the enemy shore installations off Bardia. The RN was fighting the war in the desert in addition to the now non-stop conflict to the enemy at sea.

Almost everything that followed in the ensuing action was a first and it was to end in blood, sweat and tears for both friend and foe. The third cruiser squadron was ordered with escorts to a position North of Benghasi to screen an air operation from Illustrious. It was a calm, moonlit night when, like pigeons leaving their loft, *Illustrious'* planes attacked and sank the Italian destroyer *Borea* and two freighters. Then a mine field laid by their planes sank the destroyer *Aquilone* and just to finish off a good night's work they carried out a raid on Benghasi.

The combined force then set sail for Alex. *Kent* was ordered to detach with escorts *Juno, Jervis* and *Janus* and proceed to a position off Bardia. We soon had the company of a shadow plane. Our instructions were to close the Libyan coast and carry out a further bombardment. The gallant little *Aphis* and *Ladybird* were already in position and we were to spot for our range off their gunflashes. In the faliing light of dusk actions stations, we noticed our shadow was still there, no doubt informing the enemy of our presence, who were sure to know our intentions.

It was a calm sea, a clear moon, the chain of events necessary before the launch of our barrage was systematically slotting into place. I remember the quiet, it was to be the quiet before the storm. The hour of midnight was approaching, that was zero hour, we were now all safe in the knowledge that this had always ensured our immunity from air attack. Sadly this time it was to be yet another first.

There was no warning. Before we had fired a single round of eight inch at the enemy, right on midnight, just as if they knew, a stick of bombs sent massive plumes of the tranquil Med high above our masts. From that moment *HMS Kent* was in battle, fighting for her life. The four inch AA platform was in overdrive, the twenty millimetre pom poms and the smaller Vickers 0.5 machine guns were blazing away desperately trying to keep the enemy at bay.

The *Kent* was now the sole target of the enemy, we were no longer one of a crowd, they had come to get us, it must have been preconceived.

There were now starshell and gun flashes from the shore batteries, low level air attacks from torpedo bombers. It got worse. We had fought off the initial attacks, when a new sound joined the cacophony - the staccato rattle of machine guns, clearly audible above the roar of the planes' engines. They took out our searchlights first of all. It was much different to all our other previous encounters. The night time made it doubly difficult, doubly frightening, our foe had now made it personal. The calmness of the men around me was an inspiration. The same men who, at the drop of a hat, could be as daft as a brush were now an efficient fighting unit. The enemy kept coming at us and on one occasion there was a blinding explosion. We were all hoping it was at least one of our tormentors.

Our luck couldn't last and eventually one of them got through, one plane, one torpedo and at the most two men, had put paid to the might of an eight inch gun cruiser with a crew of nearly nine hundred officers and men. The violence of the explosion seemed to lift the *Kent* out of the water and it occurred to us that we were very likely mortally wounded. It did in fact go down very low at the stern, if this motion continued in its direction, then it was a certainty that we would take to the boats in the very near future. The order had already gone out to stand by to abandon ship, so no-one yet knew if *Kent* would survive this attack.

Everything on *Kent* was still blazing away like mad in a desperate bid to blow out of the sky the men who had desecrated the innards of the ship that was our life and our home.

We were a sitting duck, a cripple, unable to move. Our turbines were idle, most of the ship was in darkness. Eventually they left, they had expended their loads on us, just one had got through. In a last defiant gesture they launched another machine gun attack and then they were gone.

Kent settled by the stern, the damage was immense and the rudder was jammed hard over.

We remained closed up, certain that they would be back to finish us off. We were doubly alert and ready for another attack. The gun crews and defences were oblivious to everything that was going on below decks, where heroics of the highest order were being enacted. Suddenly I froze, I realised that down there amongst the twisted metal there would be some of my shipmates and my thoughts went straight to my HO oppos I had joined up with. Seager, Abbey, Furness, Alex, Jock Keith. We were getting no feedback and we had plenty of time to think about our plight. Home and family were foremost in my thoughts, then it was about survival, possible capture, we were close to the enemy shore and I dreaded being a POW. I was now coping with another problem, my ears. The gunfire was definitely having an effect on my hearing. I was very reluctant to make too much fuss in case I was thought to be whingeing, an attitude I now know to be immature. It was also an established fact that you were given very little encouragement to report your ills. At that moment I was almost deaf, and had difficulty hearing anything.

A desperate battle was going on below decks to get *Kent* mobile. It had been established that the rudder was jammed hard over by the explosion and in the confines of a compartment flooded with foul oily sludge, surrounded by the horror of the detonation, men were making heroic efforts to centralise the rudder to enable *Kent* to become manoeuvrable and so make her escape from the danger of another attack that would almost certainly prove fatal. It was a race against time and for gun crews and reinforced lookouts, it was a tense time. *Kent* was completely immobile in the middle of Sollum Bay, a flat calm sea and a clear, moonlit night, just waiting for what we all thought was the inevitable.

A graphic account of events below decks is given in the personal daily diary of *Kent's* Torpedo Officer, Lt Comm, now Captain, GC Blundell CBE RN (Ret).

There were many stories of heroism, not least Chief ERA Stephens, who had rescued Leading Stoker Johnstone, who was unconscious down below. Lt Comm Blundell was thought by many to have been instrumental in saving the ship and, in the words of Leading Seaman James, "All the lads on the messdecks are very proud of you sir, and we think you deserve the VC." Lt Comm was a caring man who often publicly condemned many of the Navy's archaic practices. Had there been more men of his calibre, I'm quite sure we would have been better prepared for war.

From the personal daily diary of Lt Comm GC Blundell:

"To return to Tuesday 17th September, at some time we were detatched with two destroyers, one being Nubian, our orders being to bombard Sollum at midnight. A similar Naval bombardment had to be done almost nightly at the request of the Army in order to disrupt Italian communications and supplies which had to go by the coast road. Originally Ramillies (one fifteen inch gun battleship) had been detailed to do this but, since returning to Alexandria, I hear that the news was thought to have leaked out to the Ities and, therefore, the C-in-C cancelled

Ramillies and detailed Kent instead, thinking the Ities would learn that Ramillies had not left harbour and so would not be expecting anything.

"At 2200 we went to action stations, cleared away, then reverted to second degree. I had the first Watch as PCO which suited me as actions stations officer of the Watch. At 2315 we fell in the Watch for Ot PVs as we were now in the bay in shallow water. We were rather longer than usual in streaming and gun flashes and starshell were seen on our port bow. Then I heard a pop just like one of the exhaust valves momentarily lifting and then I heard what sounded like steam escaping from an exhaust pipe and suddenly realised it wasn't steam but bombs dropping. They fell to port. Shortly after another lot nearer. We were then firing hard at aircraft and I remember distinctly thinking we'd got a direct hit on one, but it may have been only a shell bursting. Then we had a low torpedo bomber on our starboard beam. I saw the splashes, enormous ones, as torpedoes were dropped. Shortly afterwards there was a tremendous blow aft. The whole ship reeled, then suddenly fell dead and we could feel on the Bridge as if her tail had dropped, a sort of bending, dragging feeling and the ship wouldn't steer.

"'Stop both' was ordered. All I heard Skips saying was 'CBs, CBs' (Confidential Books) and sort of turning round and round on the Bridge and groping. We were then machine gunned by aircraft that came in from ahead. I didn't really realise what it was at first except that there were loud cracks just like one hears from standing in rifle butts, whilst red worms seemed to fly all around us. At first I thought they were sparks from the funnel. It was too fascinating to be in the least frightening but when I realised they were bullets, I knelt down to present a smaller target.

"With the steering gone and the ship stopped, it felt exactly like being a man surrounded by assassins with his hands tied behind his back. I realised that the hit, being aft, had probably put both the after electrical breaker rooms out of action and that emergency cables would have to be run to get power back on to the steering motors, so I asked permission to leave the Bridge to deal with the situation aft. To my shame I first nipped into my cabin and put my tin containing cine camera and money in a safer place up a deck as it seemed the ship was settling aft. Then I went to the wardroom flat and saw the Commander pretty suiffy and told someone - it was quite dark so people could only be distinguished by torchlight - to keep an eye on him and sit him down in the wardroom. He looked like a child.

"I am completely hazy about the sequence of events; the whole of the after part of the ship was in darkness and as silent as the grave as all electric supply had failed, but I know I went to see if emergency cables were being run and yardarm groups supplied. I found some emergency cables hanging down the after engine room patch and there was a hell of a heat coming up, so I knew that all engine room fans were off. I went down and found the temperature just bearable on the bed plates. Deacon (engine room electrical artificer) was not there. I learned later that he'd fainted and gone off fo'ard. I groped to the fire end of the engine room shouting for an electrical stoker or ERA. No-one there. Going up top I met Leading Stoker Underwood and told him to make the emergency switches at the dynamos for the engine room fans. Then I shouted for the electrical (repair) party and started getting cables run.

I got hold of EA Machin to come down with me into the engine room to connect up some breakers but the heat coming from the hatch was so intense he didn't want to go, so I had to force him down in front of me. I am sure he felt that he was going to his death. It was cooler at the bottom. Then I believe I returned to the wardroom flat where I was joined by Skinner (Gunner T) and told him the cables for the steering motors would have to go over the quarterdeck, and put him in charge. I saw the whole wardroom flat filling with smoke and fumes, obviously coming from aft, so put on my gasmask, but couldn't see a thing because the eyepieces clouded over, but staggered through an open bulkhead door into the half deck.

"I couldn't see an inch, not even with my wonderful American torch. There was obviously a big fire raging inside as I could see a glow and it was dammed hot. I began to feel a bit chokey and sleepy and sat down inside the flat but realised that the gasmask was pretty well useless. I felt I could sleep for ever and I remember taking a pull at myself and saying internally 'No George Blundell', you're not going to die yet." So I heaved myself back into the wardroom flat where I recovered my breath. Then I grabbed someone else and advanced with him to shut the bulkhead door between the wardroom flat and half deck. We couldn't see each other and had to feel our way. The door didn't seem to be there but then we felt it on the wrong side to what I thought it was, felt for the retaining clips and closed it but it wouldn't shut. We had to retire and recover, then advanced again and, feeling round the rim of the door, found two hoses passing through at the bottom, so we pulled them out. I thought I'd burst and I thought the hoses would never come out, but at last they did and we shut the door. I've no idea whether the Commander was dead in there by this time or whether he had not gone in again.

"Anyhow I shouted to the four corners of the flat that the bulkhead doors were not to be opened again. Actually, I believe they were and that it was the Commander who, in a fuddled state, had gone in again to his inevitable death. His body was found outside the second staff office door (near where I had collapsed), so the poor little man didn't get far. It was terrible inside. Then I went up onto the quarterdeck to find a way for the cables to the steering motors in the steering flat. The ship was still being raked by bullets from aircraft and guns seemed to be firing at us from the shore. I nipped down into the Admiral's dining cabin through the skylight and remember a stoker saying something about spoiling the Admiral's chair covers. I tried to get through the after door but the dogs had been taken off (improperly) so I went to the pantry hatch, but its clips were on the other side. So I was done this way and climbed up onto the quarterdeck again.

"There I met Ch ERA Stephens and said 'How the hell can I get down to the steering motors?' (All normal access to the steering compartment had been blown away by the underwater explosion: in fact the decks and internal structure from the keel up had been so damaged that it seemed the stern was only hanging on by the upper deck and one side.) He said: 'There's a scuttle open down there,' pointing over the side. So I said: 'Well, I am pleased we can get in.' We got a rope and down we went, self and Stephens. I found out afterwards that Stephens had already been down and brought back Leading Stoker Johnson, the tiller flat watchkeeper who was very shaken but had been the man to open the scuttle. The ship had settled by the stern such that the sea was only an inch or two below the scuttle rim and I got jammed going in by my gasmask. Inside it was dark as hell and filled with fumes. The scuttle was that for cabin number 27. As I stepped through the cabin door I squelched on something flabby and in the torch saw it was the body of Petty Officer Masters (Messdeck PO, whose action station was at the after emergency steering wheel. He died of heart failure). I remember thinking 'That's the first dead man I've ever seen,' and feeling relieved that it didn't seem at all unnatural.

"After this we worked for about three hours down in the steering flat and nearly submerged, getting down lighting and equipment and working the emergency hand pump to supply power to the hydraulic rams to the tiller head. The steering motors being under water it was no use supplying power to them. I went up and down about three times making various arrangements and keeping the Bridge informed. The engineers were very slow in getting anybody or anything there. (I learned years later from Rear Admiral Roberts, then Sub. Lieut (E) that the Engineer Commander, who had newly joined the ship, was an alcoholic and had hidden himself away and the Senior Engineer and many of the ER staff had passed out in the engine rooms due to the heat and were out of action for some time.)

"The rudder had jammed at about twenty degrees to starboard and until we could get it amidships, or better still working, the ship was unmanageable. Eventually we got it straight by placing hydraulic jacks between the ship's side frames and the yoke on the rudder head. At one time we thought the rudder had jumped off its pintles by the force of the explosion.

"Wednesday 18th September At about 0130 we had got in tow of *Nubian*. At first it was impossible because the rudder being over to starboard and both starboard propellors being out of action, all we could do was go round in circles. Preparations were made in case we had to abandon ship. At about 0500 everybody had breakfast and later we were terribly relieved to see *Illustrious*. Almost the whole fleet seemed to come out to escort us in. (Before we could have been aided out of Bardin Bay the Italians lost a golden chance of finishing us off.) The fire aft was too bad for us to open up and get the bodies out. We put steam on the compartment to damp it out. We've got thirty three dead including the Commander and two Maltese. Had many aircraft alarms during the day. At 0900 the tow was stupidly changed to *Protector*. This lost us an hour and we'd been doing fine with *Nubian*. I had severe cramp in my legs during air attacks in the afternoon: the young doctor gave me a glass of neat lime juice."

At around 0200 we were relived to see the passing of a tow rope to the destroyer *Nubian*. To our dismay the first one parted. It didn't seem possible that one of these specially designed, immensely strong tows could part. A second tow was passed to the *Nubian* and although it held, we were going round in circles due to the jammed rudder. Again the order "stand by to abandon ship" was given as an emergency. Due, however, to the Herculean efforts of the damage control party, the rudder was middled by the use of hydralic jacks. We got under way. It must have been one of the hairiest tows ever undertaken and it was a minor miracle that *Kent* eventually made it to the safety of Alex. We were continually swinging off at right angles to the tow and at one time, we were again wallowing, adrift in the Med. At this stage the tow was taken over by the *Protector*. The after bulkhead, the one between us and safety from the tousands of tons of water, started leaking. Then the sea roughened considerably. Dawn broke and after dawn action stations we were relived to take our first eats for about ten hours or more. It was a hurried affair and we at last got information about each other. To my immense joy all my oppos were safe but one. HO 'Polly' Morgan was missing, a very quiet man and quite a loner, he was not one of my immediate associates. He was remebered as a very kind and uncomplicated character but, sadly, he was the first of our twenty to pay the supreme penalty. The Italians had quite inexplicably paid us no return visit during the night and yet made a number of visits through the forenoon, all of which were abortive. Their tactics were a constant source of amazement to the Bridge, on the other hand the attitude of the Bridge was a constant source of amazement to me. Their talk was not about the survival of the *Kent* but all about the ineptitude of our foe.

There were many more air attacks on our way back to Alex, but mercifully nothing fell very close to us. Anything quite close could possibly have taken away our stern, which was apparently holding on by a thread. By now we had the assistance of four fleet tugs, *Pharos, St Issy, Roysterer* and *No 1.* We eventually berthed at about 1400. It was thirty six hours after that fateful torpedo had torn out our innards.

H.M.S. 'Kent' *showing aerial torpedo damage.*

Chapter 21

I feel so dreadfully sorry for these men who were my shipmates and oppos, who had joined the Navy to perform their duty. Many officers and men were quite openly and coolly anticipating a surface confrontation. They were men who had, with monotonous regularity, repeated endless boring drills and assimilated action against a make believe enemy. It was their aim to become the best, and gun crew competed with gun crew to this end. They were like novice cowboys shooting cans and bottles off the wall, who were now waiting to meet the fastest gun in the West to try out their draw. They had fought off air attack, sub attack, shore batteries, but that was not what they really wanted. They wanted to meet the Italian fleet in a running battle. It was exciting and stirred the blood. No-one remembered an air or sub attack. In history it was only surface battles that were remembered. They made good reading. They epitomised the job that had been the Navy's for centuries. Ship against ship, man against man. All the other aspects of war were an invasion into a game that had been played since the days of Drake, Frobisher and Nelson.

Now, alas, they had to accept the bitter truth, that two men, one plane, and one torpedo, had brought a great fighting ship and almost nine hundred officers and men to a halt. One plane had ripped the guts out of *HMS Kent* and all the eight inch and four inch guns and the multiple pom poms and Vickers had been unable to stop her.

I knew and understood how much this was hurting them and, coupled with the loss of so many of their oppos, the mood was one of utmost dispair.

A great ship had been severely damaged. Her achievements? One plane shot down, one possible and some anonymous troops and their equipment had been destroyed, not on the high seas, but in the wilderness of the sand dunes in the Western Desert. *HMS Ken*t had just missed the successful surface action of Calabria, then ironically, shortly after we made it back to Alex, other ships of the fleet engaged the Italians and sank two destroyers. It was just not going to be *Kent's* war.

I can still vividly recall the shock of first going into that chamber of horrors down aft. The first thing that hit me was the stench, an obnosious cocktail of fuel, oil, smoke, sludge and the smell of death. It was a hugh black cavern, going from keel to the upper deck and from port to starboard. It said much for the construction of *Kent* that she survived that slow tortuous journey back to Alex in quite a heavy sea. If their bombs on the journey home had fallen any closer they would probably have dismembered the stern.

We had to wade through about three feet of black, stinking, sludge and it was necessary to close your eyes to what you were treading on underfoot. There were two bodies draped over pipes high above our heads, completely out of reach and it was dreadful to think they would stay there until a platform could be rigged. They would remain a macabre symbol of all that had gone before.

It would be great to go ashore and drink yourself into oblivion - anything to get away from this mangled metal that was once *HMS Kent*. A bed in the Fleet Club, clean white sheets, a bit of normality, a touch of civvy street, was something I could do with right now. Alas, there were still some sad duties to be performed.

The rest of *Kent's* story is one of anquish and sorrow. We first had the painful task of retrieving the bodies of our dead comrades from within the maelstrom that existed in the aftermath of the explosion. There were many harrowing stories recounted as one by one they were extricated and prepared for the traditional Naval burial survice. The bodies were enclosed in a canvas shroud, which was weighted to take it to the bottom of the sea. The poignant ceremony was porformed aboard *HMS Protector* in a bay outside Alex. What followed doubled the pain of our anguish. Within twenty four hours, twelve of the bodies were found washed up on the beach of Dekeila.

We then had the gruesome task of recovering the bodies for reburial. The bodies were now bloated and the doctor had to make incisions to deflate them. More weights were added and the ceremony had to be repeated. It was a very tragic affair and an air of despair existed throughout the ship.

There was to be a further grim twist to this catalogue of horror, two additional bodies were washed up but they had not been afforded a burial. It was then concluded that they must have washed free of the ship as we were entering harbour. Thirty three members of the crew were unaccounted for after the action, inevitably after a huge explosion in a confined space, the bodies were blown apart. The appropriate number of weighted shrouds had been committed to the deep, but fate had decreed that yet one more twist was necessary to end this bizarre episode of the *Kent's* dead. War is a nasty, uncompromising series of botch and cock-up, in the midst of which were unbelivable acts of bravery and devotion to duty by men who were at the sharp end of it all.

I was detailed for the second burial party and I admit to being wet eyed at the ceremony. The men responsible for the fiasco must have been devastated. Among the burial detail was a survivor who had lost two oppos alongside him in the explosion. God willing, this time their bodies would indeed rest in peace.

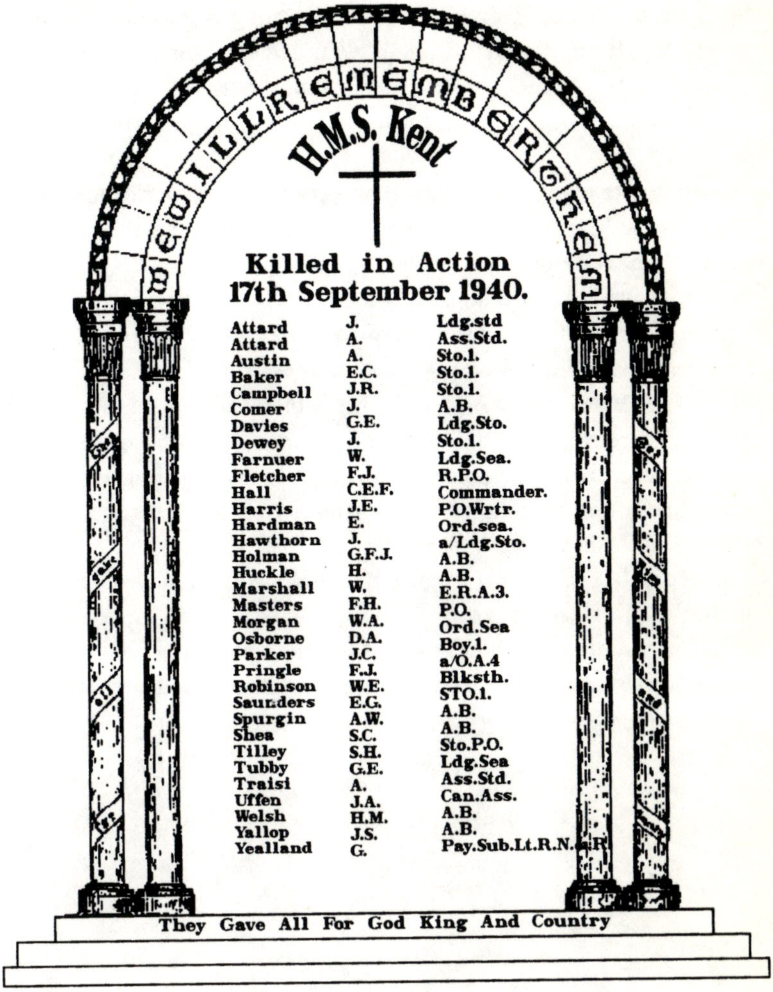

H.M.S. 'Kent' *Scroll of Honour.*

There was more tragic news to follow on our return to *Kent* after the burial party. *Liverpool* had been hit by an aerial torpedo and, like us, was limping back to harbour under tow. She was towed into harbour stern first by *HMS Orion*. What an awesome sight. The complete bows had been blown off and it was like looking at a block of flats with the front blown off. It was possible to see a complete cross-section, through the gun turrets, down through the messdecks. It appears that the initial explosion had done little damage but, through an ironic twist of fate, it had punctured the aviation fuel tank which had caused a secondary detonation. This had blown off the bows, causing twenty nine casualties and an equal number of burnt and wounded survivors.

In a couple of weeks two out of three of the third cruiser squadron had been taken out by aerial torpedo. The Italians were beginning to learn their job.

Of the fifty or so Naval ships that were operating out of Alex at the same time as *Kent*, thirty three were to be sunk and most of the remainder suffered severe damage but survived.

Ships were lost, ships limped back into harbour to be rebuilt and with a fresh crew, sailed out once more to do battle with the enemy.

There were now ten empty spaces at the mess tables, familiar faces never to be seen again. All their little foibles and mannerisms would soon be forgotten but they would all be remembered in our hearts. We were all tired with our exertions of the last two days but this was no occasion for our usual lighthearted banter. Most of us were glad just to seek the seclusion of our hammocks.

Sleep didn't come easy, in spite of my weariness. There was so much to think of, not least the news that we would be heading for home in the UK. That would not come about until major repairs had been effected. I should have been more excited about this prospect, but perhaps it was too far away yet.

Chapter 22

I was still very worried about my ears. My hearing was getting worse and I still had not reported it. I must have eventually fallen into a sleep, so deep in fact that I didn't hear the hands called. Someone was shaking my hammock, it was George and there was something strange about him. He was making shapes with his mouth but no sound was coming from it. I realised I was deaf. I was panic stricken. It was a dreadful sensation to be suddenly excluded from every sound around you.

I was on my way to Alexandria Hospital within a couple of hours. I was still at panic stations. I knew nothing about perforated eardrums but knew something about deafness, as one of my favourite uncles was stone deaf. I had visions of reading questions from a slip of paper, just like uncle Paddy had done, of being unable to hear everyday sounds like music, playing the piano. It was all too horrific to contemplate.

They kept me in hospital and all I can remember of it was pain. Whatever they did to me, they did it without anaesthetic and it hurt enough to make me cry out. I was only in hospital for two days and then attended as an out patient for further treatment. They did it, they made me hear again. How, I don't know and I didn't care. I was elated. It improved by the day, even the boring old messdeck backchat sounded great. One of my abiding memories was the sound matelots hate most, the bugle call "wakey wakey, lash up and stow". You'll forgive me for saying that it was 'music to my ears'.

Things seemed to happen fast after that. *Kent* was *hors de combat* and it gave all the officers and crew time to catch up on courses, drills, small arms target practice, etc. ABs with no non-substantive ratings could now complete a course, in either gunnery or torpedoes. I was given no option. My damaged hearing ensured that I would be taken out of the four inch gun crew. It was a torpedo course for me and my long time friend George Seager joined me on *HMS Woolwich* to do the course. I enjoyed it and qualified with a very respectable 82%. The course covered electrics, torpedoes, mines, demolitions and depth charges, much more interesting than popping off guns.

That simple change to Seaman Torpedo man was to govern the rest of my time in the Navy and afterwards in civvy street.

I returned to *Kent* on completion of the course to find the repairs in an advanced state. She would soon be leaving dock and be tiddlied up in preparation for her homeward journey to the UK. The shadow of gloom had now lifted considerably from the messdecks and there was an air of excitement aboard the ship. I soon joined in the mood and the thoughts of a Christmas with my friends and family was something to look forward to and relish.

It was inevitable that they would get *HMS Gloucester*, the sole survivor of the third cruiser squadron. The gallant *Gloucester* had succombed to the combined air attack by both German and Italian planes. The loss of life was horrendous, six hundred and ninety three young men had been sent to their doom.

Words cannot adequately describe the dimension of this loss of a fighting ship and her ship's company. It took endless practice and patience for these men to reach the required degree of efficiency. They lived, ate, slept and often died together. A special bond grew up, no-one talked of it, it just came, it was essential to trust and rely on each other. Each man was a single piece in a giant jigsaw, a very complex jigsaw.

No-one could put on a front for long on a Naval messdeck, your very soul was soon bared to all around you. You were what you were. Your strengths were exposed as were your weaknesses and there grew a tolerance of each other that was only apparent on Naval messdecks.

The third cruiser squadron was now non-existent, *HMS Gloucester* was no more, the cruel sea had claimed her; may she rest in peace.

More mayhem, damage, casualties, more telegrams, "The Admiralty regrets etc". It was endless, you sailed out through the boom and the whim of a man would decide whether you lived or died. Decisions had to be made, decisions that often were wrong, calamitous, made in a split second. Not an enviable decision for anyone to have to make, but there was no shortage of takers. Victories would be remembered in perpetuity. Disasters and failures were simply forgotten. It would all be put down to the fortunes of war, a well worn cliché that gave substance to the many pubs of that name on our street corners.

The decision that sent *Gloucester* and *Fiji* to their doom was a typical example of this continuous lottery of death. Almost an entire crew of vibrant, healthy, young men were despatched to a watery grave in the *Gloucester*, plus about two hundred on the *HMS Fiji*. The ships that were once their home had now become their tomb. There was no Padre, no weighted shrouds, no ceremony, no prayers, no white ensigns, just death and instant burial all at a stroke.

None of the grisly, macabre rituals that had been performed on the dead of the *Kent*. Perhaps *Gloucester's* was the best way, instant and arguably the more honourable, but what of the wisdom of the decision that sent her to her doom?

HMS Greyhound a G class destroyer, compliment around one hundred and sixty men, had been dispatched to apprehend and sink a couple of Greek Caiques carrying Axis supplies. This she accomplished with commendable expediency but, alas, she in turn was sunk by enemy air attacks. Someone then made the decision to send two cruisers to her assistance and so it was that over eight hundred lives were lost going to the rescue of the survivors from the one hundred and sixty crew of the *Greyhound*, which I understand numbered about forty.

What was the justification for this calamity? One thing was certain, and that is Sea Captains had altered little through the years. Right back to the old days of sail, when the scent of battle was in the air, the adrenalin begins to flow, the challenge is in the air.

"Steer one hundred and ninety degrees Number One."

"Full speed ahead both."

Bosun's whistle, bugle calls, running feet.

"Stands to action stations."

Off you went to glory or oblivion, all, as I have already said, at the whim of one man. Who would want his job? The answer is unquestionably almost every officer aboard.

More mayhem, damage and casualties, more telegrams, so dreaded by the folks at home. The envelopes were identical, it was the contents that could differ. "The Admiralty regrets to announce that your son was killed in action, blah, blah, blah." Or the telegram you were allowed to send yourself. "Safe and well, don't write." That was all, but at least it meant you were alive. Only then would the almost nightly obituary be spoken over the air. "The Admiralty regrets to announce the loss of *HMS* ...., next of kin have been informed."

"Roll on my f______ twelve."

Chapter 23

A mixture of steel, timber, cement and ballast coupled with the skill and ingenuity of the engineers, shipwrights and welders had eventually knocked *Kent* into some sort of shape and seaworthiness, in preparation for her homeward journey.

The fact that *Kent* was a cripple did nothing to excuse her from the persistent nightly attacks by air on the harbour. We were unable to answer back, as our four inch guns were forbidden to fire and this made us feel that we were now more vulnerable. It was quite on the cards that we could again be hit, but amazingly the ships in the harbour were at that time unharmed by the raids.

It was getting close to the time for flooding the dry dock in preparation for our exit, but there were a number of delays, such as leaking plates and glands, a rather serious fire, all caused by slackness on the part of the 'Gyppo' dockyard mateys. At times the air became blue with the language as well as the fire.

After all our trials and tribulations the repairs were completed. We thankfully left the dock and berthed alongside. Tomorrow about midday we would be on our way back to the UK. The farewell run ashore was an inevitability.

"D'ye hear there."

"Leave to the port Watch from 1600-1700." This would be our last run ashore in Alex, a celebration of our return home and a fond farewell to Alex. There was nothing unusual about this run ashore, it followed the usual pattern. Fleet Club, bars and the Black Cat nightclub. Long before the last stop at the nightclub, there were very few matelots on the street who were not two sheets to the wind. It was a setting in which just about anything could happen and usually did. Everyone was on a short fuse, tempers, generally speaking, were contained on the messdecks, but ashore and full of liquor it was a different story. It didn't have to be anything of importance. Big ship against small ship, Stoker against Seaman. Aussie against Pom. There were never, or seldom, anything other than fists used, fists that were fortunately usually flailing in thin air. This time it was a little more personal, it was *Kent* versus *Liverpool*. Your opponent on these occasions was just an excuse, anyone or anything could be the object of your anger. When it was over you just felt better, even thought the recipient could have left you with bruised knuckles. If you were lucky you got away before the arrival of the Naval patrols, when invariably big ship would have his arm around small ship and likewise, *Kent* and *Liverpool*, and Aussie and Pom. Very likely they would be singing the celebrated matelots' song of remorse.

"This is my story, this is my song.
We've been in commission
Too f-----g long.
Roll on the *Nelson*, the *Rodney*, *Renown*
This three funnel bastard is getting me down.
Hold your row, what'ye say
From Alex to Chatham's
A f-----g long way."

Everyone would feel fine in the morning, they had got the devil out of their system. Tomorrow would be sailing day, we would be off on our long journey home. The route of that voyage dicated by the enemy who controlled the Med, by virtue of its superiority in the air. It would mean the long boring journey through the Suez Canal and right round the continent of Africa, a journey thousands of miles longer than going direct through the Med via Gibraltar.

For *bon homie* high spirits and laughs it was a day to remember, that is until "eight bells" and the changeover of the duty Watch. Almost immediately there followed the pipe "D'ye hear there, Able Seamen Cairns and Seager report to the Divisonal Officers' office immediately."

There followed plenty of ribald comments and several suggestions as to what it was all about, sadly they were all very wide of the mark.

The Divisional Officer Lt Comm Sitwell, an English gentleman to his toes, said: "I'm afraid I've got some not very good news for you." That was the opening shot. "I have a signal requesting that I select two torpedo men to leave *Kent*."

It was evident that he had little stomach for the news he was imparting to us. "You realise that you are now both qualified torpedo men and, of course, you have only been away from the UK for a short ten months. All the other torpedo men aboard are now nearly three years away from home. I'm sure you understand, it's nothing personal, it gives me no pleasure etc, etc."

The full implication of what he was telling us took a full three seconds to register in our numbed minds.

Anything trying to describe our devastation would sound inadequate. Seager and I turned to each other in disbelief.

"I'm sorry lads," continued Sitwell. "I'm afraid you must pack your gear at once and leave the ship tonight. You do understand don't you?" he continued.

We both had to agree that it was the only course he could take. This admission, however, did nothing to alleviate our total disappointment at the news. He shook our hands and wished us well and we left his office to return to the mess and break the news to our messmates.

I'm sure everyone was just as stunned as we were. We had no time to go about ship to say our farewells; within an hour we were loading our gear onto a Naval runabout. We felt like two prisoners being recaptured and taken back to gaol.

There would only be seventeen of the twenty HOs making the journey back to Blighty, but at least we two were still alive. Polly Morgan's family would still be mourning his loss.

To say it was tough saying goodbye to my oppos is an understatement. Six of us had been together since the train journey from Liverpool Street Station to our first posting of *HMS Royal Arthur* to begin our training.

Seager and I were like two stranded whales, separated from the school, but we had no time to dwell on our tribulations. The truck driver was anxious to get away, after all he was oblivious to our predicament. We were off the jetty and away, all in a flash - perhaps it was better that way.

There had to be a sound reason for our sudden departure from HMS*Kent* but we had only been told there was a demand for torpedo men. We were given no inkling of what, why or where we were going. Thus it was that the course of torpedo man that I had so recently completed was to determine each one of my future moves through the remainder of my service in the RN. Which, then, of my new found skills would they be calling for? It was a question I was to wait for the answer to. Would it be electrics, torpedoes, demolitions or mines?

We spent the first night in the disgusting transit camp at Sidi Bish. I can tell you that our morale was at rock bottom and I spent the night heavily cursing Cornelius Finbar Driscoll and everything associated with HMRoyal Navy. No-one could be expected to appreciate just how it felt to be suddenly torn away from the security of the messdeck with its feelings of belonging to a family and the camaraderie that you shared with these men who you had lived and laughed with. Nor was it easy to forget the sadness and grief we had so recently shared.

After breakfast in this flyblown dump, we reported to the office where someone in the uniform of a CPO told us we were moving that day to another location. This was the beginning of an Egyptian safari - we still knew nothing about our destiny. Into the back of another truck and out through the back streets of Alexandria was a journey that, for me, put into perspective the traumas of my early childhood in the depressed North East of England. The abject poverty of these people and the filth and deprivation of their environment, made my childhood appear as if I had lived in Shangri La.

We skirted the bay round Alex and a crumbling potholed track took us to a coastside compound of huts, which proved to be the Fleet Air Arm base of *HMS Grebe*, at Dekeila. A sentry approached us at the gates and we unloaded our gear at yet another Army-style hut. To say it was depressing is an understatement and it was immediately memorable for two reasons. We were taking stock of our surroundings when Seager turned to me and said "Look round Phil." I turned and immediately froze. There out in the bay silhouetted against a beautiful sunset was *HMS Kent,* steaming towards the Suez Canal en route to the UK. It was devastating to watch as she steamed homeward taking the crew back to their loved ones. It was hitting below the belt and rubbing salt into our wounds. If that wasn't bad enough, I immediately contracted Gastro Enteritis, quite laughingly sometimes referred to as gippy tummy. My home was a toilet seat for about six days and I thought I would never survive and, I admit, at one time I couldn't have cared less whether I did or not.

We were on *Grebe* ostensibly to service torpedoes, but we were never to get sight of a 'tinfish' during our stay there.

Chapter 24

Stato Maggiore della Marina Militare
Il Capo dell' Ufficio Storico

Rome, 12 March 1993

Dear Sir,

here enclosed are

- a short biography of Cdr. J.V. Borghese;
- an excerpt of the book "I Sommergibili italiani" edited by the Ufficio Storico of the Italian Nay where you can find the submarine's data;
- the chapter IX of the book "I Mezzi d'Assalto" where the action again Alessandria is described in full.

I hope you will find someone to translate into your language the said documents, which are "no cost". My Office will enjoy to receive a copy of your book when pubblished.

Sincerly

Amm. Div. Renato SICUREZZA

Mr. Philip CAIRNS
20 Surrey RD.
DAGENHAM - ESSEX

Letter from Italian Archives with the 'Scire' *Captains own version of the sinking's in Alexander Harbour.*

When Lt Comm Prince Valerio Borghese left his home port, his star sign must have been in the ascendancy, he must have claimed Irish ancestry and he had certainly not broken any mirrors in the previous seven years. When he headed for the Dodaconese Islands of Leros with his submarine *Scire*, he needed all the elements of good fortune mentioned above and he got them in abundance.

The *Scire* left the port of La Spezia in Italy on a mission that was to bring glory to the much maligned Italian Navy. The surface fleet had earned the reputation of running scared from any confrontation with the RN, how much of this criticism was justified and how much of it was British propaganda we will never know. Perhaps a bit of each. Certainly this great feat of bravery and seamanship was never acknowledged to any extent at the time.

The *Scire,* a large submarine, had been specially adapted to carry three brilliantly designed small underwater craft which she picked up outside the harbour of La Spezia. They were known as Maiales, a twin manned underwater propelled torpedo with a detachable warhead and crewed by a pilot and diver.

The Captain of *Scire* had set out with the confidence of his successful mission in Gibraltar after a number of previous unsuccessful and disastrous attempts behind him.

The plan was for three Maiale craft to each attack a preselected target within Alex Harbour. The targets were the battleships *Valiant* and *Queen Elizabeth* and the aircraft carrier *Formidable*. The Italian intelligence about the *Formidable* proved wrong because she was not in harbour, but a substitute target was available.

The attack was scheduled for the night of the 17th but the weather conditions caused it to be postponed for twenty four hours. It was now that the gods began to shine down on the Captain of the *Scire*. On the 18th everything was perfect for the attack, there was a clear sky, with no moon and a flat, calm sea. *Scire* surfaced shortly before 9pm about one and a half miles from Alex Harbour and released three Maiale craft. As they neared the boom they had the amazing good fortune to find it open to allow the entrance of an H Force destroyer escort. At this time the air attack was timed to be at its peak and was one of the heaviest ever launched against Alex. They proceeded through the entrance, where one of them was nearly run down by a returning destroyer, all three then closed in on their targets, unspotted. Outside the harbour the Officer on the Watch on *HMSJervis* had a sub reported on the surface dead ahead. *Jervis* attacked and the sub then crash dived. After more depth charges were released, oil and debris were reported on the surface, the usual sign of a kill.

Mysteriously no Allied or enemy sub were acknowledged in the area. The Captain of *Scire,* which was reported safely back in Leros, claimed he had suffered no attack. The *Jervis* had apparently seen and attacked a sub that did not exist. Was it a hushed up attack on a British sub?

There was an ironic twist to the story because *Jervis* was to receive serious damage on the raid. It was not quite clear how the enemy would have gained entry had the boom not been so fortunately open.

The two Italians Martelloto and Marino headed for the oil tanker *Sagones*, a substitute target for the absent *Formidable*, and fixed their warhead to its hull. The hapless *Jervis* was now tied up to the *Sagone* which then sank with a tremendous explosion. The two Italians had safely made their escape, having got the bonus of a crack British destroyer to their credit. *HMSJervis* was to be severely damaged and out of commission for a month - that was success number one. A short distance away the *Queen Elizabeth,* now forewarned, and with her crew on the upper deck, blew up, again with a massive explosion. The Commander in Charge, Admiral Cunningham, had the anguish of being a witness. In his own words:"The *Queen Elizabeth* with flames belching from her funnels, exploded and lifted a full five or six feet in the air." This was success number two to the Italians Marcelglia and Schergat.

By all the odds, attempts to sink the third target *HMSValiant* should have resulted in failure for the intrepid Italians. As Captain Durand de la Penne neared his target of *Valiant,* his craft began to sink and he found his co-pilot was missing. La Penne had every justification for abandoning the mission but by a superhuman effort of bravery he managed to detach the warhead and place it below the keel of Valiant. Completely exhausted by his efforts, he managed to surface and heaving the mask from his face, fill his lungs with oxygen and swim to the buoy where, to his utter amazement, he found his co-pilot hanging on. It is not established why Bianchi left his craft, it may have been blind panic; remember the explosions of the *Queen Elizabeth* and *Sagones* were adjacent to where they were underwater.

The sinking of the *Valiant* was to be more prolonged, but at least one rating of the RN was on duty that night and he spotted the two Italians hanging on the buoy and opened fire on them. Now at last there was some counter action and searchlights began to scan the water. The two Italians were picked up on the order of Admiral Cunningham, taken aboard *Valiant* to be interrogated. It is easy now to understand the blind panic that must have existed when the two POWs were taken aboard

Valiant. I am not quite sure that the treatment afforded those two gallant men was strictly within the rules of the Geneva Convention that governs the treatment of POWs. The Admiral ordered that they be taken into the bowels of *HMS Valiant* and be clamped, to see if they would impart information about the explosive in order to save their own skins. It was not surprising that these two valiant men refused to do so. At ten minutes to six La Penne asked to see Captain Morgan of *Valiant*, he then told him the explosive would detonate at 6pm, ten minutes to clear lower decks.

"Where are the charges placed?" Captain Morgan asked. La Penne refused to answer and was again taken below. La Penne got there to find Bianchi had made his escape. After a few agonising moments the *Valiant* exploded and was sunk. La Penne survived the blast, fortunately. It would be interesting to know if their treatment was justified - no doubt the cliché all is fair in love and war was applied.

What was the fate of the other two pairs of crewmen? Marcelglia and Schergat steered their craft to land, then sunk it, they hid for a while among the rocks. They then reached the railway station at Alex, caught a train to Rosseta off the mouth of the Nile, where another sub, the *Topazio*, was lying off to pick up survivors. They were actually walking down the beach to await a signal when they were spotted by an alert Egyptian sentry and captured. The other two, Martelloto and Marino, pursued the same escape route but were caught at the dockyard gate. Thus it was that six gallant men took out three warships and a fleet tanker, a deed that completely altered the balance of sea power in the Eastern Med. The Eastern Med fleet was now in a parlous state, with no battleships in service at all, whereas the Italians now had seven to call on. We were hemmed in, with enemy air bases, U Boat bases, E Boat bases and a far superior Italian fleet. Add to that the terror of the German Stuka dive bombers and you will wonder how we ever survived.

The success of the two man sub attack still did nothing to induce the surface fleet of the Italians to leave the safety of their harbours and take up battle stations with the RN. It was therefore fitting that six brave Italians survived, for had they not, their sacrifice would have been in vain.

Chapter 25

Across the bay at Alex air raids were commonplace and spectacular, occurring almost nightly. This one, however, was noticeable by its intensity and was made more significant by the fact that the hands were piped to muster in the small hours.

I managed to stir some life into my sleeping frame but my aching body was still suffering from the assault on it by the Egyptian cuisine and the venom of its insects, as I also had an attack of Sandfly Fever on top of my Enteritis. I cleared my eyes of sleep and a glance of my watch told me it was the unearthly hour of 3am. I struggled into my gear, inwardly cursing, then my addled brain cleared enough for me to realise that there was something very serious afoot.

We piled into the back of the trucks and the driver sped off with a speed that had no regard for the state of the potholed road, or yet the sorry state of my innards. The buzzes were rife, including the possibility of an airborne invasion, we were very weak and the successful airborne invasion by Crete by the German paratroopers made this quite feasible.

On our arrival in Alex we saw everyone running around like headless chickens. When the reason for the panic became known, it proved to be almost as serious as an invasion. Eventually out of chaos came some sort of order and I joined the two man crew of a Greek Caiquak, a type of fishing boat. In company with three other such boats, we found ourselves patrolling across the entrance of Alex Harbour. At intervals we were dropping small explosive charges over the side. There were other crews performing even more bizarre routines. The boom was a toughened wire gate that covered the entrance to the harbour and could be opened and closed to allow the passage of boats, and keep out the enemy. A line was secured to the edge of the boom, with corks at intervals so that it floated on the water out to a Naval cutter which was anchored offshore, another such line passed between a boat anchored further out to sea. On each boat sat ratings holding each line in their hands. The hope was that any small craft would hit the floating line and so alert the men in the boats of their presence. This then was the Navy's answer to the success of the Italians in their assault on the fleet in the Alex. It was crude, it was ineffective, it was too late. We had been caught napping by an enemy we had constantly despised and the price we had to pay was an extremely high one.

It was, however, essential that something be done to make it appear that we were striking back and so alleviate the humiliation that had been imposed on the RN.

The brilliance of the Italians was quietly played down. That was the name of the game in wartime, only the enemy gave out propaganda, what we gave out was news.

Georgio the Greek engineer in my boat spent all his time singing, an oil can in one hand and an oily rag in the other. The shrapnel from the blanket of steel covering Alex Harbour from the anti aircraft guns was like falling rain and the splinters sizzled round our ears. Two sticks of bombs fell close enough to violently rock our boat and huge plumes of water rose majestically in unison into the sky. Georgio shook his fist to the sky and from the welter of abuse issuing from his lips, I could decipher "German and Italian bastards." How the Greeks hated them. As the water around the boat sizzled like a cauldron of frying chips, so did I.

The counter measures bordered on the ridiculous but they were all we had. The idea of three men in a boat holding a piece of string across the water to keep the enemy at bay sounds fanciful, but it was true. The question that needs an answer is, crude as the counter measures appeared to be, why were they not in operation before the debacle? We already had ample evidence of how devastating the Italians could prove by the sinking of HMSYork in Suda Bay and the successful sinkings in Gibraltar.

This raises the question of how the Maialis would have gained entrance to the protected harbour had Admiral Vians' destroyer force not so fortuitously been entering the harbour at the same time? This was just an amazing piece of luck for the Italians, had the boom been closed an entry would have to be found elsewhere.

The three subs would have to make for the edges of the boom and squeeze in between the wall and the edge of the net. Hence the string and cork routine already explained. It is possible the hindrance of the nets and extra time taken, could have resulted in a different story of the events being recorded.

The Italians, however, from the word go, had the luck of the Irish, everything had gone completely in their favour. Such are the fortunes of war.

I personally had about three weeks of this boring, tedious and uncomfortable routine before I was whisked away to participate in yet another bizarre, exciting and dangerous episode of the war, an event that was to again have very grave consequence for the Allies and the conduct of the war in the Med arena. It occurred to me as an after thought that, had the *Kent* still been operational in Alex at the time of the raid, because of her size she would have been an optional target in the absence of the carrier *Formidable.*

Chapter 26

The notice to leave *HMSGrebe* was as swift but not so traumatic as our departure from *Kent.* We were called to the office by a faceless CPO on the other side of the window and, once again, our gear was in the back of the truck and we continued on our safari, to where we still knew not.

We eventually hit the road running alongside the Suez Canal and continued down its length into the town of Ismailia. Two half submerged wrecks in the canal itself should have given us a clue as to our presence there, but at the time it did not register with us. We entered Ismailia and the ride down the main thoroughfare gave me the initial impression of a Wild West town, but there was much more to Ismailia than that.

We pulled up at the front of quite a large house in the corner of quite a nice square; looking up I spotted the white ensign fluttering in the breeze, above that the statutory radio mast and aerial. We had arrived at Navy House.

We were met by Petty Officer Farrell, an amiable man who, to our surprise, took us to a nearby cafe/bar on the main thoroughfare. We sat down and he beckoned a waiter. "Like a beer lads?" he enquired. The question begged no answer, we had three, it was Stella, quite acceptably cooled. He then requested menus from which we chose a meal to compensate for the total inadequacy of the corned beef sandwiches we'd had on our journey. It was all, to our relief, on the Admiralty.

We ended up on the perimeter of the RAF camp at Moasca, and so from the comfort of our bed and breakfast in town we had descended to a tent at the edge of the barren desert. We were now beginning to quickly expand in numbers, but none of them had taken the slipshod, haphazard route that we had experienced.

The reason for our presence on the canal lay in the two sunken ships we had seen on our journey down the canal road. This was to herald one of the most critical periods in the pursuit of the war on land and sea in this arena. Everything was going wrong: on land Rommel had counter attacked and driven the Allies back through the Egyptian border to within striking distance of Alexandria. Then the entry of the German Luftwaffe to the Mediterranean arena had decimated the Eastern Med fleet. The Med was virtually in command of the Axis air forces, and we were relying more and more for the supplies and the reinforcement we needed on the Suez Canal, even though this meant the long haul round the Cape for virtually everything that came into the Med.

The Germans were quick to realise the disastrous effect the closing of the canal would have on the Allies. They now had bases within easy striking distance of Suez and they launched their attacks from the Dodeconese Islands. So began the mining of the Suez Canal, not by the orthodox mines we were familiar with, but by a new and devilish type we, at first, had no answer to.

I lay on my Army issue bed, staring through the darkness in the general direction of the ridge of my Army issue tent. I was reflecting on the strange quirks of fate that had placed me along with Seager in my present completely disorientated environment. Surely they could have left the two of us in our comfortable bed and breakfast in Ismailia, at least until some more of the compliment of HMSStag arrived? To place just two of us in one of three huge tents on the perimeter of an RAF camp in Moasco was an action quite beyond belief. Here we were living like Bedouin Arabs with only scorpions, scarab beetles, mosquitoes and flies for company. Sand permeated everything; it was in our hair, our eyes, our ears, it was up our noses, between our toes and when the Sirocco winds blew, it tore at our skin. How the squaddies in the Western Desert put up with it I'll never know, without going into battle: they were each and every one of them a hero.

We both yearned for the companionship of the messdeck, meal time in the mess, always something like the Mad Hatter's Tea Party. We longed to be back on the upper deck of the Kent, breathing in lungs full of ozone as she scythed through the clear blue sea of the Med. We would gladly put up with the deafening ack ack, the calls to action stations and even the crump of the bombs. Anything, rather than the loneliness and discomfort of our present situation. I closed my eyes and sank into a fitful slumber, heartily cursing the name of Cornelius Finbar Driscoll.

Morning broke and we left our Bedouin abode. I glanced up at the sun-bleached scrawny tree outside, on which perched a number of equally scrawny vultures and I speculated that they were hoping to have us for breakfast at some future date. After a wash we joined the RAF 'Erks' for our meagre breakfast before reluctantly returning to our mess, spelt with a small 'm'. Another dawn, another day and glad tidings awaited us. At last, something to dispel our gloom. The truck from the Navy Office at Ismailia pulled up outside our tent and from it alighted a grinning PO Farrell.

"How's it going lads?" he asked with too much enthusiasm we thought. We told him in no uncertain terms how it was going. "Never mind lads, the school in Ismailia will soon be ready for us," he said. "Anyway, I've brought something to cheer you up, come with me." We followed him to the truck and our eyes lit up when, looking down, we saw two bundles of mail and a parcel. When I tell you that it had been a whole nine months since either of us had received a single letter, you can guess just how elated we were. The mail lying in that truck was now no longer news, it was history, but it was modern history, it spoke of the people at home, our family, our loved ones. It was the fragile thread that connected us to each other.

I admit to my pulse racing a little as I reached out and opened the letter from South Africa. I knew of course who it was from. I knew also before reading it that it would stir up emotions, emotions that I had quite resolutely kept under control. I had made a conscious decision not to communicate with Mary, I could only personally see heartache and grief in the continuance of correspondence.

That night my slumber was fitful, something was niggling away at my subconscious, appealing to my vanity, why not write just one more letter? Go on, boost your ego. Why was I now doubting my decision not to write? The chances of seeing Mary again were almost zero. By the time I was due to return to the UK the Med would be open, I reasoned, and I would speed home on a returning destroyer, or suchlike.

Sad to say, my vanity got the better of me and I wrote that letter, worse still, it was a very romantic letter which answered all her questions and would play havoc with her emotions. This was not the end of the story, there was more, but that was in the future.

Our spell in Moasca was short lived and George and I made our move to Ismailia where the Catholic school in the centre of town became our barracks. The school looked deceptively clean with its stone and marble structure. In fact we had to deal with rats, bedbugs and mosquitoes continually during our occupation.

On our first day in the Catholic school a young Alsation dog wandered into the grounds. A number of attempts were made to eject it but each time it would find its way back. Eventually PO Farrell, an obvious dog lover, took a shine to it and so it became part of the ships company of *HMS Stag*. It was then given the apt name of Navy and with the expert attention of PO Farrell grew into a fine healthy dog. Navy went everywhere with us. It also developed a strange trait, everyone that wasn't Naval was an enemy. No squaddie or Arab could get near him. He became a familiar part of our establishment.

The bar/cafe which was our home for a short time, we were allowed to convert into our own Club House. It was a very welcome addition to our facilities.

Some of the mine clearance party, Suez Canal (1940)
Left to Right Ted Hayward, Horace Marshal, 'Alex', 'Paddy' and Author.

Ismailia itself was a very pleasant town and the French influence was evident. There was a substantial French population in residence and many of them were known to be Vichy sympathisers. It boasted a beautiful Catholic church and two cinemas, one open air and, tucked into the corner, we discovered a delightful English tea room with the rustic name of The Copper Kettle. I don't remember its history. Nearby were some beautiful shrubbed and landscaped areas, complete with rustic bridges and water inlets. We learned that it took an operation almost equivalent to the building of the pyramids to create this oasis in the desert terrain of Ismailia. It was achieved by the transport of thousands of tons of mud from the Nile delta. The whole setting around Lake Timsah was a credit to the foresight of the Canal Company and, no doubt, the vision of the French.

The canal at this point in its history held the key to all future events, not only in the Med but it was also the key to all that happened in the Western Desert of Libya. Almost everything that was not entering the Med came or left via the Suez Canal. We were at that time on our knees and many of our problems were down to our lack of air cover. This was never more evident than on the canal where the German minelaying planes operated with impunity. Had the Italian Navy with its superior forces shown more resolve, and had the Germans not been fully stretched from the Med to the frozen wastes of Russia, Alex and the Suez would surely have fallen, the results of which would have taken the war onto an entirely different course.

It was not surprising that Churchill, the War Cabinet and all the Generals were acutely aware of the necessity to free this vital waterway to allow our shipping unrestricted passage. It is therefore very surprising to discover that little of the events that took place on the canal have been written about or are recorded in the archives.

Lt Comm Morgan Giles set about organising the counter measures against this latest deadly weapon of war. The mines dropped around the busy Thames Estuary had initiated the first attempts at a solution.

There followed many waterborne devices, but the answer to the magnetic mine was found by HMSVernon in their new Edinburgh headquarters; it was the Double LSweep.

The scheme to keep the canal clear of these devices was simple in its operation and, at first, very successful, but things then started to go awry. The reason for the failures were initially the human factor but there remained some mystery about some of the failures.

Suez Canal 1941. Mine look out post. H.M.S. 'Euryalus' *in background.*

The canal mine disposal unit had one distinct advantage over other units and that was the width of the canal, which was about two hundred yards from bank to bank. The disadvantage was it was about one hundred miles long. Our first task was to establish lookout trenches along its entire length, spaced fifty yards apart on the side of the canal. The idea was simple, but costly in manpower. Each trench contained a board with a pointer. The board was marked off round a one hundred and eighty degree radius, thus, when a mine was dropped into the water the lookout simply pointed his indicator at the splash. The lookout in the next trench would do the same and the mine marking party would then race the length of the canal. Wherever a mine had been reported, they would take a bearing of where the two pointers crossed, pull out in a rubber dingy and drop a marker buoy over the spot.

We were, however, desperately short of sweeping devices and could only boast three of the more successful of the methods, the Double LSweeps. Trials had previously been carried out the Mk I A Wellington bombers, fitted with powerful electric generators which energised a huge magnetic coil which was carried on its undercarriage. Five of these grotesque machines then flew the length of the canal, sending out magnetic waves. They had some successes, but they were deemed to be not effective enough for the time and effort they required. The situation was becoming critical and a number of canal boats, called hoppers, were urgently being converted to sweepers.

The archives say it took three and a half battalions of British troops to man the lookout posts and, I quote: "The Egyptians took over this operation most efficiently." This I know to be far from true. Initially they performed the job quite well, however, on a few occasions mines fell on the bank or at the edge of the canal in shallow water. The low water pressure on the hydrostatic valve allowed the mine to detonate. One of these detonations killed some Egyptian lookouts, which was enough for many of them to become disenchanted with keeping their heads up to observe the splashes. When the raiding planes neared their trenches, they dived to the bottom of the trench in case there was an accident. They surfaced when the planes had passed and pointed their marker at random. This had a devastating effect on the whole operation with a resulting loss of life. It is my recollection that Lt Comm Morgan Giles wanted all the Egyptians removed, but the Egyptian authorities insisted that their troops took part in the defence of their canal. I have, in fact, memories of the Commanding Officer threatening physical violence towards them.

Three ships had already been sunk in the canal before the formation of the mine clearance sqad, the *Ranee, Aghios Georgis* and the *Darwenthal.* Fortunately none of the wrecks blocked the passage of shipping.

It was, however, the sinking of the *SSRanee* that set the alarm bells ringing. It was sunk in between raids and some twenty ships had safely passed over the mine that sank her. The authorities soon realised that they had yet another problem to deal with, another type of mine actuated by a completely different set of circumstances. So it was that we were introduced to the acoustic mine.

It was to set the boffins yet another puzzle to solve. This, as its name will imply, was a sound detonated mine, as opposed to the magnetic type. The principle was that the sound waves from the ship's engines were the actuators of the detonation. As with the magnetic, the influence on the detonator was at its maximum when the ship was passing over it.

The answer to this problem was found in just one more clever but simple device. On the bows of the tugs employed, a sound chamber with a powerful compressed air hammer inside was lowered into the water from two pivoted arms. The hammers produced a noise much in excess of that of a ship's engine and in consequence the mine was exploded before the tug was in the vicinity of the explosion. To everyone's delight it worked, that is the mines were exploded, but sometimes the tugs were very badly shaken up and it was dangerous and uncomfortable for the lads on the tugs. Before the advent of these compressed air hammers there was no other method used, at the very least it was only an expediency. The Canal Company owned two very powerful launches, capable of around forty five knots. We acquired them and installed crews. The principle involved now was that the boats would approach the position of the marked mine, rev up to maximum speed, on the theory that the speed of the boat over the mine would beat the detonation - and it worked. Once again, the idea was merely an expediency. It was a deadly dangerous exercise for the intrepid crewmen and predictably it was to end in disaster. For its success it relied entirely on the buoy in the water accurately marking the position of the mine. This was the first indication we had that the Egyptian lookouts were letting us down in the marking of mines. The Dard, one of the high speed launches, had made its run, achieving maximum revs, when over the marked position it slowed down at the end of its run to turn and make another attack on the mine. The explosion was devastating, it blew the launch to smithereens. There was one very lucky survivor, the Coxswain. How he survived was a miracle, as there was nothing left of the boat and the rest of the crew.

This all happened in front of our eyes, it was sickening. The first man out there was Lt Comm Morgan Giles and the boat that took him to the scene of the disaster stopped while the Egyptian crew picked up the dead fish from the explosion. I think this incident put into perspective our relations with the Egyptians at that time.

It was after this incident that the Commander was goaded into personally confronting the trench lookouts and threatened them with violence if they didn't do the job so essential to our safety. There were other fatalities entirely due to their malpractice. One of the converted hoppers hit a mine and sunk with the loss of life and later the Tynedale was sunk.

In spite of the ingenuity of the boffins we were still having problems in clearing the mines. It was then decided to engage the services of a squad of Naval divers. I believe there were about six of them and the senior one was a Chief or PO Watson. When they learned the danger of the task they were asked to perform, they decided to ask for danger money, which they were awarded. It was only in retrospect that the attendants on the diving boats realised that they were in just as much danger as the divers. They, however, never received a bean which brought into focus the fact that the whole squad were performing beyond the normal call of duty.

The arrival of the divers added a new dimension to our activities and the purpose of their enlistment was to locate the mines on the bed of the canal in order to recover them. The average depth of the canal was six fathoms (thirty six feet) and it appeared to be a routine operation. In fact it was to become a major problem. Every marked position had to be investigated, after the orthodox sweeps and not affected an explosion.

The unreliability of the mine spotters was totally upsetting the routine, it was now doubly hazardous. The Germans had the services of a former Chief Pilot of the canal, who was obviously well versed in every yard of its geography, exactly where the bottom would be undulating would be known to them. It was believed that he actually planned the raids. Another obstacle to the divers was the six knot speed of the flow, this in spite of the Med being tideless. It was also quite surprisingly murky. The Naval divers were trained at great depth, hence their weighty, cumbersome attire. Solid brass and copper helmets and great leaden soled boots. The search would be slow and as they plodded along the bottom, they were also disturbing the silt, further hindering their visibility. At that time there were no skin divers with oxygen bottles.

The archives do no justice to the gravity of Great Britain's situation. Rommel had struck back and with superior air power his forces had driven the British Army through the borders of Egypt and was threatening the Eastern Med Naval Base at Alex, the evacuation of which had already commenced. The next target was the Suez Canal. At that time not only was the Army's transportation system in tatters, the Navy was being denied the exit of damaged ships for repairs but also the entrance of reinforcements and replacements. In addition, the Greeks and Turks relied heavily on the canal for supplies and equipment for their railways and so it was a situation fraught with danger.

Chapter 27

It was around midnight when the now familiar melancholy wail of the air raid siren sounded. At dawn we were off to tackle the results of yet one more unopposed attack. What surprises would today hold for us? What time would it be when we wearily climbed into our beds? Time alone would tell.

We marked about twelve mines and commenced the now rehearsed routine, starting with the 'Double L' magnetic sweep and the tugs with their 'Bow Hammers'. We had three undetonated and for the first time, the divers went down, it was our intention to recover the mines and bring them ashore. The diving boats were secured to the Hawser stretched across the canal. The divers donned their cumbersome gear, two attendants manned the manually operated pumps on each diving boat and down went the two divers on their search for the lethal cannisters. They found one within the hour, recovery plan was once again clever, and like most ideas, simple.

A wire hawser was shackled onto the submerged mine; alongside the canal road were a series of bollards for securing ships that might stop on their way through. The wire hawser was passed round it and then secured to the rear of a Matador truck, which then drove down the road and out came the mine. It was, however, not quite as straightforward as all that, a precaution had to be taken.

We already knew that if the mines were in shallow water they would detonate. The answer was found by the expert in the squad, the specialist who was attached to us. He is described in Admiral Poland's book *The Torpedomen* as a diver. In fact he was a Canadian, Sub Lt Cook. He it was who devised a cunning device that neutralised the hydrostatic valve during the changes in pressure as the mine surfaced on its exit from the canal. Again it was a simple device: he adapted a motor horn, the type operated by pressing a round rubber ball. By fitting a screw thread on the business end of the horn which matched the aperture over the valve controlling the mine's fuse, he could maintain a ten pounds per square inch pressure. It worked, but must have been a very critical operation. I don't think it was apparent to me at least that we could all have been blown sky high.

This particular mine was then manhandled to a spot some distance from the canal bank. It was roped off and Sub Lt Cook then began coolly dismantling the fuse structure in a quite matter of fact fashion. It was a great privilege to watch an ice cold hero in action. His bravery was an essential factor in keeping abreast of the cunning of the enemy.

There was another two incidents that involved recovered mines. Richard Green was one of the cool-headed heroes who delved into their secrets, and the first incident was quite humourous. After a few bevvies in the canteen, Richard, in company with some others in the crew, decided to play a prank on one Lieut Comm Duff. After steaming the explosives out of a recovered mine they set off in the dead of night and deposited it right alongside the Lieut Comm's houseboat. Upon arising the following morning he looked down in alarm at the mine, and immediately set the whole recovery operation into action.

The other story, which tells much about the calibre of these men, occurred when, with his hand inside the lethal chamber, he released a booby trapped spring loaded panel. The lid came down on his fingers and he calmly turned and asked for a matchbox to place under the trigger. He then calmly continued with another successful defusing.

It was a long, tiring, frustrating day and the slow, plodding progress of searching for the other two mines proved fruitless. The search area was methodically extended beyond the marked positions, which meant the repositioning of the moor line across the Canal. After about eighteen hours of non-stop work, we returned wearily to our billets. This one raid closed the canal for five days, it was a situation that was to repeat itself many times and the reasons were to become very worrying.

It was decided to carry out further sweeps and we successfully blew up one of the two remaining suspects. That's what we had got down to now, we were calling the marked positions 'suspect'.

On the fifth day the canal was deemed safe and the vital flow of shipping was recommenced without incident, until the next raid. The enemy were no doubt informed of our every move, there was no need for underground agents, spy rings or reconnaissance flights. Their intelligence was supplied by local, home-based residents.

Strangely enough, one of our own squad was arrested and charged with consorting with the enemy. The story had all the ingredients of a spy thriller including a beautiful girl, the balcony of whose house overlooked our base.

The arrested man, an AB S/T was a native of the French Caribbean and I was one of his escorts when he was taken to Port Tewfik for trial. No-one got to know any details of the case, nor did we discover the result of his trial. I will concede that the beautiful girl on the balcony may have been a figment of a Jack's imagination as far as being an agent was concerned, however the story of the West Indian's arrest was fact and the beautiful girl continued to grace the balcony.

The raids and the clearances continued and by March/April had increased in intensity and a very interesting fact emerged about the lack of air defences throughout the Med arena. At the time we were making strong representations for protection, it was stated that six Hurricanes had been allocated to Malta for her defence. Six Hurricanes. This figure is put into perspective by the claim made some months earlier after the Battle of Britain, during the London Blitz. It is claimed that nine hundred planes were lost by Britain, while shooting down one thousand seven hundred German Luftwaffe. Just one more inexplicable fact that emerges when you delve into the annuls.

The next raid was calamitous, it started alarm bells ringing from Suez to Whitehall. It could not have come at a worse time, our fortunes in the Med, in the desert and, not least, in the canal, were at the lowest ebb. The Germans were no longer waiting for us to clear the canal before executing another raid, they were now coming nightly.

For days there were no war materials, fuel, food, and the coal and supplies for the Greeks and Turks, who at the time relied wholly on Great Britain who, it must be remembered, was completely on its own. Nothing was getting through, eventually there were more than one hundred vessels held up, a mixture of merchant and warships, all so essential to the war we were conducting against all odds.

This was by far the worst snarl up that we had so far encountered, nothing about the job was now predictable. One of the hammer sweepers had got too near its prey and suffered severe damage, and more of the marked positions were proving negative to both sweeping and locating by divers. It was very frustrating, because in theory if the mine spotters were doing their job it was virtually foolproof. The canal was being kept closed longer by mines that did not exist, than it was with the genuine thing. It was driving everyone to despair and all concerned were getting frustrated. It was a problem that was being addressed in the highest quarters but no-one came up with anything to improve on the system already in use. There were some bizarre ideas mooted from barrage balloons to smoke screens. Another was the dragging of a giant drogue along the bed of the canal. I have only read of these suggestions in the archives and I have no knowledge of them being experimented with.

The best suggestion of all, which the archives say was actually put into operation, brought a smile to my lips when I read of it. It involved, would you believe, the rascally 'Jim Irish', the king of the Egyptian spivs or fixers already mentioned during my time in Alex, plus the coin divers of Port Said. Jim is said to have hired six of these divers to assist in the search for the mines.

Apparently only two were genuine divers and Jim had brought the remainder along to boost his commission and, to quote from *The Torpedomen*: "The others were observed to splash around the area of the boat and return to the boat breathing heavily and towelling themselves down." There was a lot of merit in using these skindivers because the depth of the canal was no problem to them. Also, one of the problems with the Naval divers was that their leaden boots stirred up the silt on the canal bottom, which restricted visibility. The skindivers had unrestricted head movement and no visor to restrict their vision. The fault with them, as the book relates, was their "fear and apprehension" of the lethal canisters for which they were searching. This was exactly the problem that we were experiencing with the mine spotters.

Most of our problems in locating the mines occurred in the stretches where the bottom of the canal was undulating and creviced. A theory strongly held by the mine clearance party was the possibility of the enemy dropping large objects that made an observable splash in the water. The objects, we thought, were perhaps just large sand bags that dispersed on hitting the bottom of the canal. It was a sound theory, because it was the unlocated mines that were now causing the main problems. It did substantially extend the time the canal was closed to traffic and we were now regularly opening the canal with marked mines remaining unexploded or not being located by divers.

There must have been huge sighs of relief from Cairo to Whitehall when eventually the traffic began to flow. They were nose to tail as they eased their way through and one of the first in line was the aircraft carrier *HMS Formidable*, so urgently needed as a replacement for the *Illustrious*, which had received six direct hits from one thousand pound bombs delivered by the fearsome, shrieking divebombers of the Luftwaffe, the JU87 Stukas. It hardly seemed a dog watch since *Kent*, as part of those great massed East and West Med fleets, had seen her safely through the blockaded Med to Alexandria.

Now it was the turn of the Naval casualties to make their delayed exit from the Mediterranean. It was a body blow for the Navy to lose the services of *HMS Illustrious* so soon after her entry into the East Mediterranean. She was well equipped with armoured deck, radar, the invaluable secret eye, and the latest Fairey Fulmer aircraft. *Illustrious* sadly made her exit to cross the Atlantic for repair. She was closely followed through by *HMS Dido* who was to give us some great news as she passed by. The whole nation had been stunned by the tragic loss of the pride of the RN, *HMS Hood*. She had been sunk with only a couple of survivors. *Hood* had been sunk by what was acknowledged to be the finest battleship afloat, the pride of the German Navy, the *Bismark*. Now the words written down the side of the *Dido* in large white letters, going from the bow to the stern, told us that the *Hood* had been revenged. The words read "*Bismark* sunk". Everyone instinctively cheered, we really needed that morale booster. It was made all the more poignant by the fact that *HMS Dido* was grievously damaged; her whole superstructure was wrecked and her main armaments were pointed in crazy angles. The Stukas had been out once again and wreaked havoc.

There were two more ideas being pursued to try and provide the answer to our problems, as the canal was being closed for longer and longer periods. The first was a colossal venture given the go ahead by the C in C Admiral Cunningham. It was to cover the whole of the trouble spot with nets from bank to bank. It was intended originally to cover the whole one hundred miles of the canal, a feat similar to building the Great Wall of China. It was only abandoned when someone had the good sense to get out his abacus and estimated it would require one million miles of codline to bring it about.

The mammoth task of making, installing and operating the anti-mine nets across the width of the Suez Canal came under the command of Lieut Commander Douglas V Duff.

He was quite possibly the most flamboyant of all the great characters thrown up by World War II. In his book *May the Winds Blow* he describes in detail the amazing events that took place on the canal during his period of command. He was undoubtedly the very last of the swashbuckling seadogs, his exploits were legendary.

He was the godchild of Sir Roger Casement, a novice monk, in the RNVR the Royal Ulster Constabulary, and also the Palestine Police. The Black and Tan troubles in Ireland, the rescue of fugitives from the Bolshies in the Black Sea, special service in the Mediterranean and the Western Desert, all saw his involvement. Upon his arrival at *HMS Stag* on the Suez Canal, he described it as the "craziest Naval establishment on earth". Apart from the Naval personnel, he had under his charge some five thousand Egyptian labourers. He found that there was widespread bribery and corruption among the natives who were under the control of an assortment of local Mafia-type gangsters. Gang warfare between them was rife and there were many killings. Vast sums of money were involved in the purchase of enormous quantities of goods and materials needed to complete this mind boggling feat. He claims that there were three attempts on his life, which included a stabbing, a gunshot and an unexploded grenade.

The other idea not yet mentioned was to make headline news on television and radio in 1992 when film was shown of the Americans using trained dolphins to locate underwater mines. They homed in on the mine and attached a line, presumably by magnet, to the submerged object. The showing of this startling feat prompted the Russians to claim that they had perfected the practice some twenty years earlier, which would take us back to the 1970s.

I will now quote Admiral Poland's *Torpedomen*: "The urgency of the situation on the canal prompted a number of bizarre suggestions for locating mines, such as the use of trained dolphins." This in 1941. I'm sorry Uncle Sam and Uncle Joe, but I'm afraid you were only second and third with this great idea. It was a case of a perfectly feasible plan that had lain dormant for many years.

There was no need to be bored. In the leisure time between the raids it was quite pleasant, apart from the fleas, bugs, mosquitoes and the occasional rat. There were no sprays or repellents, no-one thought of fumigation, so it was always a personal battle with the vermin. Before you retired you did what you could as far as delousing was concerned and then dived into bed, firmly tucking your mosquito net round the edges. You then lay and listened to the sounds of the night before drifting into a slumber. In spite of the mosquito nets, at "rise and shine" sometimes your oppos would be hardly recognisable from bites. Strangely enough, the mosquitoes only seemed to feast at night and 'Gyppo Mossies' must have been a vampire breed for they seemed to leave you alone during the day.

I was relatively unaffected by the mossies, compared to some of the others, perhaps careless with their mosquito nets. Some of the comedians suggested they were choosy about whose blood they drank. I can vouch for the fact that there was at least one special mosquito that wasn't choosy. I was watching a film at the local cinema, at first I thought I was still woozy from the previous night's drinking bout. Then almost without warning I had collapsed unconscious, or rather delirious. I vaguely remember faces peering down at me on occasion and from then on, although I was unaware of it, I was fighting for my life. I had caught one of the most virulent forms of malaria. It was four weeks before I was allowed to rejoin the lads. I was the only matelot in the hospital, which was a tented one for the treatment of wounded from the desert. In the last week of my recovery the staff made a great fuss of me. The doctor told me that my life had hung by a thread and that I must have immediate convalescence. I rejoined my unit and was put to work the following day. I had made the fatal mistake of standing up and it was my experience that if you were standing in the Navy, you were fit to work. I had lost a substantial amount of weight and I was to suffer returning bouts of shivering for about the next ten years. Apart from that I was perfectly fit. I am eternally grateful to the wonderful Army nurses who were instrumental in saving my life. It was at my request that they came along in numbers to make our occasional dances such a great success.

The raids continued unabated and we were to lose another of the converted hoppers which hit an unmarked mine. It was a nasty setback and was to again dent our confidence at a time when the raids had dramatically intensified. During July/August there were no fewer than thirty four night raids on the canal area.

During this period there was a major deviation in the routine mining raids. On the night of 4th/5th August the air raid alert sounded, we were quite blasé about the warnings by now, because they were always concentrated on the canal. This time the planes were over the town itself and this time they were not carrying mines, they were carrying bombs.

The raid was inexplicable. The town of Ismailia was full of Vichy sympathisers and there was only one legitimate target and that was our headquarters in the school in the centre of the town. The bombs fell near but not that close, the planes had no adversary to worry about. It was a devastating raid and it killed two hundred and seventy civilians with many more injured. Everyone was mystified, they had failed to hit their target, if indeed we were their intended target, and they never repeated the raid. It was a gruesome night as we set about helping with the rescue work. We returned to the school and it was found that PO Farrell was not with us.

What happened next was to plunge the whole unit to the depths of despair. A local Egyptian policeman came in and informed us that PO

Farrell had been killed and Navy, our beloved mascot, was also dead. It appeared they were making for the school, having left Navy Office at the commencement of the raid, they were found lying together on the pavement. The first casual examination revealed that they were apparently uninjured. In fact both had died from the freak coincidence of flying shrapnel piercing a vital organ. everyone was completely devastated, how could fate possibly be so cruel? In one blow we had lost two of the best loved characters in the squad. PO Farrell was one of the nicest men it was my good fortune to meet. It's as well, perhaps, that they both died together, for it is doubtful whether either would have come to terms with the other's loss.

There were no dry eyes at the burial party of the much loved PO. It was then decided to give Navy a Naval burial, and he was taken by boat to the middle of Lake Timsah and committed to the deep with full Naval ceremony. It is my recollection that the unit never got over the loss of PO Farrell and Navy. It was as well that we were kept desperately busy as it took our minds off our sad loss. For some obscure reason this loss, which took place on land, was different, more personal than death at sea, with all the trappings of war around you. Warships had a close affinity with death, for that is their role, to inflict death and destruction on the enemy, hopefully before he did the same to you. The recent losses had more in keeping with a civilian air raid which, in fact, is exactly what it was.

The raids continued apace and just when we thought we had got it beaten we lost another ship, the *Tynedale*. Death then, was still lurking in the depths of the canal and everyone again realised that there still existed the need for the utmost care and vigilance.

The Axis forces really had us by the short and curlies. We survived because they had stretched themselves to a battle too far. Both Alex and the Suez Canal were still gravely threatened. Nothing was going right for us on either sea or land. The mining of the canal continued unabated but we were learning all the time and we were never to have another massive hold-up of ships. The tragic loss of *Hood* was followed by a further series of disasters in the Med. In the course of a couple of weeks we lost the aircraft carrier *Ark Royal*, the battleship *Barham* and the cruiser *Dunedin*. This was followed by one of the turning points in World War II, when the Japanese decimated the American fleet in Pearl Harbour on 7th December 1941. The Americans had been caught with their pants down. "Foul" they cried, "this is treachery."

The raid on Pearl Harbour ensured that Britain was no longer alone and so it was for the second time in a couple of decades, the Yanks were fighting beside us. The playing field was now much more even and soon the Atlantic would become like a main boating lake, as men, food and supplies streamed out of the ports of America en route to Blighty.

It was now eighteen months since Seager and I had been unceremoniously dumped on the jetty at Alex when *HMS Kent* steamed for home. It was also more than two years since we left the shores of Blighty. The canal was now seldom closed for more than twenty four hours. In spite of our success with the clearance of the mines, the bizarre experiment of covering the trouble spots with nets continued. By general consent they were now considered unnecessary, but it went ahead with both tragic and extraordinary results.

On the first experiment one of the boats capsized and one of the lads got entangled in the net and drowned. The net, however, was stretched across the expanse of the canal. Unfortunately no raid took place that night so the exercise proved fruitless. Upon trying to withdraw the net back to allow shipping through, it was found that all the draw lines had been stolen by Ali Baba and his forty thieves. Bedouin Arabs had crept up to the canal banks in the still of the night and helped themselves to all the rope that was necessary to draw the net back; it was a complete fiasco and resulted in utter mayhem. But who was to know? The nets could have been the saviour of the canal. We arrived after the first mines almost completely ignorant of what we were up against or how to combat it. In the end we got there. I have spoken of the almost total absence of material about this most critical of times. There had been tragic losses, some of them avoidable, but it says much for the men involved that, in spite of our lack of resources, we won the battle of the Suez Canal.

What of my companions in the squad? As I have said, almost to a man like George and myself, we were survivors from an assortment of incidents, many of them quite horrific. Strangely there was little talk of our experiences, which were I suppose memories best forgotten. There did, however, exist quite a different relationship to that prevailing on the messdeck. There was something markedly different to living out of each other's pockets, smelling each other's breath and body odours. Atmospheres where the dangers you lived with minute by minute in the confines of waters dominated by the enemy, controlled the pattern of your behaviour.

The mine disposal routine on the canal was something quite different, you knew where the danger was, they were fleeting moments. Then again, it was mostly at the beginning when we were operating in ignorance that most of the danger existed. Now we were all quite confidently going about our duties, but about ten lives had been lost. There was also the ever present danger of new booby traps and it could have been the next mine you dealt with. Leisure time was spent differently, you were free to spread your wings and, in consequence, it was much easier to keep your individual personality.

Like went with like and it was very noticeable that there was a dearth of the usual outrageous characters.

Chapter 28

The following morning Seager and I received the great news that our reliefs were en route from Alex. We would soon be on our way home to the UK to join our loved ones. What better twenty third birthday present could I have? They arrived within a week and we were on our way home, but not before a great farewell party which, strangely, ended in tears for a couple of the lads. 'Spencer' Tracey, who was married, was one of the most affected. It must have been really tough on the married men among the conscript HOs. Scouse Harrison, Doug Gill 'Alex', Spud Murphy, and a very close oppo Tim Riley, our star football player, were all deeply affected.

We said our goodbyes and set out for Alex where we would just embark on a troopship and set sail for home.

I passed through the gate of *HMS Stag* for the last time, taking the very first steps on my journey back to the UK, my home and my loved ones. It would now be all so simple, my destination was Alexandria, where I would simply step over the gangway of a ship and sail across the sea to Blighty. Wrong, it was not quite like that, the ship proved to be a rusting hulk with a quite unpronounceable Polish name. One look at it and I could understand why it had so far not been dispatched to the bottom by the enemy. The enemy probably concluded the torpedo was more valuable than the target. It was an indictment on the authorities that they allowed the thing to transport human beings as it was not fit for pigs. The transportation of troops was a substantial part of most convoys, which made great demands on our diminishing number of vessels. The large prestigious passenger liners were ideal for the job and I had personally enjoyed the sheer luxury of one - the *HMS Andes*. The next available ships were cargo vessels which were converted to troopships by simply putting in two or three wooden decks down the holds of the ships. Access to the accommodation was by a series of wooden stairways from the deck to the lowest platform, and it was generally the policy to mess the RN ratings in the lower holds. You need little imagination to visualise what would happen if the ship was struck by an explosive of any kind. The complete hold was a wooden tinder box and you would have had as much chance of escape and survival as a sardine has of getting out of its can.

On the third day we limped out of Alex Harbour and on succeeding days we were either limping along or stranded with silent engines. The wonder was that we ever made it to our next port of call. It should have been a joyous voyage but both Seager and I found ourselves remembering our lost oppos on the *Kent* whilst we were in Alex and our oppos who had perished in the now relatively safe Suez Canal as we limped through into the Red Sea.

There was to be no swift dash home for us on the short cut through the Med, but a perilous journey round the Cape of Good Hope. Some twelve thousand miles lay ahead of us.

Seager and I knew the canal almost as well as the pilots that took us through and we spent the one hundred miles reminiscing about incidents both humourous and tragic. It was a solemn moment when we passed the spot where the high speed launch *Dard* had disintegrated into a mass of matchwood before our very eyes when the mine exploded. The *Ranee*, *Darwenthal* and the *Aghios Georgiou* were still there and would remain a monument to the perseverance of our enemies and our own inability to restrain them. Thousands of servicemen would pass them and wonder why and how they had been sunk in the narrow, vitally strategic waters of the canal. Perhaps they would also be fooled by the dummy planes and guns along its bank.

Looking back on my twenty days in that heap of Polish scrap I still marvel at the resilience of the British servicemen in those wartime days. In truth we were all mostly servile, subservient peasants. This was manifested by the arrival on the scene of the Americans. They had far superior pay, uniforms, food, equipment and rights. They were made to feel important; we were made to be fully aware of the yawning gap between officer and man in every single aspect of service life. However, in pursuit of the necessary product for the prosecution of a hard and dastardly war, the British and Commonwealth product usually emerged as the best for the purpose. Hard living made hard men and to that end it worked. I honestly believe that the Americans would never have subjected their men to the conditions on that rusting heap.

We stopped officially at Aden and Mombasa and, yes, we ended up at Durban. They were the official stops, the unofficial stops were three times as many as that, in what were now hostile waters. I'm quite sure that we owed our survival to the quite inexplicable behaviour of the Italians in this conflict. Time and again they failed to take advantage of strategically superior situations that could have wreaked havoc on the Allies on numerous occasions. I for one was eternally grateful, for we were continually broken down and wallowing helplessly, a sitting target. I believe we ended up under tow as we entered Durban. We tied up on the jetty at Mayden Wharf and it was quite significant that the entire compliment was transferred to another ship, the *Niew Holland* by train, passing right around the perimeter of the harbour, but not before we had spent one more night aboard the Pole.

This time it was different, there were no happy, welcoming faces, waiting to whisk you away and take you up homers. This time we had arrived, not in a glamourous RN cruiser, but in a quite anonymous hulk, a marked contrast.

I had struggled with my self-imposed dilemma about Mary and decided not to phone her and make my presence known. In any case she might well have someone else.

With Seager and a new found townie oppo Ken Ferrier, I left the Pole and taxied into town to once more savour the delights of Durban. We went straight to Thomas Cooks travel agents to change our currency into South African. Inside Cooks we met some young South African Army officers who insisted that we joined them in seeing the town. This, of course, was no more than a pub crawl, during which I became aware of the large presence of Aussie troops. We had arrived at the same time as a contingent of Aussies en route to Egypt. You didn't exactly feel their presence, it was imposed on you, at no time more than the amazing spectacle of hordes of them in the City Square. We closed in on them to see what was going on. There in the middle of the throng were about ten rickshaws, all were occupied by the very colourful Zulus and in the shafts were ten husky Aussies. One of their number was running a book with varying odds on the occupants of the shafts. It was an amazing sight. They were meticulously lined up in the square and at the order, set off down West Street, which was about the equivalent of performing the same act in London's Regent Street. No-one in authority intervened as they weaved their way through traffic, turned at a given point and raced to the finishing line in the City Square. It was quite unbelievable, they appeared to be in control of the city and some of them had perpetrated vandalism to such an extent that forced some premises to close when they were in town. It was as well that the wildness of their behaviour was controlled on the battlefield, where their reputation as fighters was high.

We were having a great time and it was inevitable that we would end up eventually at the *Regal* where the paths of Mary and myself had first crossed. I freely admit that my eyes had been everywhere for the whole day just hoping to catch sight of the girl I could so easily have contacted by phone. Once inside the *Regal* I scarcely had time for my own companions as I constantly screened the new arrivals as they entered. I gradually, however, relaxed under the influence, and began to banish the maudlin thoughts from my mind and to enjoy my company. Suddenly we were off and two taxis took us to one of the luxury blocks on the lovely Durban seafront. The lift took us up to an apartment of sumptuous luxury where we were to enjoy a great party with food, girls, music, the lot. There was also the inevitable piano to add to my enjoyment. It was after midnight when taxis were called and we were all saying our farewells, when suddenly from the landing outside the apartment came a horrified scream, followed by shouting and general pandemonium. A horrific tragedy had occurred; a couple of the girls were skylarking by the banisters, with them were one of the South Africans and Kenny Ferrier. One of the girls had fallen over the banisters, three floors to her death. In two dramatic seconds joyous laughter had been turned into sheer horror. A tragic accident had taken the life of a lovely young girl.

A doctor appeared, followed by an ambulance and then the police. Everyone was interviewed and made statements. A distraught Kenny Ferrier and the other man and woman were detained, the rest of us were allowed to leave. Seager and I returned to the Pole, we were dumbstruck, a chance meeting in Cooks had turned our run ashore into a horror story.

George and I were still talking into the small hours about the tragic event but eventually I forced myself into a troubled sleep. Then someone was shaking my arm and quietly calling my name. I stirred and found myself looking into the ash white face of Kenny Ferrier who was quite obviously still in deep shock. In spite of the time, he wanted to talk, when he did it was in an agitated voice. We learned that he and the South African went outside the apartment to say goodnight to their girlfriends. There was a bit of horseplay but Kenny and his partner withdrew to engage in a quite snogging session. The other two continued with their skylarking, during which the girl tragically toppled over the banister and was killed. The police accepted his version of events, but Kenny would have to report once again to the station. We were genuinely sorry for the unfortunate South African, but greatly relieved that Kenny was absolved of blame.

We spent most of the next morning on the very enjoyable chore of transferring from the abominable hulk to the much more agreeable *Niew Holland*. We were mustered on the dockside, checked for name and number and then boarded the train which took us to the other side of the dockyard to our new ship. We were about to move off when there was a banging on the other side of the carriage. A glance out of the window revealed four matelots asking for entry into our carriage, chosen no doubt because there were only four occupants in it. We assisted them aboard the train, then took our seats and awaited their explanation. What followed was as bizarre as the story of Albert RN, except this incident involved getting someone in, not out. We had agreed to participate in a plot that could quite conceivably have landed us all behind bars in chokey. For one of the four was in fact a young woman, dressed as a matelot from head to toe. We had about fifteen minutes to attempt to execute our plan, it certainly got the adrenalin flowing and the situation was tense as we disembarked from the train.

It was a situation borne of this strange effect the city of Durban was having on so many of its visiting troops. Liaisons both passing and permanent were almost the order of the day. Married, as well as single men, were caught up in this mad whirl of romances, most of which could only end in heartache and disaster. The only people on the right track were the matelots with the philosophy of having a girl in every port and 'love 'em and leave 'em'. They were the sensible ones, not the most thoughtful and considerate ones, but definitely the sensible ones. I should know for wasn't I up to my neck in it, the spell of a fantastic city, in the midst of a drab and violent scenario of war?

John Sharpe was a Leading Stoker and he was most certainly caught up in it - his story was a carbon copy of mine. Ship calls into Durban, boy meets girl, romance blossoms and a chance return to Durban once more fans the flames of love. It was quite remarkable that in those days of general orderliness and obedience, so many young men took such dramatic measures as desertion. It was, in fact, one of the most heinous offences you could commit in wartime, yet here were men oblivious to all the consequences. Such was the power of the mood at the time.

This escape went even further in the cause of love, for 'Sharpey' was about to attempt to bypass all the international laws of immigration and smuggle his girlfriend out of South Africa into the UK.

The plan was simple, very simple. She would just walk up the gangway and aboard the *Niew Holland*. There was no worry about her appearance as she adequately fulfilled the part and she had even sacrificed her hair in the name of love, an action that on its own could have put some women off the venture. Nevertheless, we had a plan and it simply entailed her walking up the gangway, nicely screened between two of the hammocks slung across our shoulders. The illegal entry was made easy due to the fact that everyone had been checked onto the train but not onto the *Niew Holland*. There were a few hundred of us and it would have taken much too long checking us on boarding. There was therefore just a casual visual inspection before the illegal immigrant was over the gangway. It worked like a dream and in minutes she was anonymous among hundreds of men on the Naval messdeck.

We had no idea how long it would be before the Niew Holland sailed. I personally would have settled for hoisting the gangway inboard and sailing full speed ahead for the UK as soon as the last person was aboard. Was it impatience to get back home or was I anxious to leave the subject that was still troubling my mind safely behind me? Compared to Stoker Sharpe and the number of men who had deserted ship in the cause, I showed up as a coward. Mary was still only a phone call away, assuming she was still in town and, more to the point, still in circulation. I didn't even necessarily have to see her. I could just chat to her on the phone, surely there was no harm in that? Secretly I admired these men, they hadn't pussy footed around, they had gone for it, full steam ahead and here was I dithering about whether or not to make a phone call.

The ship's tannoy made up my mind for me. It told me there was shore leave until 2000 hours. I showered, dressed and rushed down the gangway inside the hour, and made my way to the phone box, my resolve almost melted away. I was nervous as a kitten as I picked up the phone and dialled. As soon as I had dialled the last digit I was hoping there would be no answer. Then my pulse would return to normal and the saliva would return to my dry mouth. "Hello," said the voice on the other end of the line, and when I answered I'm quite sure my voice was an octave above normal. I managed to splutter out my identity and so it was that my tenuous romance with Mary continued. I remember what can best be described as a shriek when Mary had identified the caller. It told me that I was still on her calling list. Twenty minutes later I was nervously sipping my beer in the familiar venue of the *Regal* awaiting Mary's arrival. I was still wrestling with my thoughts, had I taken the right course, should I have broken off the line of communication and let it all fade away in the distance of time? The first sight of her immediately eliminated all my doubts but I was not prepared for what I saw. I was expecting to see her in a cool summer dress, that would emphasise the lovely tan of her fair skin, the tan that all the ladies of Durban acquired by right. That is why she was upon me before I knew it. To say she looked stunning was an understatement, as she stood before me in the blue uniform of the South African Armed Forces. The chances of this meeting taking place here were minute. I never dreamed that was remotely possible, yet here we were together once again.

I couldn't believe that there was still no-one serious in her life. I was glad for my own selfish reasons of the moment, but I now had some explaining to do. She would be unaware that I had been in town for forty eight hours or that I had already been ashore. Nor was she aware that I had been present at the tragic death that had occurred only twenty four hours ago. The story had been reported in the local Durban newspaper. I didn't lie, I told her and she was stunned into silence when I told her of my presence at the scene of the tragedy. Mary didn't question my motive for not contacting her immediately on my arrival in town, which put both our situations into perspective and made the remainder of our time together that much easier. We now both knew that would be the way of it, if we were ever to meet again it would be chance, it would be entirely up to fate for we lived on two different continents and there was still a war to be won. We had a wonderful day together and after a meal in the WVS canteen, we finished off the evening on the dance floor at the Emerald Gardens.

It was no different to the first time we met in the City Hall on the occasion of the reception for *HMS Kent*. We were going through the whole gamut of emotions of a couple deeply in love, each of us knowing the sad futility of it all. It was a love story of the times, for there were thousands of these scenarios being enacted throughout the wartime world we were then living in. There were no torrid sex scenes or one night stands, no quick gratification down that dark alley, or in the back seat of a car. All these things were commonplace enough and I had listened to men recounting their conquests since my first week in the Navy. In spite of this there was undeniably a bulk of the young and eligible who, at that time, firmly believed that you should 'save it' for each other until you were betrothed. A woman was then more protective of her virginity and it was reflected in the films and novels of the time.

Thus it was that our farewell embrace was once again to reflect the mood of the times. We both still had the lifeline of the written word to communicate our thoughts to each other but now that was all. Everything else was imponderables. Would I ever return to Durban, would Mary, now in the services, ever sail to England, would I return to South Africa after the war, more to the point would I survive the war? Questions that time could answer, but 'hope springs eternal'. We were both desperately trying to be casual and in control as we alighted from the taxi at the dockside. We kissed tenderly and parted, but not before the final brush of her cheek told me that she was once again crying. I turned at the top of the gangway and with a wave of the hand, Mary boarded the taxi and was gone.

Any despondency that I was feeling about my own romance was instantly dispelled when, on entering my messdeck, Kenny Ferrier rushed up to break some news to me that was to make my problems pale into insignificance. By the cruellest of all cruel tricks of fate John Sharpe and six other stokers had been taken from the *Niew Holland* to make up the crew of a destroyer that had been under repairs at Durban. It was not unknown for home-going matelots to crew RN ships returning to the UK. In fact I was hoping it would happen to me, as it could mean the short cut home through the Med. However, for Sharpey to be picked out among the hundreds on the Niew Holland, was to suggest someone had blown the whistle on him, the odds were so great against it happening. It appeared that the girl had given herself up and was now in the hands of the authorities and Sharpey, after a court appearance, would be dealt with by the Navy. Another Durban romance was on the rocks.

There must have been some outright winners, they certainly were not among the deserters, who must for ever be looking over their shoulders, nor yet me, or the unfortunate Stoker Sharpe. The messdeck was buzzing with the story for days, we needed something of the kind to relieve the soul destroying boredom of the wartime messdecks of the troopships. There was compulsory PT quizzes which we organised ourselves, and a certain amount of deck games. One such game, the basket ball final, resulted in me acquiring torn ligaments in my right ankle and I spent the remainder of the voyage in the ship's hospital, where they feverishly worked to get me walking again.

The *Niew Holland* was a marked improvement on the Polish heap, but it was still a wartime troopship and even on our new ship animal rights protesters could have put up a strong case on our behalf.

The *Niew Holland* was carrying troops from the three services and women and children who had managed to escape the horror of the Japanese invasion of Singapore. We were twenty four hours out of Freetown, our next port of call, when the alarm klaxons sounded in the early hours of the morning. There had been two full scale rehearsals for boat stations and, in theory, everyone should have known exactly where to go. This one was for real and the time was about 3am It turned out to be one of the most distressing incidents of my war. The *Niew Holland* had been challenged as to her identity and for reasons we were never to find out, the Captain decided to run for it. He was obviously unhappy about the nature of the challenge. What followed was both frightening and very deeply disturbing. A shot was fired across our bows, at which point the *Niew Holland* came to a slow halt.

There was panic and distress as the women passengers and their children clung to each other in sheer terror. It was awful to witness, no-one knew what was going on and, as far as we were all concerned, the craft that was approaching us was the enemy. I remember everyone trying to reassure the women and children, but we were no more wise to the situation than they were. A ship approached our beam, suddenly a searchlight pierced the total darkness and as it neared us the silence was broken by a voice on the loud speaker. The language was unmistakable and so were the words, which were not for women's and children's ears. They were a string of profanities issuing from the Bridge of a RN escort vessel.

It was all something to do with the identification code for the day. For whatever reason there was a cock-up and, to be fair, the Captain of the *Niew Holland* was no doubt doing what at the time he thought was best for us. I will never forget that experience as this was a different ball game to being alongside 'hairy arsed matelots'. It was frightening to witness the fear of the women and their charges. It was an entirely different concept of the war and one I have no wish to experience again. My descent through three decks to my mess once more brought into focus the precariousness of our situation - if we were ever to be attacked, it would be mayhem down below. There were, in fact, a number of troopship disasters, but this was war and there were, in reality, no alternatives. We could still have done without women and children coming into the equation though, and we were now, as we left Freetown, in the thick of enemy U Boat activity and it must be remembered that we were of course unescorted during the whole journey and, like many other ships with a reasonable turn of speed, relying on our good fortune to get us through.

Fourteen days after the *Niew Holland's* altercation with the Royal Navy South of Freetown, the liner *Laconia* was set on the same course. This time it wasn't the Royal Navy and there was no challenge. Two torpedoes from the German submarine U 156 struck the *Laconia* with devastating effect. It was to become the worst troopship disaster of the war, aboard were three thousand people including eight hundred and eleven British servicemen and their wives and children, one thousand eight hundred Italian prisoners of war guarded by one hundred and three Poles. One of the British survivors was my oppo Tim Riley, with whom I had had a sad farewell drink when I left for the UK, two weeks before he set out to follow me home on the *Laconia*. Tim was taken prisoner of war when he was picked up in the South Atlantic by a Vichy French destroyer. He was incarcerated in a French foreign legion fort in Casa Blanca before being released by the Yanks. Tim and I had a great reunion when we met through an advert I placed on Channel 4's *Service Pals*. The amazing story of the *Laconia* disaster is told in the book *U Boats to the Rescue* by Leonce Peillara.

Our twelve thousand mile marathon voyage was coming to a close and for the first time there was an air of excitement and expectancy. The service I had joined to do a swift six months training had already taken up over two years of my life. Two years of self discovery, of humour, tragedy, thrills and visits to undreamed of lands and islands of magical beauty. Two years that had taken me to the dream world that I had envisaged in those far off days when I was anchored in front of a huge steel mangle, rolling sheets of black rubber for eight hours a day, six days a week and then emerging into the squalor of the East End docks, to pedal on my long ride home to Dagenham. How much more of my life was the RN to take? More to the point, was the RN going to take my life? Could I ever possibly go back to Henleys when it was all over?

The *Niew Holland* entered home waters and headed for the River Mersey and the great port of Liverpool. The Liver Building came into view with its twin towers, a sight now so familiar to thousands of homecoming sailors. The remainder of our journey would be a combination of train, bus and taxi, but there was a story to tell before I eventually crossed the threshold of my home at Number two Lawrence Crescent, Dagenham, Essex; nothing was ever to be straightforward.

Chapter 29

Walking down the gangway onto the dockside, I could now understand for the first time the feelings of the returning sailor. We left Lime Street Station and boarded a conveyance that in times of peace could have been described as a train, now it was just a container for storing troops, it was unbelievable. Men and women were just piled aboard regardless, the only consideration was that the doors could be closed. The heap of humanity wound its way slowly Southwards and eventually somehow we arrived at Chatham. Having completed my rejoining routine, I was now homeward bound to see my loved ones. A privilege denied to all my oppos who had perished.

There were four of us in our immediate party and we set off, not directly to home in our respective areas, but to London, the big city, where we could down our first pint of British beer and then go on our separate ways. It would not, however, be quite like that. Before we left Chatham we all sent telegrams home to announce our arrival; these telegrams were important because they were the only means of rapid communication, as no-one in our walk of life then possessed telephones. The train ride from Chatham was completed in high spirits and, on arrival at Charing Cross Station, there were handshakes and good wishes as the lads broke up and went their separate ways. A group of us found our way to the adjacent *Griffin Arms* public house in Villiers Street; that first pint lived in our memories for some time for obvious reasons and within an hour most of us were so engrossed with our immediate needs and enjoyment that we temporarily forgot the completion of our journey home. We were excited and our stresses and cares were fast disappearing as the drink took charge of all our decisions.

It was only the guv'nor's cry of "time gentlemen please" that alerted us to the hard fact that we had trains to catch. The farewells were now noisy, boisterous and much more affectionate. I remember Seager and me holding each other and vowing eternal friendship, he left to find his way home to Tottenham, I was in fact never to meet up with George again; thus ended a friendship that had survived two and a half years and four ships and establishments. Such was the way of friendship in those wartime years.

Before setting out on our binge we had all deposited our gear in the left luggage department at Charing Cross Station. We were not prepared for what followed. First of all we enquired about our left luggage. "That office closes at 8pm," said the porter. Calamity. While we were discussing this bad news we were informed that the underground train to Upminster on the District Line was the last, and it left at 10.15pm. We had decisions to make, major decisions and only minutes to make them.

Our party consisted of Ferrier, a Canadian matelot whose name escapes me, and myself. Ferrier was playing host to the Canadian in his Ilford home, adjacent to my own in Dagenham. We made our way hurriedly to the District Line entrance, but I was a hindrance to progress with my injured ankle, which I suddenly realised was hurting like hell. We scrambled down the stairs and the guard obligingly waited for me to board, then we were off. We sat back and drew our breath, we would have to return on the morrow for our luggage. None of us had given any consideration to our families who were sitting at home fretting about our late arrival.

The remainder of the journey would be a doddle, we would alight at Barking and each get a taxi, one to Ilford and another to Dagenham. Identifying rail stations in the blackout was difficult enough, but add to that the heavy downpour of rain and you will understand why we missed Barking station and went on to the next station at Upney. No problem, we'd get taxis at Upney instead. We alighted at Upney and climbed the slope to the exit. We asked the ticket collector about taxis, he looked at us with incredulity, eventually he spoke. "Taxis, are you having me on?" he enquired. We told him of our plight, pointing out that I was now almost *hors de combat* with my injured ankle. He was completely unhelpful, his attitude was appalling. He had us outside the station and the gates shut as he spoke to us in a totally disinterested voice. It was a farcical situation, I was only about three or four miles from home, yet I knew unless I had transport, I was stranded and my ankle was killing me.

Kenny was worried about me and suggested I get an ambulance to hospital. I turned to the ticket collector and once again explained my situation and told him the only solution was to let me sleep on the station. It was now past midnight, I was tired and in pain. I was now quite aggressive, I could easily have hit him. He reluctantly agreed and we walked wearily to the men's waiting room.

So it was that my twelve thousand mile journey home had come to a grinding halt a mere three miles or so from home, an implausible, but absolutely true story. I hardly slept at all and with the snores of my oppos for company I waited for the dawn. I had plenty of time to reflect on my behaviour of the previous twelve hours, and I now realised that my family must be feeling some concern about my non-appearance. In spite of my feelings of contrition, we reasoned that in the circumstances it made sense to catch an early train back to Charing Cross and retrieve our kit from left luggage. This we did, and for the second time we made for home.

What emerged increased my embarrassment about my late arrival. Practically the whole family had gathered to welcome me home. I had some explaining to do when I crossed the threshold of number two.

I entered Lawrence Crescent where my mind went right back to the day war broke out and the apprehension that followed that very first air raid warning when we were in fear of poison gas canister tumbling from the sky. Dagenham, however, did not escape the attention of the enemy bombers. The family reunion was heartwarming but tearful and my thoughtless behaviour was scarcely mentioned.

Chapter 30

Three or four days into my leave I was quite unaccountably feeling restless. During my long absence I had thought of little else but my return to the nest and life within the family fold. We had been through most of the reunions and parties and once again I was just another serviceman on leave. It wasn't that, I'm quite sure I was happy to be anonymous. In fact if I had any civvy clothes left I would have been wearing them, but due to rationing and the advent of clothing coupons, all my civvies had long since been used and worn out by my brothers, a common occurrence within all wartime households. I had given my restlessness a good deal of thought and I had come to some personal conclusions. Chief among them was the undeniable fact that I was now not the man who had fled the nest so long ago. The quiet, home loving and very unsophisticated lad of pre-Navy days perhaps would never be the same, was this possible? My horizons then were very limited, football, cricket, the Saturday night tanner top, a night at the flicks and I had once spent seven days on holiday on the Isle of Wight. When I tell you that this was an achievement at that time, you will better understand things as they were then.

If I had found the confines of the messdeck a bit claustrophobic, I was now having even more problems within the four walls of home. For almost three years I had sat on a wooden form, leaning on a wooden table, opposite my oppos who were doing the same thing. That was it, day in, day out, when you were off Watch, there was no escape, no front room with easy chairs, carpets and curtains. The language, behaviour and topics of conversation were on an entirely different plane. Each day at home on leave I was off at lunchtime to meet Kenny for my midday beer, but I soon realised that beer wasn't the chief component of my needs. No, it was the company of matelots that I needed, I had become, for want of a better word, institutionalised. This manifested itself in other ways. I found myself walking up and down the garden path at home, just as I had described earlier, the matelot's habit of pacing the deck for exercise. This habit continued on station platforms and bus stops. It is only in hindsight that I realised my behaviour must have appeared odd to my family and friends at the time. It was no consolation to say that this practice has, for decades, also been the province of inmates detained at Her Majesty's Pleasure in institutions of correction. So there you have it, prisoners and matelots as kindred spirits.

Most evenings my tracks took me straight to the other lads on leave and my first venture into the all enveloping blanket of the total blackout was to end in complete humiliation. I was crossing Beacontree Heath when ahead of me out of the night, a very youthful voice gave me the challenge "Halt, who goes there?" Someone having a joke I thought, but to my utmost surprise I was confronted by a lad in khaki holding a rifle. He demanded my identity card, or in my case, my pay book. I had left home without it and to my deep embarrassment I was escorted by this slip of a lad across the playground and into a classroom inside the Beacontree Heath school, where an officer of the Home Guard severely admonished me for my failure to carry my pass. He then ordered a corporal to escort me back to my home to pick it up, whereupon I was allowed my freedom. Secretly I was infuriated, I had been on leave just two days and on each of them I had been in confrontations, first with a jumped-up ticket collector at Upney Station and now a pink faced, wet behind the ears kid had apprehended me not more than a couple of hundred yards from my home.

This was not the homecoming welcome that I had envisaged. I was a returning hero and should have been spared these affronts to my dignity, or so I thought.

I eventually located the lads in the *Angel* on Ilford High Road. We were the only matelots in the bar, which was full of Americans. They expressed themselves freely and most of them appeared to be bold, big headed and brash. We were, by comparison, introverted and withdrawn. It was going to be a clash of the two cultures, but if we were honest we would admit to being jealous, jealous of their immediate success with our women, jealous of their slick uniforms, their pay and their easy outgoing attitude. It was no wonder the ladies went for them like wasps to a jam pot.

The American attitude to their servicemen was light years ahead of the British. They paid heed to the needs, the comfort and the appearance of their troops, they were made to feel good, look good, to feel important, even superior. I felt particularly sorry for our squaddies, they looked by comparison like POWs in their drab, heavy, shapeless khaki; take away the 'putties' and it had hardly changed since World War I. However, the main ingredient was the man inside and not the uniform and, once again, our boys were to prove themselves matchless. "Clothes maketh the man" runs that well worn cliché, but in times of war "that ain't necessarily so".

After going to the Plessey Social Club Kenny and I walked home solo. Kenny was courting strongly, Haggis, who had approached every woman in the club, left with a female, both of them would probably regret it when they were sober. The four or five mile walk to Beacontree Heath gave me plenty of time to ruminate on my first couple of days in Blighty. The populace was working hard and it looked like they were playing hard as, for the first time in decades, they had a few bob in their pockets. They were assured of regular employment, plenty of overtime and they could earn more by joining the Home Guard. I resented their new found affluence and fumed at the thought of my miserly one pound eight shillings a month that I had to survive on. I was forced by law to allocate half my pay to my mother, regardless of the combined incomes of the household. There was plenty of overtime in the Navy, but that was for King and country. To be fair, the government did put by a sum of money, payable as a gratuity at the end of my service. I can still clearly remember receiving my payment book upon demobilisation. It contained the princely sum of eighty seven pounds, after more than six years' service.

My leave had taken on a predictable pattern, it was a daily repeat of a mindless preoccupation with immersing ourselves in each others' company, almost to the exclusion of all things that were not Naval. It is only in hindsight the true sublimity of my behaviour becomes obvious.

Perhaps it had to do with that modern phenomenon, counselling. Everyone must now have counselling for the birth of a baby, a bereavement, plane, train, bus, marine incidents, living in flats, incompatibility of workplace and, of course, marriage. The marriage one was easy, don't get married, it's better to live in sin and leave if it doesn't suit you. This, then, could be the answer to why we were all drawn to each other, the herd instinct, we were kindred spirits, perhaps this was how we got our counselling. We were all experts in traumas, perpetually with us for twenty four hours of every day, while we were sailing in hostile waters.

Both Kenny and I had witnessed the horrors of war at first hand, we had seen men die in front of our eyes, right alongside us. Shipmates, oppos, personal friends. So what? This was considered the norm, men were expected to die. Hard luck. If you survived, a wash and brush up, a new kit, a new ship and off you went, there were plenty of vacancies to be had. Counselling! What was that? Kenny Ferrier was a good case for counselling. He lost the *Kipling* in the Battle of Crete, was picked up by another K Boat that got sent to the bottom, and he came back to Alex in the AA cruiser *Calcutta*. This was all in the space of a few hours. The *Calcutta* had no ammunition left to defend itself but it mercifully arrived safely back in Alex. By any stretch of the imagination Kenny was a hero, but let me tell you how he was rewarded.

You may remember that Kenny was witness to the horrifying death of the young nurse who accidentally fell to her death in Durban. In the confusion he had dropped his wallet with his pay book, which was also his identity card. Kenny didn't realise his loss until he was out of Durban on his way home. On his arrival in the UK he was charged with losing his pay book, but after some discussion he was allowed home on leave. However, on his return to barracks he was charged and given fourteen days stoppage of leave. So much for a returning Naval hero. The Yanks would have awarded him a string of decorations and a civic reception.

Kenny's story was only one of the many things that had changed me from an open mouthed, green eyed and unquestioning patriot, into a cynic, who now looked at events around me with a very jaundiced eye. My patriotism was still not in question, but I was now aware of such things as draft dodgers, men in and out of the services who were trying to 'work their tickets'. There was a host of fiddles and fiddlers with exemption from the forces in the reserved occupations. Rackets in food and clothing coupons, spivs who at the drop of a hat could rustle up almost anything in short supply, providing the price was right. The playing field was now very uneven and it would be doubly difficult for me to face and accept what lay ahead of me. It could be long Atlantic convoys, bitterly cold and horrendous Russian convoys, or the deceptive blue seas and sunny skies of the totally beleaguered Mediterranean Sea. This while dodgers, fiddlers and con men were living it up in the comparative comfort of home.

I sincerely believe that Jack had a strong reason for feeling aggrieved about these skivers. The Army's and Air Force's call to arms was sporadic throughout the six years of war. The Royal Navy, however, from the moment of Chamberlain's declaration of war was in the thick of it fighting for its life. It is an established fact that Germany had her ships and submarines already strategically placed and on a war footing from the very start. So the task of the Royal Navy was to continue for every hour of every day for more than six years, there were no phoney wars or lulls in the fighting. It was continuous, relentless, you left harbour and they were out there, the bomb, the shell, the mine, or the torpedo. There were no green fields, country lanes or village pubs, just a grey hostile expanse of water. End up in the 'hoggin' on a Russian convoy and you had about four minutes to live.

Returning to ship after your leave, you crossed the gangway into a steel casket of angle iron, rivets and nuts and bolts. Your home was a wooden mess table and enough room on a wooden form to park your backside. That was it, on most ships there was nowhere else to go.

Your bedroom was a hammock, slung in the air if you were lucky, otherwise you just unrolled it on the deck wherever you could find space. All ships in wartime carried more men than there were billets for. This was in order to cover the Watches when you were at sea. The idea was to split the crew into two Watches, but it never worked out like that. Once you went to action stations everyone was closed up and if the action was prolonged you just lost your time off Watch; if it was your sleeping period, hard luck. It was an unremitting burden on your mind and body, and add to that the times when you were wet, cold and being tossed about like a cork in an angry sea, you may wonder, as I did on many occasions, how they got men to volunteer for it.

These were the thoughts that filled my mind on that long walk home, angry pessimistic, despondent, perhaps whining thoughts, but above all the thoughts of a disillusioned man. It hurt me just to think of the thousands of men and women who had sacrificed their lives for these unscrupulous parasites. The irony of it all was that if I showed cowardice in the face of the enemy my punishment could be death. I arrived at the door of number two and entered the house as quietly as I could, but I knew that Mary Anne, my mother, would have one eye open and one ear cocked, awaiting my safe return. Nothing had altered, I was still her baby.

My leave was rapidly coming to a close, the thirty five days had simply sped by. It worked out at roughly fourteen days for each year abroad. Not really very generous when you consider that I had not even had one weekend off over that period of two and a half years while I was overseas.

The family get-togethers were at that time held in the *Eastbrook*, a pub that still today is a perfect example of the fine craftsmanship and style of the times. The beautiful walnut panelling, cornices and colonnades have survived the attention of pseudo interior designers and is still a pleasure to behold. The interior's unchanging face makes it easy hostage to the ghosts and memories of those wartime days. However, any surviving wraith might wonder at our sanity, as we coughed up three pounds sixty pence, which during wartime was a whole week's wages, for the two pints of Bitter that sat before us at the table. The sparsely scattered customers were in sharp contrast to the jam-packed interior of those days. The lights, the warmth and the atmosphere were a necessary release from the pressures of war and the unremitting drab darkness of everything outside. Homecoming, as well as farewell parties, were a constant ingredient of the scene. Uniforms abounded, there were happy faces, voices ringing out in song. The age old recipe of a piano and a singer to lead, hardly room to lift your elbow to down your drink, from the glass that you never let out of your sight because it was yours personally. There were no glasses, you brought your own. Beer and spirits were often in short supply and consequently you never knew which pub would open on any particular night. There was, however, a grapevine, and I have seen queues outside the *Eastbrook* long before it opened.

Each day of my leave was virtually a carbon copy of the last as we enjoyed our pursuit of what we thought was a great leave. Was it though? Or was it that anything we got up to, no matter how mundane, was infinitely preferably to the rigours of the mind and body sapping routine of the Navy at war. After a month in the trouble free luxury of civvy street, I knew that I was a changed person who now didn't comfortably belong to either the Navy or civvy street. This manifested itself clearly when my return to Chatham at the end of my leave was arrived at without any particularly dark thoughts. There was no farewell party, I returned resigned to the routine of a barrack stantion. All night leave, every other night, and alternate weekends off. All I had to do was to work my way into a quiet number from the Chatham Mafia, sit back, relax and enjoy the green fields, leafy lanes and country pubs of rural Essex and forget all about those grey, hostile and inhospitable waters somewhere out there, at least for a while.

The minute I left home at the end of my leave, I knew that it was the beginning of yet another journey into the unknown. It could be waiting for me on the end of my mess table in Chatham the moment I arrived in the form of a draft chit or a brief announcement on the tannoy. "D'ye hear there, ABST P Cairns report to the Drafting Master at Arms." I would then be off to anywhere in Britain, or anywhere in the world. On the other hand I could land a quiet number from the Chatham Mafia, become a barrack stantion and commute between Chatham and home. Another remote possibility was the cessation of hostilities and victory, in reality a victory that was far into the distant future. It was, in fact, half time and I had another three years to go. Three more years of drama, death, destruction, elation, depression, highs, lows, humour and tragedy.

Chapter 31

My entry through the portals of Chatham Barracks was made in a mixture of dismay and anticipation. Once again I was a piece of flotsam and of no fixed abode. There was nothing nice about Chatham, it wasn't like a ship or an RAF or Army barracks. It was mostly men on arrival, men in transit, that was its main function a kind of travel agency. But this travel agent told you where to go rather than giving you the choice. Then again, it was some soft of detention camp; there always seemed to be more offenders on the parade ground than there were men under training. Add to that the Dickensian quarters and the foul smelling air raid shelters and you would begin to wonder why men in Gibraltar or Malta would spill their life blood defending the place against the 'tiddy hoggy' and 'pompey' ratings in barside brawls. Such is the perversity of human nature.

The long row of imposing figureheads of our distant sea heroes seemed to look down on me with approval, and why shouldn't they? I was no longer a sprog O/D but a Naval man of some stature, or so I thought.

I jauntily climbed the stone steps to Nelson Block, my mess in Chatham. I stowed my gear into my locker, a voice said "Don't bother to lock it up Lofts, there's a draft chit for you on the table, probably be Russian convoys, I heard there's an acute shortage of torpedomen in barracks," said my tormentor.

"What about you, you idle fat bastard?" I returned, "You haven't tasted salt water since your old woman put too much in the cabbage water."

"Well I'm one of them dumb gunnery ratings ain't I? I ain't got the brains for a torpedoman," he came back swiftly.

I snatched the chit of paper from the table. It was innocuous and merely said AB/ST P Cairns, C/JX 167723, report to the Drafting Master at Arms Office at once.

What of my piece of paper? It was a false document to shanghai me onto my next ship and two years of hell. You don't argue with the Drafting Master at Arms Office, you are allowed perhaps one question. "Where to?" I asked. "Devonport for Western approaches," I was told. "Not bad," was my first reaction, at least it was in home waters with a chance of an occasional leave, "I'll settle for that" I decided, at least I'm not going on foreign service again. I'd had enough of sun, sand, flies and mosquitoes.

For the first time I was a lone traveller en route to join a new ship, it was a learning experience. I looked down in dismay at my baggage, however was I going to manage it? My luggage consisted of my six foot long hammock with my oilskin inside, a full kit bag, an attaché case, a gas mask and my overcoat. It would be handy to just raise your hand and call "porter", but that wasn't on, it was down to 'larkins'. The total weight was around one hundred pounds, almost a hundredweight, we managed it all somehow. I alighted from the train at 'Guzz' and lugging my 'home' with me, I left the station and threw it all into the back of the waiting truck that whisked me away into the Naval dockyard. It was dark, empty, cold and uninviting. The driver pulled up and pointed to the dockside. "It's one of them," he said. I looked across and my heart sank, there were eight, what looked to me like biscuit tins, shaped at the front to make them look like ships. They were tied up in two rows of four. I was looking at the thirteenth mine sweeping flotilla, eight Bangor class fleet sweepers, and one of them, the *Felixstowe,* was the reason for my hasty departure from Chatham. I made my way across three sets of gangplanks, *Felixstowe* was on the outside.

Fleet mine sweeper H.M.S. 'Felixstowe'

I met the Coxswain and we shook hands, he didn't beat about the bush. "Have you been paid?"

"No," I replied.

"Have you had your leave?"

"Leave?" I said with a query in my voice. "Why no." The third question was the killer.

"Have you got your tropical gear?" I was slow but it was gradually beginning to sink in.

We are leaving for foreign parts on the morning tide, he told me. I immediately remonstrated with him. "It was clearly told by the DMAA's Office that it was a home posting on Western approaches, furthermore I have just returned from two and a half years in the Eastern Med." I demanded to see the Captain. "OK" said the Coxswain, "Captain's request men, tomorrow." To say I was upset was to put it mildly. "We are sailing first to Dunoon on the Clyde to pick up our convoy, so all is not lost yet." I was completely crestfallen as he took me down to introduce me to the lads in the mess, where they had just returned from embarkation leave. They were all sympathetic, but the most hurtful blow came when one of the lads said "It'll only make it worse, but you've got to know sometime, you are relief for a yellow bellied bastard who's deserted. He went on leave with the first batch and didn't return." That was all I needed, I have already made my feelings known about these 'jackals' and now I was about to suffer at the hands of one. The Captain was sympathetic and sent a signal requesting another replacement. Sorry, said Chatham in reply, but we are completely out of ABSTs at the moment. Nothing was forthcoming about the deceit of the Drafting Office and so it was that I headed straight back to the Med, albeit this time it was the Western end.

I had been shanghaied aboard *HMS Felixstowe* by barefaced lies and there was nothing I could do about it.

"See you on Thursday," I had told my family. On Thursday I was battling my way up the West coast of England on my way to the Clyde. I now knew it would be many a Thursday before I saw them again. For a long time I was a very unhappy and disgruntled member of my mess, for I quite rightly felt I had drawn the short straw.

My first visit below decks did nothing to raise my spirits, they really were unbelievably small and basic. The seamen's messdeck was about the size of a large dining room in an average house, but it served as both bedroom and dining room for over thirty men. It was no good, I just had to stop making comparisons, it was not helping at all.

I met my messmates, they were all on my side, to a man they agreed the deserter was a doubled dyed bastard. I found I had a townie in the stokers' messdeck and yet another stoker lived in neighbouring Romford.

That night they took me on a run ashore in Guzz. Needless to say I got well and truly drunk. It helped at the time, but the king sized hangover didn't help, when before the light of dawn we slipped and went to sea.

The flotilla joined up with a small convoy, rounded Land's End and headed North, a strange direction to be sailing in view of the tropical camouflage of the ships. I got my first taste of sailing in a six hundred ton biscuit tin, battling against one of the wildest of waters, the Irish Sea It was very harrowing, but according to one of my oppos, "you ain't seen nuffing yet".

A typical exchange of words between two matelots could go something like this:

"What ship Jack?"

"Hardships," would be the reply.

"Hardships, you don't know what hardships are," he would answer.

In that short journey from Devonport to Dunoon, I had soon found out what hardships were. It was sailing on the *Felixstowe* in the turbulent Irish Sea. Little did I know what the future had in store for me.

Before we went too far North, we made a right and sailed up the Clyde to Dunoon. I went straight ashore and cabled my family who would already be wondering what had become of me. Censorship limited me to the briefest of messages. "New address *HMS Felixstowe,* c/o GPO London." That was it. I could have been a young married rating with a pregnant wife, there was no sentiment, no favours, no appeal, once that little piece of paper appeared on your mess table that was it, you were on your way.

It was my first visit to Scotland, a country renowned for its scenic beauty. It was also famous for the Gorbals, Sauchiehall Street, and a bar where for the price of a chaser, a glass of ale and a dram of whisky, you could get to shake hands with the famous Scottish boxing champ Benny Lynch. Being a matelot it was no contest, and in the company of Harry the Skipper's Steward I made for the latter, and had a thoroughly good evening.

We sailed the following forenoon, passing the mighty *QE II,* three battleships, no less than five carriers plus an awesome array of cruisers, destroyers and escorts. Something was definitely afoot.

When I stepped off the jetty at Dunoon, and on to the deck of *Felixstowe,* it was to be the last time for eighteen months that my feet would stand on the soil of the UK.

We left the 'bonnie banks of the Clyde' and 'sailed across the sea to Ireland, berthed at Londonderry and shortly afterwards sailed with a convoy, heading South in the company of the destroyers *Boadices, Bulldog,* and *Boreas* . We were at sea for nearly five days and it was hell. The little Bangors were not equipped to fight these mountainous seas, most of the crew were violently seasick and those of us who were not physically sick still felt poorly. Efficiency was at zero and I won't even attempt to describe the appalling state of the *Felixstowe's* messdecks and flats, they were foul. Anyone suffering this malaise ashore would warrant a darkened room, an attendant nurse, probably in intensive care.

The first new fleet of mine sweepers to be built were launched in Belfast at the beginning of 1940, although they were designed and ordered in the pre-war depression which affected the ship building industry very badly. The ship's architects were virtually told to design and build something cheap and nasty, and they conformed to the word. Proof of the total disregard they had for the men who were to serve in them was ample. They were built and designed to sweep mines in coastal waters. The Admiralty knew the peacetime compliment was around forty men, and in wartime double that number, in spite of the fact that most of them were built after the outbreak of war, they never altered them one iota. For example some were equipped with diesel engines which required much less space than the bigger reciprocating engines. Instead of utilising the extra space for the comfort of the crew, they made them twenty feet shorter to save a few quid. They were very bad sea ships, and leaked like sieves in bad weather. It was then decided to convert them to perform as submarine hunters, which meant the addition of ASDICS and depth charges. It also meant that they would now have to operate as convoy escorts in addition to sweeping mines. This would mean long days at sea, but the crew of ninety were provided with an ordinary, household size fridge to store fresh food. We were always without fresh food, and living on corned beef and Ship's biscuits on regular occasions, again nothing was ever done to alleviate this position. They were without a doubt the toughest of all Naval ships to serve on and I have spoken to sub mariners who told me in no way would they swap, after all it wouldn't do for subs to leak like sieves would it? And I was assured that they seldom ran out of food in normal circumstances.

The Admiralty's insensitivity didn't stop there, I found two of my shipmates on *Felixstowe* had an even greater grievance than me. 'Taff' Whittle, one of the seamen, had been torpedoed in the Atlantic and was adrift for twenty days before being picked up. It was criminal that he should be at sea at all, never mind about the ship he was on. His nerve had completely gone, and he spent most of his time on the upper deck, his lifebelt constantly around his waist. It was so obvious that he was unfit for sea, yet no-one went to his aid. This puts clearly into perspective the total disregard the powers that be had for the serving man.

The other case is equally heartless, my opposite number on *Felixstowe* 'Torps' Harris, suffered from sea sickness, he was far and away the worst case I had encountered. He was ill even in a swell inside the harbour, and most of the time at sea he was *hors de combat,* but no-one gave a thought to getting him a swap to a shore base, or at least a much larger ship.

The middle Watch was bad enough in itself, at 'eight bells', you had quite conceivably already been without sleep for sixteen hours. Try to envisage starting work at midnight in a warm comfortable factory or office without sleep for sixteen hours. Now imagine climbing an iron ladder and opening a hatch to step out onto a rain lashed, windswept deck, which was alternating between pitching backwards and forwards, and rolling from side to side not necessarily in that order. Suddenly the bows slicing through the angry tormented seas, plummet into a hole in the water, because of gravity your body follows, with the exception of your stomach, which is making desperate efforts to leave via your mouth. The bows are now pointing towards the bottom of the sea, which now rushes along the deck and crashes against the bridge superstructure. The *Felixstowe* would be completing this manoeuvre through all of the next four hours of my Watch, it was sheer hell.

I was sharing starboard lookout with a character called 'Pongo' Waring - Pongo because of the famous Aston Villa centre forward, who must have been in the Army before becoming a Pro/footballer, and matelots referred to all soldiers as Pongos. Pongo Waring was some character, he was a soft spoken Lancastrian, and a wise old owl. However, what he told me on that Watch should have induced me to quietly push him overboard and then wait ten minutes before reporting it. Pongo was a deserter, a persistent offender who had been on the run, or in detention since the day of his call-up. I have no need to tell you that deserters were not flavour of the month for me. I had started the Watch with murder in my heart, and when we came off Watch together, he had convinced me that having met Mary in Durban I should have had no hesitation in deserting to be with her. I was now utterly confused. Here was a persistent deserter telling me, who was only on the *Felixstowe* because of a deserter, that if I'd had the guts to desert, I would now be in sunny South Africa with the lovely Mary, instead of being tossed about like a cork in the middle of a stormy Irish Sea. It says much about life aboard *Felixstowe,* that Pongo insisted Naval detention, the hardest of all service chokeys, was infinitely preferable to what we were now enduring.

It was a feat of superhuman effort that kept the ship at all functional. The one saving grace about sea sickness as far as sufferers were concerned was the rapidity of the recovery, almost as soon as the 'spirit levels' in your ears righted themselves, it was gone. You won't travel many more troubled waters than the Irish Sea and the Bay of Biscay when they were in tumult, but at least it usually kept the U Boats and hostile aircraft at bay as well.

However, as soon as the weather abated, we were attacked by enemy aircraft, the raids were, fortunately abortive. The weather continued to improve, the sun got warmer, the skies and seas were bluer, conditions long familiar to me.

To starboard my night glasses picked up a subtle change of light on the horizon, the tell-tale glow of a city bathed in the lights of peace. Something my shipmates had been denied in the UK ever since the first day of war. Soon the full blaze of light would reveal the city of Tangiers, in Spanish Morocco. We entered the Straits of Gibraltar, and prepared to enter harbour.

It was my first visit to Gibraltar, that guardian of the Med, and together with Malta and Egypt, it was the only reason we had any sort of foothold at all in this theatre of the war. A foothold only achieved by calamitous losses to both the Royal and Merchant Navies.

The blue Med with its sun, and mostly placid waters, could paint an inviting picture if you were 'shipping them green' in the Atlantic, or out on Russian convoys. The Med, however, was an enclosed arena, completely surrounded by the enemy. It was also infested with minefields that had already claimed many victims. Minefields that the thirteenth mine sweeping flotilla were about to confront, much to their cost.

The town of Gibraltar was 'Mickey Mouse' and totally dominated by the towering Rock, but it possessed a fine Naval harbour. It was a garrison town, it was also a matelots' town, a good run ashore, not perhaps so much in matters of the flesh, that is unless your tastes were for male rather than female company. It was something we soon found out on our first stroll through the infamous Alemeda Gardens where low hisses and whistles invited you into the bushes, and it wasn't for botany lessons. Here we were also introduced to the Barbary Apes, peculiar for the fact that they were the only apes resident on the continent of Europe.

The great harbour was jam packed with the Royal Navy. Everything from battlers, carriers, cruisers, down to the diminutive fleet sweepers. The thirteenth mine sweeping flotilla had proudly made its entry into the company of its more illustrious seniors and berthed alongside the Mole, under the towering stern of the cruiser *Sheffield*. We must have appeared to them like toys on a boating lake.

Most of my oppos had never seen anything like this array of sea power before, they had commissioned *Felixstowe* from new and had been paddling up and down the South coast of England. They had enjoyed night leave and weekends at home and on occasional long leave, but this was a new ball game, there would be no weekend leave out here, although there was leave tonight until 11.00pm.

The waters of the harbour were a spectacular sight, the small boats were like ants, everything from the Admiral's barge, to the dart-like 'skimming dishes' were weaving intricate patterns on the water's surface. Wake crossed wake, as each boat homed in on its target. It was like a water ballet as the imperceptible touch of the wheel avoided what looked like certain collisions. Boats ferrying top brass to conferences, coded information from ship to ship, courtesy calls for the quaffing of pink gins, vital stores and supplies and not the least our boat, among many others, that were carrying liberty men on a run ashore. There were so many squaddies and matelots in town, that those on the outside of the crowd were in danger of falling into the sea.

There was an aura of excitement about Gibraltar, a tenseness, a feeling of anticipation, even foreboding, you could feel it, smell it, even taste it. An awesome assembly of sea power was ensconced within the harbour. Tomorrow, the next day, soon, anyway, it would all disgorge from the harbour, like sauce from the neck of a bottle. A new conflict was about to commence, somewhere out there, it could be anywhere, remember every beach out there was either neutral or enemy. There were men drinking in those crowded bars that were having their last run ashore, squaddies who would launch themselves naked onto a beach, a son, a husband, a father, then die without making a single contribution to the conflict except, that is, to die.

Chapter 32

The *Universal* and *Trocadera* bars had been emptied of their feuding occupants, this was an ongoing one. It always started with the Allied forces throwing their arms round each other and ended up with them throwing bottles and chairs at each other. The patrols would move in and toss the miscreants they could capture into the back of the trucks, or they would end up in the local nick to sober up. A few would end up in hospital, a barside brawl would deny them the doubtful pleasure of participating in the forthcoming Operation Torch and, quite feasibly, save them from adding to the list of casualties.

The air defences and anti sub patrols would already be in operation, as first the leader on *Rothesay,* left the Mole and headed for sea. *Felixstowe's* Captain eased her round the bow rope and ordered half astern both on the telegraphs. Everyone waited for the counter order, half ahead starboard engines to swing her round into the stream astern of *Rothesay*. The order never came and so it was that *Felixstowe* became the very first casualty of Operation Torch. No-one knew why, but the 'brakes, were not applied and *Felixstowe* came to a halt only after scarring the face of the wall by the Governor's Steps, caving in her stern and redesigning her sweeping rollers, bollards and davits. The impact was enough to throw some of us, unaware of what was happening, right off our feet.

We were second in command in the flotilla and the collision was to relegate us to junior ship. We never saw the Skipper again; a car arrived alongside and whisked him away. Rumour was now rife as to the whys and wherefores, but without any proof, suffice it to say he was a sick man.

The collision gave immediate promotion to one Geoffrey Powney Lt RNVR who was First Lieutenant (Jimmy the One). It must have been a profound shock to find himself having the mantle of Captain thrust upon him in a matter of minutes. He would now have to perform the same duties, make the same judgements, and sometimes split-second decisions as the Captains of the capital ships around him. A responsibility taken at the time of one of the most important sea offensives of all time.

His first duty was to get *Felixstowe* secured alongside and signal headquarters as to the seriousness of the damage sustained. Within the hour there were dockyard mateys swarming all over the ship, compressors, burning gear, welding gear, rivet guns were everywhere. In the space of a few hours, *Felixstowe's* sweeping stern was brand new and functional.

Almost before the last dockyard matey was ashore we were under way to join the flotilla. We had the best part of two days to catch them up and that meant that we could burn up the Med going flat out at fifteen knots.

Two hours out of Gibraltar we closed up at dusk action stations. We were alone, just the *Felixstowe* against whatever the enemy had in store for us.

I had traversed thousands of miles of ocean in *HMS Kent,* always with a feeling of security and confident we could handle any situation with which we were confronted. Right now as I meticulously scanned the waters of the Med and the ever darkening skies with my binoculars, I had a feeling of uncertainty about my fellow shipmates. The whole set-up on *Felixstowe* was more relaxed than on *Kent,* this was considered normal on small ships. However, I didn't think that this should apply to lookout duties - the importance of seeing the enemy first was of paramount importance.

It was the custom of the Royal Navy in times of war for the Captain to inform all his crew of any special mission in which danger was above the average. We now knew that we were part of a massive sea force that was to make landings on the coast of North Africa. There were to be three separate assaults, on Morocco, Algeria and our particular venue - Tunisia. The 'thirteenth' was part of a centre force which was to attack the beaches in and around Oran. The whole mission was to be known as Operation Torch, at that time it was the most powerful sea force ever mustered in the history of Naval warfare.

Darkness rapidly closed in and in my mind the *Felixstowe* took on the dimensions of the *Ark Royal,* we were, I felt, alone and vulnerable. A clear starlit sky, a flat calm sea and a full moon shining down on *Felixstowe,* like the floodlights in a football stadium. That moon, so indispensable to writers of romantic fiction, was both feared and hated by all matelots in the Med. It made you appear like a new sixpence on a sweep's backside. Then again the phospherance of your bow wave and the wake astern seemed like an arrow indicating to any lurking sub exactly where you were and even the direction you were steering. In truth any U Boat in the vicinity would be much more interested in the convoy that *Felixstowe* was desperately trying to overhaul.

The clatter of the Aldis lamp and the 'password' of identification told us we had made contact with our objective. There followed shouted orders, the sound of engine room telegraphs and some deft manoeuvres as we eased our way into our allocated niche in the convoy.

Dawn action stations showed the convoy numbered about two dozen ships and the morning Watch was just ending when the after lookouts reported ships dead astern. Four destroyers soon came into sight, elegantly performing their anti sub sweeps, ahead of a mighty force of sea power: the battleship *Rodney,* aircraft carrier *Furious,* two escort carriers *Biter* and *Dasher* the anti aircraft cruiser *Dehli* and the cruisers *Aurora* and *Jamaica,* plus two submarines and other destroyer escorts. The total landing force was a spectacular sight and was to number seventy ships. The main landing force was housed in thirty four troop transport ships. Centre Taskforce was under the command of Commodore Trowbridge in the headquarters landing ship *Larqs.*

The allies were unsure of two things in particular about this mammoth undertaking, the first was the continued neutrality of Spain and the other the fear of the French fleet emerging from Toulon. Either scenario would have posed major problems for the project. These eventualities had to be prepared for, therefore a strong Naval force was detailed to protect our rear. It comprised three battleships *Nelson, Renown* and *Duke of York,* the carriers *Formidable* and *Victorious,* four cruisers, seventeen destroyers and air cover from Gibraltar.

The enemy were expecting this huge force to proceed further into the Med to relieve Malta, and to reinforce the troops in Libya; they guessed wrong. Centre Taskforce made a one hundred and eighty degree alteration to course and headed toward the port of Oran, on the North African coast. It was first round to the Allies and Operation Torch. Torch was an entirely different proposition to the landings in Panterlaria, Sicily and Salerno, on mainland Italy, which were to follow. These were to be on unmistakably enemy soil and were subject to intense aerial and sea-borne bombardment. This took away the element of surprise, but was considered essential to the success of the operations.

The Torch landings were spared this onslaught in the hope that it would make it easier to get the co-operation of the wavering French.

Centre Taskforce was to land in the region of the Royal Navy's assault of the French fleet, when, after its refusal to surrender, it was decimated by the Naval force under Admiral Somerville. The French had never forgiven us for this attack.

Worse was to follow, the American General Doolittle, famous for his air attack on Tokyo, devised a plan to dispatch American paratroops from airfields in Britain, to fly the one thousand mile journey then drop and capture vital airfields in the vicinity of Oran. To say it went wrong was an understatement.

Every British voice was raised against the scheme, but it was proceeded with regardless of the dire warnings that it had elicited.

The Americans had no previous experience of airborne invasions and no such attack had ever been attempted more than four hundred miles from the objective. This venture was to involve a journey of one thousand miles, some of which would also violate the neutral territory of Spain.

Every conceivable thing went wrong with the operation. Of the thirty nine transport planes that set out from the West of England, not one achieved its objective. They were to land in no less than five different countries, Gibraltar, French Morocco, Spanish Morocco, Algeria and Tunisia. Some were forced down by the French Air Force, others were captured by French Police. Only fourteen of the C47s that took off remained operational. It was seven days before the surviving troops, just over half the number that set out, were mustered to join in the battle for Tunisia.

Bad planning, bad luck and bad weather all played their part in this fiasco, but even without this bad fortune things could not have been more chaotic. A British destroyer lay on the course to their target with a secret homing device aboard, which would guide the oncoming planes to their targets. Unfortunately the signal from the device on the destroyer was tuned to a different frequency to that in the planes - a slight oversight that rendered it completely useless.

If the airborne assault had ended in disaster the same could not be said of the two brilliantly organised armadas that had left the shores of Britain and the USA. Both arrived at their objectives, almost without incident. In fact it was the enemy that suffered the loss of two U Boats that were sunk by the strong air cover over the convoy.

The day of the 7th November 1942 was warm, sunny and calm, it was incredible to see the awesome array of Naval and Merchant shipping, just quietly nosing towards the enemy coast. What a dramatic change had come over these hostile waters, where high level torpedo and divebombers had so recently wreaked havoc on the gallant seamen trying against all the odds to sustain Malta and further afield the Eighth Army in Libya. Zero hour was near as the huge force moved ever closer to the beachhead, so far everything had proceeded with clockwork precision and the element of surprise had been achieved.

Aboard the headquarters ship, *Larqs,* stomachs would be knotting, muscles would be tightening and bowels would be loosening. Specialists, highly trained commandos would soon be lowered gently into the waters of the Med and silently approach the key obstacles they were to take out. It was bad enough for them but what of the thirty nine thousand Yanks who were to follow them in? Once on the beach their fate would be decided by luck. The squaddie went in naked, unprotected, they were the real heroes, psychologically the sailor had his ship around him and the pilot his plane.

The thirteenth mine sweeper flotilla detached itself from the main force and took up the pole position on the grid. The little sweepers were always the first in and we headed for our location just off the beaches in the Bay of Arzue where the main landings would take place.

The flotilla split up into three units as there were three landing points, it was to be a line abreast sweep, the most dangerous of sweeps. *Clacton* marked the Channel to be swept with dan buoys. We pointed our bows to the enemy shore, which looked dark, still and ominous.

"Sweeping party muster on the quarter deck," the order was given in a modulated voice, as if the enemy was in hearing range and suddenly would flood the sea with light and blast us out of the water. It was no good modulating the voice, I thought, because the *Felixstowe's* powerful engines seemed to be twice as loud as usual. It was all imagination, of course, but there was an atmosphere of expectancy aboard. Suddenly the whole scene of quiet calm took on an air of panic stations. First of all a small convoy of French boats appeared on the scene, something that was always on the cards. What happened next was just one more example of the catalogue of cock-ups that had plagued this venture.

This error was unforgivable, suddenly out of the darkness the huge hulk of the *City of Bermuda* loomed into view and very nearly ran down half of the flotilla. From then on things really started to go awry. Assault craft were lowered and sailed merrily on towards the beach through unswept waters. Some of them made it, others hit a sand bank some distance out, the ramps were lowered and men and vehicles found themselves in about five feet of water. Most of the men made it, the vehicles didn't. Then the weather suddenly took a turn for the worse, engines were water-logged, vehicles were badly loaded. Many that made it to the beach made no headway in the soft wet sand. Fortunately there was no immediate opposition, although shore batteries were now in action over they bay and heavy gunfire could be heard from the harbour and city of Oran.

Tragic happenings were taking place in the harbour of Oran. Misguided information had led the Allies to believe that if they sent in two ex-American destroyers, flying the American flag and telling them over megaphones it was a friendly invasion, all would be peace and tranquillity. Tragically it was not to be. *HMS Hartland* and *HMS Walney* came under withering point blank fire from the French. It was a cold blooded massacre which inflicted carnage aboard the two heavily laden ships. Three hundred and eighty five Army personnel and one hundred and eighteen Naval personnel perished and two hundred and forty five men were wounded.

The whole concept of Torch was based on the assumption that the recalcitrant French would, as D Day approached, soften and fall into the arms of the Allies. Nothing, as it turned out, was further form the truth. Practically the whole show was run by the Americans, partly because the name of Great Britain was anathema to the French and mainly because of their strength in numbers and equipment.

Voices had been raised against aerial and sea bombardment, were they justified? We were at war and the French had been given the opportunity to make the invasion bloodless and had refused. We sacrificed the lives of five hundred highly trained men to the guns of the very people we were trying to free.

Mightier pens than mine have tabled the exploits of the French Resistance movement, men and women who put their lives on the line in the constant fight against the aggressors on their soil. Their courage surpassed even that of the serving men, for they were fighting two enemies, the invaders and the traitors who were collaborating with them. Others had joined the Free French Force and continued the fight against the enemy on land, sea and by air.

As the result of the landings of the Torch operation they would be the first to experience the immense thrill of participating in the first victory on French soil. Sadly the joyful celebrations would be followed by retribution against the many who had thrown in their lot with the enemy. That was in the future for there were still many battles to be fought and won and friend and foe would continue to perish in their pursuit.

The landings, after the initial bunglings, took on some sort of order and the Bay of Arzue became a huge harbour. Once away from the soft landings on the beach head fighting became fierce and the ships in the bay were getting plenty of attention from shore batteries, hostile aircraft and the U Boat.*Rodney* was knocking seven bells out of *Mers el Kibir* as if seeking retribution for the massacre of the *Walney* and *Hartland*. So fierce was the resistance in Oran that it took over two days before it capitulated.

The burden on the mine sweeper was unrelenting, sweeping for mines by day, sub patrols by night, escorting convoys. *Stornaway* went in pursuit of a merchantman and came under heavy fire from shore batteries. *Polruan* got a sub contact, the *Geranium* was sunk by a U Boat, the liner *Viceroy of India* was sunk by a U Boat. Outside the bay the U Boats were reported in packs. "*Clacton* in attack on U Boat", so it went on, there was little respite and sleep was at a premium. Inevitably it was taking its toll, in no way could men continue to operate efficiently under this stress.

Felixstowe and *Clacton* had completed a sweeping routine and were assigned to the long boring hours of anti sub patrols around the periphery of the huge array of shipping at anchor. It had finished my Watch in the 'last dog' (6am to 8pm), swinging into my privileged position of a slung hammock - most of my shipmates put their hammock down wherever they could. My head hit the pillow and I was asleep before my tired frame had straightened out.

The thundering crash almost shot me out of my hammock, I had been in the land of nod for a very brief one and a half hours and my scrambled brain was trying to reason out what had happened. Was it a bomb, a torpedo, or a mine? I swiftly gathered my senses and pulled on my boots, the only part of my attire that I had removed. I suddenly realised that so far there had been no pipe over the speakers. Diving through the messdeck bulkhead I crashed headlong into figures racing into the space I had just left. I was then that I learned of our problem, the *Felixstowe* had crashed headlong into the stern of our sister ship *Clacton*. The party I had collided with leaving the mess were rushing forward to see if the bulkhead was intact between our mess and the cable locker flat on our fo'castle.

The *Felixstowe's* bows were now some four feet shorter, collisions were becoming a habit with *Felixstowe,* for this was our third. So far it was the bows, stern and then the bows again that had been disfigured, in that order. Within an hour I was back in my 'flea pit' and soon I was sound asleep.

Chapter 33

For six days we continued the grinding routine of protecting the landing beaches. Troops, stores and the paraphernalia of war continued to pour ashore from the supply ships. The empty vessels gave us a break from the boring routines and soon we were off escorting convoys to and from Gibraltar. There was now intense U Boat activity and constant air attacks to contend with, mostly from torpedo bombers.

The Med, as I have already stated, was virtually one huge minefield, there were so many narrow channels that were easy to control by mine. There were, I believe, four flotillas of F/M/Sweepers operating, plus the gallant little trawlers. Their workload was quite staggering, enormous enemy minefields were being cleared, all of it hard, boring and dangerous work.

In addition to the thirteenth mine sweeping flotilla, the twelfth, fourteenth and fifteenth flotillas were also much in evidence. Many names spring to mind, and others. Each one performing heroics of the highest order in the dangerous and arduous task of clearing the sea lanes of lethal mines. Few of these gallant little ships will ever be remembered, except perhaps by the surviving crew members and the next of kin of the huge number of casualties.

The main hazards were in the opportunist enemy mines, mines that were laid in previously swept channels overnight by the enemy mine layers, E Boats and minelaying subs. It meant that often even the previously swept channels were not necessarily safe. The battle on land was for ever running into difficulties, but fortunately the RN commandos and other troops fairly soon had control of the coast and seaports.

Relentlessly we pushed ahead clearing channels to capture the harbours and one by one they fell, Oran, Algiers, Phillipville, Bougie, Bizerta, Sousse, Sfax and so on to Tripoli. All this was achieved under constant attack from a determined enemy, with bombs, torpedoes, shore batteries and submarines. Very little was made of the enormous achievements of these small but tenacious terrier like little ships, which bore a disproportionate part of the danger of these operations. An exception was the excellent book *Out Sweeps* by Paul Lund and Harry Ludlam. *Out Sweeps* deals in graphic detail with the operations in the Med by the sweepers. Unfortunately, for reasons not known, they failed to mention the thirteenth who were there from start to finish and lost two of its number in the process. In consequence they missed the story of the *Sidi Bel Abbes* and other equally interesting yarns.

We were once again on the endless, gruelling, treadmill of escort duty, in company with *Stornaway*. The convoy consisted of the *Empire Buckler*, the *Empire Dace*, and the *Findra*. One of these ships was on her last voyage. The Commander in the U-boat made one more adjustment of range and deviation, tension would be high aboard the U-boat, they were going for the kill.

The *SSFindra's* crew would be unaware of the missile of death that was about to blow her apart. There would be jubilation aboard the U-boat as the torpedo exploded and blew the guts out of the *Findra*. Men that a second ago were either asleep, or in animated conversation, would now be dead or fighting for their survival in the sea. One second, that's all it took to turn calm into calamity.

The scene was now commonplace, a cryptic entry in the *Stornaway* diary reads, "The *SSFindra* turned on her end and sank beneath the waves."*HMSStornaway*, fleet minesweeper and U-boat hunter, was about to become a lifeboat and a hospital ship, as she went about the rescue of the stricken crew of *Findra*.

With her engines stopped and her boats lowered she would be a prime target for the lurking U-boat.

Biff Finlayson in the A/S cabinet on the bridge of *Felixstowe* suddenly stiffened. The monotonous 'ping, ping, ping' from his cabinet turned to the sound every operator wanted to hear, the returning echo from the hull of a U-boat.

"Strong echo bearing 300, right deviation," he gave out, the ever present uneasy calm of the bridge suddenly changed. Shouted orders, course alterations, engine room telegraphs asking for maximum speed, all upped the tempo.

Right through the whole ship's company, adrenalin would flow, tension would mount, we were going into battle, black pennant flying on the mast, it was thrilling. The echo was still loud and clear.

Felixstowe keeled hard over, the constant exchanges loud and hasty gradually subsided to a level of calmness. We were seeking retribution for the loss of one of our charges.

The fragmented innards of the *SSFindra* brushed against our sides as we passed the bobbing figures in the water, the eyes of the survivors could have been saying, "Why did you not protect us?"

Aboard the U-boat the air of jubilation would change to one of concern as the Commander gave the orders to crash dive as he made his endeavours to escape.

Felixstowe at maximum revs closed in on our target and fired the first set of six cannisters of destruction, the U-boat was now fighting for its life. Who would want to change places with the brave men encased in that black, noisy, steel casket, desperately trying to escape from the frightening explosions that were seeking to 'rend it asunder'?

During the seven attacks *Felixstowe* dropped twenty-six depth charges. The enclosed report claims it was the second pattern of five that severely damaged the U-boat and the third, fourth and fifth pattern that eventually sank her.

There the story of *Findra* and the U-boad was to end, but when collating the archieves, reports of the incident, something caught my eye at the top of the written report. It read:

(Date 23 Feb 43) Latitude:36° 58' 15" NORTH

(Time 1406hrs) Longitude 03° 40' 54" EAST

It was the date, the time and the exact position of the attack, pinpointed somewhere in the Mediterranean Sea.

With hindsight perhaps I should have ignored it, but curiosity got the better of me, and so it was that for the second time I contacted Horst Bredaw, curator of the German U-boat archives in Cuxhaven. Little did I know that I was unearthing a can of worms that threw doubt on the authenticity of archive material, and the veracity of some of the claims of RN successes against U-boat.

The Germans' report of the *Findra* incident is completely baffling. They show that the *Findra* was torpedoed by Commander Mehl in U.371 and claim that no attack was made on U-boat 371 and it made its escape. They do admit however that U-boat 443 was sunk in almost the exact position as claimed by *Felixstowe* and on the same day (23rd Feb 1943). This can only mean that there were two U-boats in close proximity at the time, and we had assumed it was the one that sunk *Findra* that we had sunk. That wasn't the end of it, the U-boat archives claim that the destroyers *Wheatland*, *Laverton* and *Malvern* had sunk U.443, there was no mention of *Felixstowe* whatsoever.

The enclosed written report will confound the findings of the report from the U-boat archives.

Felixstowe first made ASDIC contact with the U-boat at 1406hrs, less than one hour later the captain had claimed it as sunk (1455hrs). It was nearly three hours later (1745hrs) before *Wilton* arrived, *Laverton* is not mentioned.

Stiftung Traditionsarchiv Unterseeboote

U-Boot-Archiv

Cuxhaven-Altenbruch, 07.12.1996

Mr.Philip Cairns
20 Surrey Road
Dagenham
Essex RM10 8ES
England

Dear Mr. Cairns,

To answer your request:-

(1) It is impossible to find out what boat was attacked by H.M.S. "Felixstowe" on 07.02.1943.
On this date we lost two boats, both in the Atlantic. I cannot look through all the U/Boat war diaries to find which boat was attacked and not damaged.

(2) The SS "Findra" was sunk by Commander Mehl in U/Boat 371., she was not attacked and sunk by H.M.S."Felixstowe" on 23.02.1943.

(3) On the same date 23.02.1943 the U/Boat 443 was sunk at position $36^{o}.55'$ N. $02^{o}.25'$ E. It was sunk by R,N. Escorts "Bicester, "Lamerton" and "Wheatland".

(4) I helped you because the German Embassy in London asked me, as you needed the information to include in your book.

With best regards,

With best regards, sincerely

Horst Bredow

Stifter und geschäftsführender Vorstand: Horst Bredow

Anschrift: U-Boot-Archiv · Bahnhofstraße 57 · 27478 Cuxhaven-Altenbruch
Telefon: (0 47 22) 3 22 · Telefax: (0 47 22) 25 75
Bank: Stadtsparkasse Cuxhaven (BLZ 241 500 01)
Konto 154 203 - nur für steuerlich absetzbare Spenden

Information re. sunken U/Boat from German U/Boat Archives.

Copy of Official Report

At 1349A, 23 rd Febuary., 1943. H.M.S. Felixstowe was screening to starb'd of the Convey (consisting of three Merchant vessels in line abreast) in position C. When S.S. Findra (M.V. port side of convey) was observed to have been apparently torpedoed, and commenced to go down by the stern, sinking shortly afterwards. H.M.S. Stornqway (S.O. Escort) who had been screening to port, altered course to close Convey, and H.M.S. "Felixstowe" closed Convey on course of 130 degrees.

The two remaining M.V.s made an emergency turn to starb'd from the original Convey course of 264 degrees, and increased to full speed. "Stornoway" then ordered "Felixstowe" to carry on escort Convey. Course was altered to port 180 degrees, and when ships head was pointing just clear of the starb'd quarter of Convey, A/S operator reported Echo bearing 350 degrees, range 1500yds. Time 1406A/23. Altered course to 350 degrees,- hoisted Black Pendant Echo was sharp, extent of target 12 degrees. Propeller H.E. was clearly recognisable. Classified S/M.

Target was moving right, inclination opening. Attack carried out as previously indicated in report,-speed 15knots. Contact was held, and a second attack carried out (with inclination closing) which it is opined, resulted in severely damaging the S/M to such an extent as to cause her to finally sink after the 5 th attack.

Contact was held after 2 nd attack, slight Propeller H.E. fading out at 900 yards. Contact became weaker and was lost at 200 yards before 3 rd pattern was fired (stop watch) Contact was not regained, and 4 th pattern was fired on position of 3 rd attack.

Contact regained at 1455A/23, echo bearing 170 degrres range 1700yds. Went into attack, fired 2 Throwers (500ft) which were ready, by recorder. Air bubbles observed. Contact was held but with difficulty, and was lost at 700yds when going in to carry out 6 th attack. Pattern fired by stop watch.

Contact was not made again, and after searching 50 minutes without result, one D/C set to 500ft was fired at 1609, on box thrown overboard in position of 3 rd attack.

"Felixstowe" then proceeded to carry out box search from position of sunken M/V. Total area covered during attacks and solo search, was between the following parallels.

37 degrees 03 minutes North. 36 degrees 56 minutes North.
03 degrees 40 minutes East. 03 degrees 45 minutes East.

H.M.S. "Wheatland" joined and took over search operations at 1745A/23. H.M.S. "Wilton" joining at 1800. H.M.S. "Wheatland", "Wilton", "Felixstowe" carried out box search of the following area: Between

37 degrees 12 minutes North, parallels 03 degrees30 minutes East and 04 degrees East, and a line Joining Following positions, 36 degrees 53 minutes North, 03 degrees 30 minutes East., same latitude, 03 degrees 41 minutes East and 37 degrees North. Negative results,- one non-sub echo at 1815A/23.

H.M.S. "Felixstowe" received orders; from C-in-C Mediterranean to return to harbour, and discontinued search at 0810A/24.

Official report on the sinking of the U/Boat.

On what grounds did the three destroyers claim the U-boat? It may have had something to do with 'pecking order' in the RN - three majestic destroyers against one humble minesweeper.

The reader will see by the evidence provided who was the justified claimant, as for myself, in retrospect, I am sorry my curiosity got the better of me now, I would sooner not have known.

The weather was worsening by the minute, it is hard to persuade people just how volatile the Med could be. For the last two weeks the sea had been on its worst behaviour, it didn't need much of a sea to upset the equilibrium of the little *Felixstowe*. Now we were being tossed about like a cork.

Tired men had endured endless hours of the anti-sub patrols, continuous sweeping of enemy minefields, the continual convoys into the Atlantic, and from Gibraltar, replenishing supplies and returning the empties. In these conditions there was only one word to describe the inside of the *Felixstowe*: appalling. Whenever high seas came over the bows there was no way of keeping the messdecks and flats dry, water was swilling about everywhere down below. Men were violently sea sick and just wanted to die, they were wet, cold and hungry, in these heavy seas, driving rain and howling wind. If action stations was sounded there was no way the ship would have been manned with any efficiency, by the same token, it was very unlikely the enemy woukd be sporting any subs or aircraft, so it was deuce.

It was in circumstances like this that a time honoured ritual of HM Royal Navy called for the consummate skill of an expert. In the calmest of waters the duty of the Rum Bosun was an onerous one, inasmuch as he was duty bound to measure each tot into the cup with the precision of a pharmacist, right to the nearest milligram. Now imagine the burden that was on his shoulders when the deck he was standing on was constantly swapping places with the ship's side. 'Nelson's Blood', the matelot's tot, the elixir of life, the *sal volatile*, that could almost revive a corpse, it was guaranteed to lift the spirits and square the shoulders of the most moribund.

The opium of the Naval messdecks eased the pain of all that hurting, and the boom of Algiers Harbour continued the process as we made our way to the harbour wall and secured alongside. A change of clothes, a shower and a level place to put your two feet, and the past few days are all forgottenn. This was Algiers, a real town still intact, so a run ashore was in sight. The other ports, Bizerta and Bone, etc. were a shambles of gutted buildings, sunken ships and dead bodies floating in the water, the grim tokens of war. It was nineteen days since that pre-invasion run ashore in Gibraltar and we needed this break badly, for our workload had become intolerable and out of all proportion to our size and the numbers in our crew.

There was little evidence of the disaster that had befallen the gallant destroyers *HMSBroke* and *Malcolm,* who had been sent into Algiers Harbour in a repeat of the foolhardy plan that had earlier been attempted in Oran. They had also gone in flying the Stars and Stripes in an attempted peaceful occupation of the harbour. Again, the French blasted them at point blank reange with a horrendous loss of life.

If there was one thing the Yanks excelled in it was looking after their fighting services. Algiers bore testimony to this. Once the weapons of war had passed through the next equipment landed was bulldozers and mobile cranes. The Americans were brilliant at this aspect of war. All the buildings on the waterfront were razed to the ground by bulldozers. In their place grew a complete township of giant wooden cases. Row upon row of them were formed into avenues and numbered. Inside them was about every conceivable item of food that was non-perishable and could be tinned, also clothing and other sundies. They were light years ahead of the British in this aspect of the conflict.

The sharp conflict in attitudes is clearly illustrated when comparisons were made between two mine sweepers, one American, one British. The American BYMS sweepers were much smaller than the Bangors. They were wooden and used for shallow water in shore sweeping. In spite of this the refrigeration space aboard for food was nearly the size of our messdeck. Bangors built in 1942, three years after the commencement of the war, had one household size fridge to care for a crew of over eighty men.

We were continually on the scrounge for food from any ship in reach, it was an unnecessary hardship inflicted on possibly the hardest working crews in the Royal Navy.

Salvation this time was in the hands of the Yanks. A sentry guarding the crated city on the jettyside passed by and explained that he would not return for about an hour. "you've got that long to store ship guys, so move it." We had just spoken to Santa Claus, it was all our Christmasses in one short hour. Every spare hand spilled out onto the jetty and participated in the looting. It was the beginnings of 'marshal aid' and 'lease lend', two American initiatives that rescued starving Britain at the cessation of hostilties. There was no need to even say the magic words Abra Cadabra, Alladin's cave was already open, hams, spams, jams anything that wasn't perishalble and could be tinned was there for the taking, or should that read thieving. Toilet sundries, socks, underwear and items of uniform, boots, some of us were storing ship with provisions, others were setting up as Marks and Sparks and flogging gear to the willing Arabs, to whom you could sell anything in the way of clothing. That sentry had done a great Anglo-American relations job and any belief in their shortcomings soon dissipated, but what the American Quarter Master thought of it leaves little to the imagination.

The *Felixstowe* was now closer to being a merchant supply ship than a fighting ship and I'm quite sure there were those amongst us who would have gladly put our ammunition and depth charges over the side to make more room for the loot. It was strange, the officers who would have you on a charge for stealing a ship's biscuit were all suddenly afflicted with blindness, or perhaps they thought the Admiralty had suddenly realised that the men were bloody starving, which they were at times. No, I don't think the latter thought had enterd their minds, they just knew where their bread would be buttered.

It was a long, long time since one Cornelius Finbar Driscoll had warrented an accolade, but right now he was coming close to receiving one. We were in harbour, we were getting overdue rest for our weary bodies and there were ample supplies of food we had only dreamed of. The sun was warm and shining, we were clean, dry, refreshed and lined up as liberty men ready to enjoy the sights and sounds of newly liberated Algiers.

How would we be received by our French hosts? One thing was for sure, the French might know who was amongst their compatriots but we certainly would not. Would there be confrontation? Both sides had scores to settle: how would Jack behave? We had lost a lot of oppos in both Oran and Algiers at the hands of the French. Would the vino be the catalyst? We would soon know. We entered the first bar and were warmly welcomed, there was no doubt that it was genuine and it became a celebration of there newly won freedom. Surprisingly there was no animosity evident. We became firm friends with Henri and Suzette in the *Bar Mistral* and it became our up homers when in Algiers. We returned aboard, happy with our day's relaxation, it was something we had earned, but after a good night's sleep we would be outside the boom and away on the hard business of war once again.

Chapter 34

Every time we left harbour it was getting tougher and tougher, the landings had given us a false sense of security. All three task forces had arrived on the beaches almost unmolested, the absence of sub and air opposition had been mystifying. Now they were back with a vengeance and the number of contacts made by the flotilla was remarkable. The enemy must have mustered every available sub to try and disrupt the supply lines between the beach heads and Gibraltar. In the air they were now showing a marked superiority, they still had unlimited access to airfields which were modern, hard surfaced and adjacent to the action.

It was a period of unparalleled enemy activity at sea, they made desperate efforts to disrupt the flow of supplies to the ground forces in Tunisia, where things were going very badly for the Allies. There was a powerful force of enemy submarines in operation and the flotilla was in almost daily battle with ASDIC contacts. There were daily air attacks from high level divebombers, and aerial torpedo. The most persistent at the time were the torpedo bombers who at times came in droves. However, they had little relative success and this was mainly due to the strength of the escorts and something so badly lacking during my time on *Kent* - air cover. Some ships were inevitably lost but at a high cost to the enemy.

We left Oran with a Gibraltar-bound convoy. It had become like a 'Parcelforce' delivery service, the workload was incredible, Gib to Oran, Gib to Algiers, Gib to Bone, Gib to Phillipville, so it went on week after week. It seemed we were closed up day and night, there was no respite, but what a difference it made to the conflict, when the playing field was more even. The anti aircraft cruiser *Carlisle,* powerful destroyers and fighter cover, were a boost to our morale, we were about to find out how much the air attacks were escalating, they were brave, daring and persistent.

It was no great hardship to leave the harbour at Bone as it was getting constant pastings from enemy bombers. At least at sea you were a moving target, Bone had already become a marine graveyard and was littered with sunken ships.

This convoy differed in no way from the previous ones in size or importance, but for reasons unknown to us it was to receive special attention from the Italians' latest torpedo bombers, the SN79, which made the Navy's Swordfish, Stringbags look like objects from an ancient air display. The men who manned these machines showed great courage, they were almost kamikaze as they pressed home their attacks.

The weather once again was atrocious, heavy seas and driving rain made the job of convoy escort doubly difficult. It affected the essential task of keeping station, particularly at night when there were frequent near collisions and hasty alterations of course. There was, though, a plus to sailing in these foul conditions, as it made the operations of subs equally difficult, and usually grounded all enemy aircraft.

It was the middle Watch, I was starboard lookout and looking forward to my relief, only about an hour to go. The weather had subsided but was still poor, although clear. It was always the same, one moment all is quiet and orderly, routines are being studiously followed. One second, that's all it needed for the whole scene to change to one of mayhem. On every Bridge frantic orders would be shouted in rapid succession, "action stations", speed adjustments, course alterations. The whole ship's company from the upper deck to the engine room would be roused from their middle Watch torpor, that dreadful battle to keep your protesting senses alert and your reluctant eyes awake.

The anti aircraft fire was the most impressive I had yet seen, the anti aircraft cruiser *Carlisle* packed a bigger punch than the whole of the rest of the escort. There were three Italian torpedo bombers, my mind went back to the *Kent*. This was different, I was now an idle spectator, and my powerful night glasses gave me a grandstand view of the whole action. One of the Italians veered off on the starboard bow, the tracers followed it like filings to a magnet. It zoomed away to safety. One torpedo track was visible, well away from any target, the raid was abortive and the three planes escaped to safety. There was a flurry of activity among the convoy and escorts, normality had to be restored, stations picked up and distances checked between ships. Minutes earlier ships and escorts were taking evasive action and for a short period chaos reigned. Any ship altering course is involved in a very complicated operation, needing the utmost precision and judgement as they were not fitted with brakes. At last all was peace and calm, the middle Watch ended, reliefs closed up. I kicked off my boots and swung into my hammock, tomorrow we would be ashore in Gibraltar and having a respite from the action.

I was staring at the deckhead and winding down before snatching some shut-eye. The klaxons sounded, "hands to action stations" sounded; they were back. This time there were six of them. They had no regard for the fact that we had just come off Watch and were about to enjoy a well

Chapter 35

We entered Gibraltar and tied up alongside the Mole, just astern of the cruiser *Sheffield*. A run ashore beckoned and although it was a temptation to just jump into your hammock and sleep, the opportunity to get off the claustrophobic messdeck was too good to miss. We got quietly drunk, returned aboard and then we slept. We were lucky, the other Watch didn't get the opportunity. The next day we were off to sea and this time we turned right and went into the Atlantic. It wasn't very hospitable, it hardly ever was, we closed on a convoy, the Skippers of the convoy ships must have looked askance at the swap of escorts. It looked as though half the US Navy had brought this across the Atlantic and the 'minnows' were taking it into the Med.

It was a large convoy by Med standards and with escorts numbered almost seventy ships. It was slow, about seven knots, and was zig-zagging in deference to the ever present threat of marauding enemy subs. All the pieces of the jigsaw were now in place and we proceeded with the convoy in nine lanes of fifteen towards our destination. Oran was roughly three hundred nautical miles away and all was peace and tranquillity, as we slowly homed in to our port of call.

The day had passed without any incident of note, but the odd lapse of concentration would interfere with the smoothness of the keeping of stations, a job which required complete concentration on the part of each individual ship. I was roused to commence the morning Watch, in which I was sharing tricks at the wheel (helmsman). The dawn had broken into one of those warm, sticky days with a clear blue sky and matching sea. The Med was a millpond with a shimmering haze, not unlike the tarmac of the road viewed through the windscreen of a car on a hot summer day. The haze in patches was thick enough to call a fog which hung about above the water's surface.

My morning Watch was almost at an end and I looked out on a scene of peace and orderliness, my mind marvelled at the transformation that had taken place in these waters. A few short weeks ago such a convoy would never have been attempted, such was the enemy's supremacy at that time.

The quiet of the morning was suddenly shattered by the sound of explosions, immediately the whole scene was transformed. Ships' sirens pierced the air, "hands to action stations" was sounded. *Felixstowe* wheeled sharply to port and was now on a reverse course to the convoy. Three of the escorts detached themselves from the convoy which in all circumstances carried on its course. *Felixstowe* and *Foxtrot* were the recovery boats and *Fantome,* the leader, was issuing instructions. *Fantome* left to rejoin the convoy. It was conceivable they didn't anticipate the scale of the mayhem it was leaving behind for only *Felixstowe* and *Foxtrot* to deal with.

The thick sea mist was still shrouding the water when suddenly to starboard through a break in the mist we saw the first casualty, the Yank *Michigan* was going down by the stern. We picked up the crew of her lifeboats, they all looked unharmed but in a state of shock. The sea mist was now clearing rapidly, but there was still only the evidence of the sinking *Michigan* to account for the three explosions. Ahead we could now see a widespread mass of flotsam floating on the water, and it was then concluded that the *Michigan* must have received two of the torpedoes and the debris ahead was the result of the explosions of her cargo. The Skipper lowered his binoculars to issue an order, I suddenly froze, I said something like "Jesus Christ Sir, there are hundreds of bodies out there floating on the surface." We didn't know it then but we were homing in on one of the Med's most horrendous troopship disasters. The *Sidi Bel Abbes* a French foreign legion troopship had been blown to smithereens. There was little or nothing floating on the surface larger than a human body, it was quite unbelievable.

Felixstowe and the trawler *Foxtrot* were the crash boats, thus they began the most trying, heart rending six or seven hours they would ever experience. The enemy might have us in their sights, and it was the duty of every Captain to make sure he did not endanger his ship and crew. It was an impossible situation, as we needed every available man for the rescue operation but the ship still had to be manned with gun crews, depth charge parties and lookouts. For once the flat calm of the Med came to our assistance, you could almost pick up a matchbox in your binoculars, it was so flat and calm and a periscope would easily be seen.

Felixstowe was operating with three boats and we set to work in one of the most horrific scenes of carnage it was possible to imagine. It was a nightmare, the piercing screams of men who were severely burnt, men who were limbless and dying in agony. Brave men, silent men, uncomplaining patient men, terrified men beseeching you in French to pick them up next, praying men, crying men, it was heartbreaking. Each man picked up was selected, it was necessary to make choices, we were unwilling judges and juries. In the middle of the carnage a white sergeant

Stiftung Traditionsarchiv Unterseeboote

U-Boot-Archiv

Extracts from the captains log-book " U - 565 "

20.04.1943

0730 Convoy in sight.
The leading group of destroyers are not aware of my presence.
The convoy is sailing in three rows.
I set my sights between the middle and starboard rows of the convoy.

0745 Number one fired - target reached in 15 minutes.
Terrific explosion. The stern mast breaks away. The quarter-deck, lifeboats, loading equipment and other parts of the ship fly high into the air. Engines stopped, ships stern sinks quickly and deeper. The stored ammunition in the stern hold detonates in small but continuous explosions.

That was the "MICHIGAN" 64 men, all rescued.

0747 Two torpedoes fired at large transporter. Two hits, one front and middle. The second torpedo did not detonate despite reaching the target. Tremendour explosion. Red ball of fire, jets of flame and black cloud of smoke. The transporter disappears behind the cloud of smoke, only the broken mast is visible.

That was the "SIDI-BEL-ABBES" 1131 soldiers, 611 rescued.

That completes the report, should you need more please write.

The "That was the Michigan and Sidi-bel-Abbes" were not part of the report but written by letter writer.

U/Boat Captains report of 'Sidi-Bel-Abbes *and* 'USS Michigan' burnt on the hands and face, refused to be picked up before his men and was calming, encouraging and admonishing the pitiful specimens of humanity around him.

The sheer physical effort of getting one wounded and terrified man into the rescue boat was enormous, they were wearing heavy khaki clothes and canvas and cork life jackets. Each single rescue was a feat of strength.

The filled boat would then pull towards *Felixstowe* where the same physical effort was required to get them up the scrambling nets over the ship's side. We were returning to *Felixstowe* once when, without warning, the order "full ahead both" was given her and *Felixstowe* was gone. Two men waiting to be dragged on board from the scrambling nets were thrown straight into the ship's screws and massacred. The horror of war knows no limits, we had unwittingly selected them to die when we picked them up.

One of the lookouts had picked up the tell-tale feather of water made by what he thought was a periscope, it was a false alarm, it turned out to be the bottom of an upturned lifeboat.

Aboard *Felixstowe* every square foot of space was gradually being occupied by the survivors, everyone was giving artificial respiration, dressing burns, lending comfort, making tea. We were taking turns about aboard and in the boats. This went on for an unbelievable five hours. We desperately needed expert medical help, men we had managed to rescue were dying for want of skilled help. The method of life saving was then by the 'Holgar Neilson' method. The victim lay on his stomach, head on one side, the first aider straddled the survivor on his knees, placed both hands around the patient's back and pressed at regular intervals.

Temperatures were now well into the nineties and everyone was reaching a point of total physical exhaustion. We had given our all. It was an incredible feeling, your brain was giving orders that your body was unable to carry out. It was difficult to envisage your body being driven to this state in any other circumstances, circumstances where men crying out for attention drove you to almost demented action as you struggled to speed up your efforts.

The *Felixstowe* had reached a point of saturation, the little Bangors built to house a total compliment of about forty, already carried a crew twice that size. Now we were carrying over two hundred survivors, scattered around our upper deck, messdecks and flats, most were lying down taking up much more space than standing men. Fortunately *Stella Carina* arrived to help in the rescue.

Amidst the horror of war, men grew to new dimensions in their infinite capacity to show care and compassion, ordinary men performing extraordinary feats, with no help or guidance. They were just rolling up their sleeves and getting stuck in, no-one had either told them this is what happens in war, or what to do when it did.

How to quick march, turn about, correctly salute an officer, yes. Pull a terrified man out of the water with his burned flesh coming away in your hands, no!

It was the last one I remember most, he was a young French officer, apparently uninjured and unburned. He was alive, just. I worked feverishly on him, but he died on me. It left me frustrated, angry. He should have lived, I felt guilty I had failed him, I rolled off his body and with my head in my hands I cried unashamedly.

It was probably an accumulation of all the trauma and emotion that day of horror had evoked.

I had closed his eyelids and crossed his hands, this one at least would get an honourable burial. He wouldn't be unceremoniously pushed over the side like the others. He had booked the last berth aboard *Felixstowe,* for there were no more survivors to take his space. Eight hours after Kapitan Lnt Wilhelm Franken in U Boat U565 had blown the *Sidi Bel Abbes* to smithereens, we were on our way to Oran with our sad cargo of humanity. There were still scores of bodies held on the surface in the indignity of their death by the very life jackets that were supposed to save them. *Foxtrot* remained to make the final check for survivors. I didn't envy them their job, for I had seen enough headless, limbless and charred bodies. Bodies that would float willy nilly on the surface of the Med until they washed up on some distant shore I had an awful feeling that their eyes, in the future, would come to haunt me, I was not to be disappointed.

ORAN's NAVY
COMMISSION OF THE ADMIRALTY
No. 153 2A/3

REPORT

SUBJECT Torpedoing of the "SIDI BEL ABBES" 20-4-1943

ENCLOSED: ANNEXED 1. Report of "DJEBEL AURES"
ANNEXED 2. List of survivors.

1. The "S.B.A." has been torpedoed the 20th April 1943 at 6.53am in the indicated position by the report enclosed. The ship has sunk in 3/4 minutes.

2. At its departure from Oran on the 12th February 1943, the "S.B.A." had a civilian crew of 87 men and a team of "A.M.B.C." of 6 men. The changes arising at Alger and Casablanca are still unknown.

At Casablanca the ship had - according to the wireless cables loaded a detachment of Colonial troops (39 Officers, 164 Sub-Officers and 768 troops - 971 in total) as well as a load of 542 tonnes of peanut oil. We can estimate a total of about 1065 men present on the **"BEL ABBES"**.

3. There are 418 survivors at the moment and have been brought back by the follows methods.

	Military personnel	Crew	A.M.B.C.	Total
At 1400 fast American Launch carrying some severely injured and badly burned personnel	14	2		16
At 1500 English **"FELIXSTOWE"** J.126	178	17	4	199
At 1630 British Minesweeping Trawler **"FOX TROT"** T.109	114	11	2	127
At 1800 British Minesweeping Trawler **"STELLA CARINA"** 352	69	6	1	76
	375	36	7	418

4. The military passengers have been collected by the military base of Oran. The wounded sailors have been evacuated to the military hospital BAUDENS. The names of the surviving sailors are listed in an annexe.

5. The men brought back by the **"STELLA CARINA"** have been in the water for about 3 hours. There were at the scene of the disaster, according to the Commander of this patrol boat , many dead personnel supported by their life jackets. The ship only evacuated the area after many hours of searching.

List of survivors 'Sidi-Bel-Abbes'

The Skipper did what Naval Captains had done through the centuries on special occasions, he piped "splice the mainbrace" and issued a second tot of rum, in recognition not of a famous victory but rather as a tonic after the traumas of our day.

I went below decks to see for the first time the total congestion of the flats and messdecks. To my delight I spotted the intrepid sergeant who had refused to be picked up before his men. I went over to him and said "Bravo." I couldn't shake his hand for they were both bandaged, as was his head. To my surprise he had only one eye, something from *Beau Geste,* I mused.

On our arrival medics were crawling all over the *Felixstowe* and there was a string of ambulances on the jetty. The pitiful survivors were gradually driven away and suddenly a strange silence prevailed throughout the ship. The tired and traumatised crew were slumped with their heads over their arms, trying to normalise their shattered minds.

It was made public through the messdeck buzzes that we were to prepare for sea, ready to rejoin the flotilla.

The Skipper must have known that we were in no fit state to efficiently man the ship to an acceptable level of safety. This, however, was the Royal Navy. England expects, etc, but what the Skipper didn't know was the *Felixstowe* would be unable to go to sea. Something had gone mysteriously wrong with the main engines. Anyone on the messdeck could have told him it was a clever piece of sabotage. Someone down below had taken it upon himself to immobilise her, he was a hero and may very well have saved *Felixstowe* from herself.

Every available man immediately crashed out wherever he could and no-one needed any rocking, they slept the sleep of the just.

What the archives reveal about this incident makes interesting reading and says much about the attitude of the French at that time. They were still nursing grievances about the incidents involving the British and French Naval forces after the fall of France. Whatever the rights and wrongs of both sides, in no way could the Allies leave the French Navy in a position to harm our cause. They were given a choice, join us or be immobilised, no clear thinking Frenchman could argue with the logic of our case. In the event they divided down the middle and many Frenchmen joined the enemy instead of continuing the fight against the Nazis.

French opposition to the Allies in Operation Torch was in many cases fierce and they inflicted huge casualties on the landing parties.

Felixstowe, Foxtrot and *Stella Carina* didn't stop to ask the survivors of *Sidi Bel Abbes* if they were Vichy or Free French. Any one of them could quite conceivably have been fighting against us a few short weeks ago.

One of the greatest assets available to the writer of wartime events is the archives and often the most revealing of them are in the hands of the old enemy.

The serving man in the frenzied tumult of war has little or no knowledge or perception of the part he is playing in the events surrounding him and even less about what is in the minds of the enemy.

In the case of the sinking of the *Sidi Bel Abbes* our Allies in the shape of the Free French were not entirely complimentary.

Vice Admiral Rioult, the Naval Commander on Oran, made the following observations about the *Sidi Bel Abbes* incident: "The escort of the convoy was limited in both numbers and quality, a better quality and more considerable force should be employed in future."

Thank you Admiral, but I don't think your remarks would have been appreciated by the men of *Felixstowe* at the time. These ungracious remarks may have everything to do with the fact that the French Naval authorities had packed a load of high explosives and palm oil into the hold of a troopship carrying nearly one thousand two hundred men, which was the reason she disappeared in little over one minute with the loss of six hundred and eleven lives. A fact corroborated by another ship in the convoy. Lieutenant Sangeren, the Chief Officer of the *Lorrain* said: "Two torpedo tracks headed for the *Sidi Bel Abbes*. When they hit her, the explosion sent flames reaching about two hundred metres into the air. She went down bows first in little over minute, as a result of the cargo of explosives she was carrying."

Another signal a little more gracious from Vice Admiral Morean to Admiral Cunningham, read, roughly translated: "Convey our thanks to the British Marine for their gallant assistance in the rescue operations after the sinking of the *Sidi Bel Abbes* with a special thanks to *HMS Fantome*."

HMS Fantome left the scene after giving orders to *Felixstowe* and *Foxtrot* and rejoined the convoy. He went on to apologise for not knowing the names of the other ships involved in the rescue. I am sure it would have taken little effort to find out had he really been interested.

The engine room breakdown had given the crew about six hours' rest after the exhaustion of the *Sidi Bel Abbes* rescues. We left harbour in the middle Watch to rejoin the flotilla. There followed three weeks of intensive sweeping from Bone to Bizerta and on to Cape Bon, where a massive minefield occupied the attention of the thirteenth flotilla.*HMS Fantome,* one of the sweepers from another flotilla clearing this massive minefield,had her stern blown off. She was towed intoBizerta by *HMS Cadmus.*

The magnitude of this epic sweeping operation is revealed in an Admiralty communique which states; "probably their toughest job in the Mediterranean was opening up the war channel from Bizerta to Tripoli. The distance between the two harbours is about four hundred miles and the sweepers had to sweep some thousands of miles to clear thisminefield. They did it in less than three weeks, this meant working from dawn 'til nightfall." It also quotes ships of the flotilla steaming more than 50,000 miles in little over twelve months. This entailed being at sea for two hundred and fifty six days during this period. There were constant air attacks and bad weather often forced us to take shelter in the lee of a promontory. It was on Cape Bon where we were to witness through our binoculars the last desperate tank battles of the retreating enemy. It was spectacular stuff for us to witness, while going about our business of clearing the minefield. Eventually the waters were declared safe for shipping and we gratefully left for pastures new.

Chapter 36

We anchored off Sousse and at dawn the whole flotilla sailed with thirty landing craft, a number of destroyers and nostalgically the gunboat *Aphis*, our companion of Tobruk on the fateful night that the *Kent* was torpedoed. Our destination was the island of Panterlaria, which we were about to invade, the first stepping stone across the Mediterranean to mainland Italy.

At 0900 Panterlaria was clearly visible, we were joined by two larger forces which comprised the cruisers *Newfoundland, Orion, Aurora* and *Mauritious.*

There was a blanket of air cover overhead, enemy aircraft came in to attack but were driven off by our own fighters.

We were now clearly in sight of the coast and the whole flotilla majestically went to the front of the huge armada. The order "out sweeps" was given. Once again the little sweepers were at the forefront of a major landing, tiny in size against our peers but giants in the task of ensuring the safety of the mighty landing force behind us. We were so close to the shore that we could count the daisies in the fields. So far there was no opposition, there was a remarkable calm and quiet, but not for long. First there was the piercing scream of the shells as salvo after salvo passed overhead, the crump, crump, crump of the landing shells was clearly audible and we were close enough to the island to worry about the bombarding force being short on their rangefinder. The skies were then suddenly black with Allied bombers. It was merciless, one moment the fields were clearly visible along with the buildings, I remember a large white building which, for some inexplicable reason, had SOS painted across it, there were figures clearly visible. The bombing was stupendous and when the dust settled into flames and smoke there were no buildings or figures. What did that SOS mean on the white building, was it a hospital?

The saturation bombardment and bombing ceased, it had to allow troops to disgorge from the landing craft and, not surprisingly there was little opposition to the assault from the enemy forces.

The escorts, both destroyers and sweepers, now took up the boring routine of anti submarine patrols. The massive armada of shipping at anchor of Panterlaria had to have constant protection from marauding subs. There were constant air attacks and one in particular concerned at least a dozen of the screaming, nerve racking JU87 Stuka divebombers, they really did set the nerves jangling and always appeared to me when we were under attack to be aiming straight between my eyes.

One of the Stukas suddenly spun away and hurtled straight into the sea - the crash was spectacular. Many of the shot down pilots were picked up, friend or foe, but this was a cremation job, it hit the water and exploded in flames. I thought of the pilot, young, brave and, like me, doing the bidding of his masters. We were trying to blow twelve JU87s out of the sky, while they were hoping to send twelve of us to 'Davy Jones' Locker'. That's what this war was about at the scene of the action.

One of the convoys took us into harbour in Algiers, a town in Algeria that had not been decimated, a town that was still intact, vibrant and living.

This time, instead of departing immediately on another task we tied up alongside and both Watches enjoyed a very well earned night's leave and that is an understatement. It was essential, the human frame can only take so much, and the lack of sleep and inadequate sustenance was taking its toll on the seamen in particular. Seamen bore an unequal proportion of the strain, tempers were frayed and the men openly voiced their protests. It came to a head one forenoon, we had suffered three days of almost continuous sweeping and action stations, yet we were still being mustered to do the routine jobs of cleaning ship. All the seamen know that in these situations there were some of the crew who were having a comparatively easy time. Strictly speaking what happened aboard Felixstowe that morning amounted to mutiny, an offence that carried serious penalties for the culprits. To a man we refused to carry out our instructions to clean ship that morning. It fell to me to make our protest vocal and direct to the Captain. I should perhaps at this stage point out that right from my first day aboard *Felixstowe* I had enjoyed a very good relationship with the Skipper, partly because of his genuine concern at the skulduggery of Chatham that had landed me aboard *Felixstowe* in the first place, and modestly because I was a loyal and very conscientious member of the ship's crew, in spite of my grievance. It was all settled in a very short space of time, no-one was charged, although I was very severely reprimanded and warned as to my future behaviour. We won, if that is the right word, the Skipper saw the justice of our case, I had a feeling that he would, otherwise I might have thought twice about sticking my neck out. Lieutenant Commander Geoffrey Powney RNVR was, in civvy street, an industrialist, he was not a dyed in the wool professional Navy man and hide bound to the memory of Nelson.

That decision meant that we all obeyed the orders for that morning and fulfilled our duties, but henceforth many of our mundane tasks were undertaken by the assortment of ratings who were not seamen. Pongo Waring had the last word when he said to me "I told you in the first place when you joined us that it was better in Naval chokey than what we were suffering on the Felixstowe." I now heartily agreed with him.

Chapter 37

There are cities and ports throughout the world that have played host to Jack on a run ashore, many amongst them heaved a sigh of relief when the Captain took in the last rope or wire that held the ships to their jetties. I can only speak of the Royal Navy in war in the Med, both Eastern and Western ends. I have spoken of the enormous workload of the little sweepers and its affect on the crew. The sheer relief of stepping ashore on terra firma is a feeling too exquisite to explain, the stress and strain simply disappears through the soles of your boots, you are a bird out of a cage, a prisoner out of his cell, a school boy going on a treat.

Most of all you are a vulnerable human being whose resources both physical and mental have been stretched to the limit. This was the reason for some of our excesses ashore and I am sure many of our hosts quickly forgave us.

I still remember the dark, thick, sickly Muscatel that we drank in quantities in preference to the grim, yellow onion water that the French sold as beer.

We returned to the ship suitably anaesthetised from our cares and woes. There was a slight commotion behind us as we were about to board. Looking round I saw three of the lads in the company of a white robed Arab, they all four clambered aboard.

The Arab was complete with white robe and red Fez. When the altercation between the four ended, the Arab took off his Fez to reveal the puckish countenance of our 'Ace' ASDIC Op Biff Finlayson. This quite outrageous behaviour was typical of the man, he had the blackest countenance of any white man I have met, his skin was undeniably white but it was covered in black spiky hair, a permanent black stubble even when he had shaved, bushy black eyebrows and the darkest smiling beady eyes I had ever seen. The little turned up nose completed a face hard to forget, a face always wreathed in a broad toothy grin. Biff got away with it, this was symptomatic of the general relaxed routine aboard the Felixstowe. He, of course, had his uniform complete under his gown, but this didn't prevent him presenting himself to the Officer of the Watch as an Arab. Furthermore he wore his garb on Watch for the remainder of his time on Felixstowe. He was already famous for his 'buzz aerial'; he smoked a foul Sherlock Holmes pipe and across the bowl he had rigged two miniature aerials with three wires stretched between them, from which he claimed he was the first to pick up the latest buzz.

Below decks it was some time before the messdeck finally settled down to catch up on its lost sleep. It was an incredible sight below decks aboard Felixstowe on a night like this. We were in harbour and just now that in itself was an occasion, there was a minimum of crew on Watch, it meant every space on the messdeck was covered in sleeping bodies. Every hammock space was taken, there were bodies on the mess tables, bodies all over the deck, they were in every nook and cranny. It was not a pretty picture, the air was foul from body odours, beer, and stale 'baccy', it was unhygienic and even in wartime undignified and degrading.

This is how the Admiralty had decreed that we would live, on a ship that was built to fight a war but designed to comfortably carry only half the wartime crew. That was the way of it and there was sweet FA we could do about it, but like I said nights like this were rare.

Chapter 38

The following is a copy of the daily diary of the Cox'wain of HMS Stornaway, one of our flotilla and in it you will get the picture of our tremendous workload.

26.3.43. 0300. Hands to Action Stations, convoy attacked by torpedo bombers, no hits.
0410. Another attack, planes driven off, good barrage by convoy and escorts.
0450. Planes come in again, very low, about 50 feet above the surface, torpedo passes ahead of us. Six planes in attack, one merchantman hit.
1100. Passed Algiers, weather fine but dull.

27.3.43. Bad visibility, very hazy.
1030. Hands to Action Stations, six Italian torpedo bombers come in to attack and let all fish go. S.S. EMPIRE ROWAN goes up in flames after being hit. We close EMPIRE ROWAN and pick up injured from boats and two from the sea. Our own fighter planes arrive, good barrage from convoy and escorts.
Italian planes on the turn, fighters shoot down four and one shot down by flak. Injured people all badly burnt, ZETLAND sends doctor over.
1130. Working on injured, injected morphine, peeled and cleaned them, this lasted until 1630. Three dead by 1800.
1800. Entered Bone and secured alongside OAKLEY. Landed Dead and injured whilst OAKLEY landed Italian airmen from aircraft shot down.

28.3.43. 1900. Left Bone with convoy bound for Algiers.

29.3.43. Weather bad and an uncomfortable sea running, visibility bad.
0830. Hands to Action Stations, twelve torpedo bombers making attack, planes about 100 feet above sea level and among the convoy, each dropping two torpedoes. Convoy scatters and takes evasive action, ships putting up good defence.
Four more planes come in to attack, two dropping thier fish near STORNOWAY, planes driven off by our own gunfire. Not one hit on convoy. Fighters come to our assistance and report a bag of two planes.
A nice start for a Monday morning!!
After this attack, several heavy underwater explosions were heard, these being from the torpedoes as they are self destroying at the end of thier run.

30.3.43. Weather glorious, sun shining and sea flat calm.
0500. Left convoy and entered Algiers for fuel and stores.
1000. Left Algiers and speeded on to catch up with convoy.
1130. Took up position with convoy.
1900. Hands to Submarine Action Stations, one merchantman hit with two torpedoes and breaks in half.
1910. Large oiler on our portside hit by another torpedo.
Escorts turn round to try and pick up U-boat on asdics, no luck.
1920. Another explosion as oilers cargo explodes, when smoke clears she is lying on her port side.
Proceeding with escorts on asdic sweep, still no success.
1930. TYNEDALE orders us to take up position in convoy, trawlers standing by sinking ships for survivors.
2000. Rejoined convoy.
2045. Trawlers report that tanker and freighter have sunk.

31.3.43. Same glorious weather.
1430. Passed Oran, six more ships join up with convoy.
2030. TYNEDALE makes depth charge attack, no results.

1.4.43. 2000. Entered Gibraltar.

9.4.43. Entered Dry dock.

17.4.43. Practice bombing flight in a Wellington over North Africa.

20.4.43. Undocked.

21.4.43. D.G. trials and swung compasses.
1800. Secured in pens.

22.4.43. 1000. Left Gibraltar for Bone, BRIXHAM and two trawlers in company. Weather cloudy with rain squalls, sea calm.

23.4.43. At sea, weather glorious.

24.4.43. 0700. Entered Algiers and secured alongside oiler.
1000. Left Algiers with convoy of Tank Landing Craft. Weather good.

25.4.43. 0700. Outside Phillipville, T.L.C.s entered and we carry on for Bone.
1130. Entered Bone and secured alongside.

26.4.43. 0800. Left harbour with BRIXHAM for search sweep.
1600. Entered harbour.

Excerpt from 'Stornaway' *Diary.*

The day had begun so well, even though we were in the devastated port of Bizerta. For a start our mail had arrived and this was an event in itself. The method of delivery was bizarre in the extreme, this post was delivered by HMS Sturgeon one of HMS submarines. Sturgeon had made an undersea journey of more than one thousand miles to make the delivery. Mail no less than anything else in transit was often a casualty of war.

With the arrival of the mail the messdeck was a sight to behold, oblivious to all around them most of the lads were devouring every word, words that would be read in many cases again and again, men with young wives, young children back in the UK facing the bombs, rockets and doodle bugs of the enemy with news and communication so drawn out and sketchy. This could only but add to the daily traumas they were already enduring. As far as three of my letters were concerned, far from re-reading them, I hardly bothered to finish them, none of them were exactly destined to send my pulse racing. One of the letters from home told me that a doodle bug had ripped the roofs off most of the houses in my street at home, fortunately there were no casualties. It must have been pretty close, and, finally, a single letter from South Africa told me what I knew was inevitable. Mary had now married a South African Air Force pilot. For a short time my mind would wander back to Mary in South Africa and what might have been, but reality soon returned, it just became a wonderful wartime experience that would, of necessity, have to fade away in the passage of time. That was not the end of my woes because one day out of Bizerta I had one of my worst attacks of the recurring malaria from which I was to suffer for some years.

In company with Polruan and Stornaway we left Algiers with a small convoy bound for the very inhospitable port of Bone. It was always with reluctance that we now left harbour, there was never going to be a run ashore at the end of the run, unless it was Gibraltar. Most of the ports had been flattened by the Americans. It seemed to be their policy to raze everything to the ground and then send in the troops. The journey proved uneventful apart from the atrocious sea that was running and just before we entered Bone, two ME109s dived out of the clouds and strafed us with their guns. There was no damage and their shells set up regular patterns of plumes on the water as they banked away and disappeared in the clouds.

Once again an invasion force was massing, right across the North African ports, Naval Merchant and assorted landing craft would shortly embark on the task of establishing the third stepping stone, across the

Med to mainland Italy. Operation Husky was about to get under way. The object was the beaches of Sicily.

It wasn't the worst weather we had encountered by a long chalk, but it was blowing hard and the sea was angry enough to rush through the hawse pipes and splatter onto the fo'castle screen. It was not the weather for sea and airborne landings.

I looked across at the orderly rows of landing craft and my heart went out to the thousands of Desert Rat veterans crammed into their very inhospitable holds.

Before embarking on this operation I became aware that my brother Vic was in town, I endeavoured to contact him, but was denied the opportunity. He was conceivably ensconced in one of the craft we were escorting. The weather which was bad enough to cause a cancellation of the whole operation, like it did so often in the Med, rapidly settled down, and the sun made a welcome appearance. We were at times quite close to the landing craft and I optimistically looked at the faces of the cheering, waving men therein. Aside from my brother, I felt a strange affinity with these brave men of the Eighth Army. On my old ship, the Kent we had sacrificed thirty three of our oppos whilst bombarding their opponents in the desert. I had also spent nearly a month with them in hospital tents outside Ismailia where they fussed over me like hell, when I was winning my battle for life against the malignant malaria, which I had contacted on the Suez Canal. I was the only matelot amongst the hundreds of wounded Desert Rats.

Footnote: My brother Vic had a soft landing on Sicily, but was among the fourteen lucky survivors from his unit in the battle for Cassino, where he was wounded.

It was, in reality, the wrong time to be thinking of a brother who I was escorting to a rendez vous with the enemy on a rapidly approaching beach head. It was the wrong time to think of family at all, my thoughts should have been concerned with my own fate perhaps. It may have been that I was now blasé about the whole business. What was different about the forthcoming landings to what the sweepers had endured since we first entered the Med? Nothing, apart from some additional hassle from shore batteries.

To the men crouching uncomfortably in the cramped holds of the landing craft, the escorting sweepers took on a significance far beyond their size and capabilities. They trusted us to guard and guide them to their destiny. It was their Royal Navy and they cheerfully waved as we patrolled along their columns, I hope we didn't disappoint them. At least this time Naval commandos had surveyed the gradients on the landing beaches. This hopefully would eliminate the fiasco of the Centre Torch landings where many of the craft hit sand bars far short of the beach, resulting in chaos.

The unmerciful battering of the enemy's defences prior to the landings may have softened up the enemy, but it had taken away the valuable element of surprise. The intrepid squaddies would expose themselves naked to the enemy, as they launched themselves on the landing beaches.

It was approaching zero hour when the crossing, which had surprisingly been uneventful other than the weather, was thrown into some confusion. There was the sound of aircraft approaching, it was mystifying, they were approaching from the rear. Among the escorts fingers were on the trigger ready to engage the enemy for that is what we took them to be. There was, however, something strange, even eerie, about the first ones we saw, they were silent, black and had no engines. One after another they crashed into the sea around us. Someone suddenly cottoned onto the grim truth about what was happening. They were our own gliders, tragically released miles short of their dropping point. It was horrendous, the nearest one to us hit the sea with a tremendous force, more like a divebomber than a glider, and disintegrated. The full horror of it all was gradually registering among us, but we had to carry on with our landing force and ignore them, it was heartbreaking. Someone reported little bobbing lights on the water astern, it would be the lights on their lifejackets, mercifully they would be picked up. There is more about this later.

The twelfth mine sweeper flotilla had swept the channel in, most of the thirteenth were with a decoy landing fifty miles North of Sicily.

The transition from the calm of the approaching task force to the mayhem of battle takes only seconds. The marine commandos must have landed, as suddenly all hell was let loose.

We turned away from our charges as the beach became ominously nearer, I wondered if many of them had any sort of training for what lay ahead of them. This was a different ball game from what they had encountered in the desert, where tough as it was, it was at least fairly predictable. Here the ramps would drop and they would surge forward, first through the shallow water, then onto the soft sand. Many would not even make the soft sand, they would be passed by and jumped over, lips tight, mouths dry, knuckles white on the grip of their weapons, chaos, calamities, cock-ups, they would all be in evidence, eventually something would give and some sort of order would prevail. They were heroes, each and every one of them, I was still thinking of my brother Vic as was inevitable.

We were once again on the treadmill of anti submarine patrols around the invasion armada, but this time the enemy made sure we were not bored. The Warspite and her attendant cruisers were still pounding the enemy defences and the enemy gave their answer as shore batteries took up the offensive. Soon it was all reminiscent of a fairground at night, smoke, steam, an unseemly crescendo of sounds and flares illuminating the whole scene. Tracers, coloured, and chasing each other across the sky in arcs, like the lights at a disco. Above, all the bombs, often described as like the approach of an express train, that was a perfect description. The dawn broke over a massive armada of shipping, ships of every size, shape and purpose were busy defending themselves against the diving, lunging planes. It was obvious both friend and foe were in our sights in the dogfights above; no-one could distinguish friend from foe. The golden rule was never zoom around the Royal Navy. It wasn't so much that we were trigger happy. Admiral Cunningham had, it is written, instructed all Allied planes not to approach from overhead in the vicinity of the fleet. There was no such thing as a friendly bomb and the thought of one entering your funnels very quickly concentrated your mind.

Chapter 39

The port of Syracuse was quickly captured and as usual the sweepers were the first in to test the waters. In the harbour of Syracuse pending air attacks were always announced over the tannoy system as 'Red Augusta', something quite new to us all. Another innovation was the blanketing of the whole harbour area in a black, choking and oily smokescreen. This tactic was understandable in certain circumstances at sea, but in an enclosed harbour it was virtually lethal, it penetrated everywhere, down on the messdecks, on your clothes, down your throat and into your eyes. I had been in dozens of ports subject to air attack, but never was this foul obnoxious exercise deemed necessary. The perpetrators should have been stuck in an open boat, naked in the centre of the harbour to engage in the folly of their behaviour.

In the foreword of his book Slaughter Over Sicily, Charles Whiting writes:"Roosevelt and Churchill, aided by their military advisers, Eisenhower and Montgomery, decided to follow up the defeats of the Axis forces in North Africa by invading Sicily. To launch this attack on 'Festung Europa' an initial airborne invasion was planned, to be backed up by the greatest seaborne invasion ever launched. Those responsible for planning this great assault on the Nazi empire were at loggerheads from the outset. The eventual outcome was, in hindsight, inevitable, but the immediate result was catastrophic, and one can only be amazed that individual bravery and brilliant leadership at and below battalion level, was able to overcome the basic flaws which underlay the whole concept."

He goes on to refer to the fact that the lessons learned from the chaos of the initial landing were already forgotten when a similar disaster befell the same airborne division in the bloodbath of Arnhem, a mere twelve months later.

The facts revealed in Slaughter Over Sicily make chilling reading. The book, written by an American, is about American forces taking part in Operation Husky, the invasion of Sicily by the Allied forces. It is an indictment on the American top brass, and severely criticises their flawed judgement in almost every aspect of the operation. Emotive words like cowardice are used, and this gives the answer to the horrific spectacle we had witnessed aboard Felixstowe, when gliders of the airborne landing forces were crashing into the sea around us. According to the book, almost all of the American pilots in the towing planes were completely untrained, many straight out of civil airlines. Apparently they were unable to navigate, as they were only used to being guided by beacons. Most of them panicked when they neared the landing zone and saw searchlights and gun flashes, resulting in the gliders being released about two miles from their target. Others are reported to have turned tail and headed back to North Africa with the gliders still behind them. The writer reports that, in complete contrast, two companies of British troops towed by the RAF flying Halifaxes, dropped gliders right on target near their objective, the Ponte Grande bridge. This is just one more aspect of war, revealed by the archives, that ridicules the images shown in the countless American films made after the conflict.

Malta, that wonderful little island fortress that had withstood the full onslaught of the enemy bombs, protected by three ancient Biggles-type biplane gladiators. They were affectionately known as Faith, Hope and Charity: in Malta there was plenty of faith and hope, but very little charity. I had been past it, in action off it, but never had the privilege of entering the great walled harbour of Valletta.

To venture to call this a Malta convoy is to slightly denigrate the heroic convoys that fed the lifeblood into this gallant island, convoys that we had on occasion screened from the safe side. The most famous by far was not even termed a convoy, it was an operation, none less than the ill fated Operation Pedestal. History tells us this was the one that saved Malta and ensured the continuation of the Battle of the Med. It was one of the most gallant of the many heroic exploits of our incomparable Merchant service, who were to suffer enormous losses in ships and men, as were the Royal Navy. Much has been written about these memorable exploits, but by general consent it became inextricably linked with one ship, the *Ohio*. In her bomb-scarred holds were the vital oil supplies to sustain the battle. It was nothing short of a miracle that she ever made Malta; she entered harbour proud and battle-scarred and, on her superstructure was a shot down enemy plane, one of five survivors from the nineteen that had set out on this ill fated operation. The Naval losses in men and ships were equally grevious.

The air assault on our convoy was fierce, but not of the persistence of Pedestal, the reason was simple strong air cover. Pedestal had begun with a fairly successful twenty four hours, but the strength of the Stukas and torpedo bombers, plus massed U Boats was too much.

Telephone: 071-938 1712
Telex: 261102 MLT LDN G
Fax: 071-937 8664

Our Ref:
Your Ref:

MALTA HIGH COMMISSION
16 Kensington Square,
London W8 5HH

7 March 1994

Mr P Cairns

Dear Mr Cairns

MALTA GC COMMEMORATIVE MEDAL

Please refer to the form you sent indicating your preference to receive the above medal at the Malta High Commission in London. A Presentation Ceremony will be held at the High Commission on Thursday 24 March at 12.00 noon. In case you are not able to attend you could call for the medal in person at any time during normal working hours. In this connection kindly phone my Personal Secretary, Miss Portanier, beforehand. Otherwise you could request to attend a subsequent presentation ceremony.

With best wishes and looking forward to seeing you.

Yours sincerely

Salv J Stellini
High Commissioner

Award of much coveted Malta Medal.

We lost one tanker, but were otherwise unscathed. We entered Valletta and by a strange quirk of fate tied up with Stornaway alongside the heroic *Ohio* which we considered a privilege.

Felixstowe slipped and went through to Sliema Creek, then left for St Paul's Bay, where I recently holidayed and peered seaward towards distant ghosts.

It was every matelot's desire to boast that he was at Malta during the trouble and talk of 'Jose' and his dhaisao. His chest, however, really expanded when he related his exploits during his run ashore down Malta's famous 'Gut', perhaps in the Black Cat or the Egyptian Queen, two of the well known dens of iniquity. Malta, of course was a famous Naval dockyard then, and the Admiralty controlled its economy, consequently it was the matelot's dream run ashore. It was the time of the Relief of Malta and there was a wild feeling of celebrations abroad. It was equally good for Jack and for Jose, but one thing was sure, they had thoroughly earned it. We were there for three days, but true to form we were still working, Malta was encircled with minefields and the thirteenth set about the now gratifying task of making the waters a safe place for the lawful pursuits of peacetime. No island in history had better deserved the freedom from its fetters than Malta.

Chapter 40

The convoy back to Bizerta got a little sporadic attention from the air, but was making good progress in perfectly calm weather, when a bizarre incident took place. Without warning the placid surface of the water directly on our port beam, midway between Felixstowe and the nearest merchantman, erupted into a tumultuous cascade of boiling foam. It was caused by a surfacing enemy sub, for a few moments everyone was frozen, what was it all down to, a malfunction, sheer audacity, or a complete cock-up? The twenty millimetre cannons responded first, in seconds they got the conning tower in their range, but it wasn't very effective and it was some time before the forward armament was closed up and ready. The Felixstowe was initially in the prime attack position, but its armament was completely inadequate for the job. The next few moments were sensational with course alterations, hoots of Naval craft, ships' sirens. Incredibly the sub got off her 'Tinfish' and dived, they missed. A destroyer, like a bat out of hell and firing her forward guns, surged forward on ramming stations, the sub won that round also.

The convoy gradually got on course again and the crump of the depth charge explosions gradually subsided. We were never to find out the results and the attack could last another two hours. It was still feasible that it had escaped. It very seldom happened like they depict in the films with John Wayne at the helm.

On arrival in Bizerta Bay we were met by the sight of another massive array of shipping, Naval craft and landing craft. Traffic lights would have helped to guide us into harbour, so densely were they packed. Felixstowe oiled, stored ship and replenished its sweeping gear. We were at La Peckavie when one of those fierce Siroccos started blowing. At their peak the sand felt as though it was tearing the skin off your face, and your hair from its roots. However, did the Desert Rats come to terms with them? We left harbour on anti sub patrol round the huge armada. The flotilla left in the forenoon with Yankee mine sweepers and the monitor HMS Crombie for the Salerno Landings and the very first tentative foothold back onto European soil

For three whole years the continent of Europe had been under the Nazi Jackboot, now the slow painful fight back to freedom was under way, millions had already perished and the slaughter would continue before the halcyon days of peace were to return, many mothers were still destined to lose their sons. "The Admiralty regrets..."

In conditions that were flat calm and sunny the invasion force took up formation and the thirteenth mine sweeper flotilla once again took up a line abreast sweep leading. It occurred to me that a whole free world was waiting for the moment when the first foot of the invasion force touched down on European soil.

On D Day minus one the invasion force heard the news that every invader in history would like to hear and that was the unbelievable fact that Italy had just signed an Armistice with the Allies. There was wild jubilation throughout the task force, many thought that it would be just a matter of walking up the beaches and shaking hands with the old Italian enemy. That is exactly how the Italians would have wanted it, if only to save the carnage on their soil, but their German masters had other ideas.

In fact, history and biographies tell us that had it not been for the relentless and accurate fire of the Royal Navy guns, Salerno might well have been another Dunkirk.

Most serving men were aware that the nightly BBCbulletins on most fronts throughout the war were a pale shadow of the truth. Salerno was no exception and was hailed as a great victory of arms.

It was with great difficulty that troops accepted that the Hun was waiting for him a few short miles ahead. Operation Avalanche was under way.

In historical terms it would be the landings across the Channel from the shores of Britain that would be remembered as the day we returned to Europe. In truth it had all begun at Salerno on mainland Italy.

I looked along the line of little sweepers with their sweep wires stretching out as taut as rods of steel off each port and starboard quarter. The Oropesa floats bobbing along in unison on the surface of water astern. No-one would remember that it was the thirteenth, that led in the mighty invasion force. It was indisputable really, this was the first and therefore the only D Day. These were the little 'biscuit tins' that I had looked at with derision and despised on that first night in the dockyard at 'Gus'. I was wrong. These little boats were the solid backbone of the wartime Royal Navy but inevitably it would be the Kellys and the Ark Royals that would be stamped indelibly in the minds of future generations.

The heavy drone of the bombers approaching from land broke the continuing silence of the night, the fireworks were about to commence. We were still about twelve miles from shore. It must have been terrifying for the troops in the invasion force. This, General Mark Clark said, was to be a secret landing, so there would be no Naval bombardment. Some secret, the scene was from fairyland, the darkness of the night was illuminated by brilliant flares, the crescendo of noise was deafening. Hundreds of anti aircraft shells long and short range were reaching into the sky in search of a target. Bombs were falling like confetti, huge columns of water towered up from the surface of the sea as the bombs cascaded down. It was 2100 hours and the raid continued for about another two hours. It says much for the strength of the anti aircraft fire that only one LST had been sunk.

Normality returned in the form of orderly lines of craft homed in on the beaches. The thirteenth detached from the main force, lookouts had picked up the green light fixed on the periscope of the sub HMSShakespeare, lying offshore.

It was Shakespeare that had marked the course and also informed us of the density of the minefield we were now sweeping. Mines were already bobbing to the surface, then a menace to the oncoming force.

Everyone from the cooks to the officers, on every ship in the flotilla would be firing off the 303 armour piercing bullets at the surface mines to sink them below the water to safety. It was a moment of relaxation in the stress of the operation that everyone thoroughly enjoyed, especially when a lucky shot hit the contact horn, the explosion was always spectacular and generally shook the ship from bow to stern.

Search lights were scanning the water from the shore, huge explosions were towering into the sky ashore, we didn't realise then the implications of those explosions, which were caused by the Germans destroying the vulnerable munition and arms dumps as they regrouped to face the oncoming Allies. They were now alone on Italian soil, ironically to defend Italy for the Italians, who had laid down their arms and were now a cause of great concern. The enemy had been just as wise as the Allies and correctly forecast exactly where General Mark Clark's 'secret' landing was to take place and in consequence had laid hundreds of mines. There was little we could do about it, miraculously nothing within our immediate vicinity struck one, and we gradually disposed of them. We were then ordered to widen the swept channel to facilitate the speed of the landings. The sweep took us right up to the entrance of Salerno Harbour, which appeared to be deserted. We were now running the gauntlet of both bombs and shore batteries, but fortunately their accuracy left much to be desired.

The moon rose over the mountains ahead and threw that strange metallic hue over the whole scene, it was a time of subdued silence, no-one spoke an unnecessary word. The throb of Felixstowe's engines, the swish of the bow wave, the indeterminate sounds of a ship in motion. Adrenalin would begin to flow, mouths would be drying out and men, many of them agnostics and blasphemers, would be reaching out for support from whoever. The slight adjustment on the wheel or the alteration to speed would be delivered in subdued tones, lookouts would be desperately trying to pierce the dark mass ahead.

The flotilla wheeled away and one after another the landing craft ground to a halt on the soft sands of the Bay of Salerno.

One landing was much the same as another, they varied only in size and in what they confronted from the enemy. This one was obviously the biggest by far. Gradually the vast landing force slowed down and massed right across the bay.

Suddenly the war began in earnest. The battlefield was illuminated by countless flares, many threatened to land inboard. Bombs cascaded down from the skies, among the new immobile armada. Shells reached up to the skies searching out targets, enemy shells screamed across the water, Naval shells whistled across the fleet in the opposite direction. All the flotilla suffered near misses and probably every ship in the bay had been near to disaster from falling bombs and shells. However, a new lethal and sinister weapon made its appearance in the Bay of Salerno, a remote controlled missile that was to strike with devastating effect at major Naval targets. The missile was guided to its target from a parent aircraft by radio control, it was rocket boosted and carried about six hundred pounds of explosives at a speed of six hundred miles per hour. The first victim was the *USS Savannah* which was hit and sustained severe casualties. Next *HMS Uganda* was severely damaged, *HMS Nubian* and *Loyal* both suffered near misses.

Such was the intensity of the demands on the Naval force that many were running short of ammunition, but they could not leave until relieved. An urgent message to Admiral Cunningham, The C in C, saw the departure from Malta of the battleships *Warspite* and *Valiant*, together with a force of cruisers and destroyers. The air attacks were incessant and such was the speed of the fighters involved, a bizarre method of identification was used, RAF Observer Corps were dispersed over the shipping, as planes dived out of the clouds the observers held large yellow boards in the air, some were in the shape of diamonds and others were circular, one denoted enemy planes, the other friendly. I can't believe it worked because on one occasion the *Felixstowe* along with other escorts followed a couple of hopefully enemy planes with anti aircraft fire and as they dived and swooped along the shore line the gun fire from the ships raked the bridges of at least three of the in-shore ships, with God knows what casualties.

The hit and run air attacks continued relentlessly and there was little respite for the Navy's anti aircraft gunners. Ashore things were going badly wrong, the beach heads were in chaos which appeared to be the norm for most landings. British regiments with household names found themselves isolated and leaderless and facing crack German Panzers with superior equipment. They disbanded and retreated to the beaches in disorder. Elsewhere the Americans were similarly placed and found themselves facing their own NCOs' guns to get them back in the firing line.

Evacuation was given serious consideration, such was the parlous state of the troops and time and again in the archives it states that it was only the deadly accuracy of the Naval bombardments that saved the day. The *Warspite's* fifteen inch salvoes were dropping with unerring skill wherever the shore-based radio control demanded it. All this from the staggering distance of around ten to twelve miles

The wrath of the Royal Navy's guns came to bear even heavier on the enemy, when their planes lunged out of the sky to make a horrendous attack on the three Allied hospital ships. These ships, protected by the Geneva Convention, were painted completely white with huge red crosses and were very brightly illuminated.

At dawn a group of enemy planes swooped down on the three hospital ships and rained down their bombs. *Leinster* and *Somerset* suffered near misses but *Newfoundland* received a direct hit amidships causing many casualties, she was soon blazing from end to end. The German pilot was heard boasting of his success on his intercom. After valiant efforts to save the ship, the survivors were evacuated and *Newfoundland* was sunk by gunfire.

Worse was to follow when three wisps of vapour turned out to be radio controlled missiles, one of which scored a direct hit on *HMS Warspite* inflicting grievous damage and many casualties among her crew. Sadly she was to take no further part in the conflict and was towed to Malta for major repairs. The action ashore bore no resemblance whatsoever to the unctuous 'pap' put out by the nightly bulletins of the BBC.

Gradually the remorseless Naval bombardment forced the enemy to retreat and the supplies and reinforcements began to take on some sort of order on the beaches.

The order to set sail for Malta came as a very welcome relieve. Three of the flotilla set out in very heavy weather, it worsened to such an extent that we were only proceeding at about six knots. To everyone's surprise we were ordered to return to the beach head, where we learned that the land forces had come to a halt in their advance. The Allies and the German forces were now divided by the River Volturno.

The thirteenth mine sweeper flotilla was ordered to carry out a sweep along the enemy side with a view to landings being made. The sweep was made in the middle Watch under the light of a full moon. The mission was fraught with danger, and we were afforded the protection of a destroyer escort in case we were spotted by the enemy. Imagine sweepers entering the Thames at Southend where the Allies occupied one bank and the enemy the other. The first sweep took us deep into the mouth of the Volturno, surprisingly without incident. The next sweep took us right along the enemy bank this time the shore defences were engaged by our escorts. Once again we made our escape to safety and the landings were successfully accomplished.

The thirteenth then set about clearing the approaches to Naples Bay, this was followed by an operation that left the flotilla leader with a red face and could have led to disaster for the leading three ships in line. We made our entrance into the bay of Naples between the Isle of Capri and the picturesque cliffs of Sorrento. Suddenly it was panic stations among the flotilla, we were third in line and were looking down at the amazing sight of the water around us full of mines, clearly visible below the water, many of them new and painted sky blue.

The whole manoeuvre threw the flotilla into chaos, there were very fortunately no collisions as we all took avoiding action. I remember *Felixstowe* making a safe exit, with lookouts on the fo'castle giving shouted orders to the wheelhouse. We were never to find out why the flotilla had so nearly met with disaster, it was just another inexplicable cock-up that was to be a constant factor throughout the conflict.

The beautiful Bay of Naples; Capri, home of our own Gracie Fields married to an Italian Count; Sorrento: Pompeii embalmed for ever in the molten lava of Vesuvius, all of these places are now the playgrounds of countless world holidaymakers, but were then just another theatre of war that could have spelt disaster for the thirteenth mine sweeper flotilla.

The relentless workload of these versatile little workhorses continued, we came straight from the minefield off Naples to escort a convoy bound for Gibraltar.

My thoughts turned to my shipmates, all of them now men of steel. No ship's company could have given more, no ship's company could have endured more. Ordinary men plucked from a wide variety of civvy jobs and all of them turned into hardened professional men of the sea, 'Taff' Whittle no less than any of them. Taff who spend most of his time stalking around his territory just aft of *Felixstowe's* funnel. Perhaps he was the bravest of them - all the terror of his experience when adrift in an open boat was still in his eyes for all to see. My opposite number 'Torps' Harris, had suffered agonies every time a heavy sea was running. The irrepressible spirit of the young time serving members, Larter and 'Curly' Plant and, of course the outrageous Biff Finlayson. The Watch ashore was ready for liberty men before we had tied up on the Mole, strangely once again in the shadow of the stern of *HMS Sheffield* and it was to provide me with a most pleasant surprise.

In the company of Taff Whittle I was walking off the Mole taking the longer way into town when a voice from the upper deck of the *Sheffield* called out my name loud and clear. "Phil wait at the gangway." I didn't recognise the caller until he was half way down the gangway and my face lit up with pleasure. The voice was that of Kenny Ferrier, my companion of the fateful journey home, when at the stop-off in Durban the young nurse had tragically fallen to her death. The same Ken with whom I had spent a wonderful thirty five days' leave in the UK before I was shanghaied onto the *Felixstowe*.

We hugged each other unashamedly, and after a few exchanges arranged to meet in the town. The venue was a bar in Main Street that promised, on the cessation of hostilities, 'Free beer for all' in huge letters on the wall behind the bar. Ferrier duly arrived and an assorted mixture of *Sheffield* and *Felixstowe* ratings set about the task of drinking Gib dry. In this they had the assistance of men from the Commonwealth, Yanks, Free French, Poles, Norwegians and others, each seeking respite from the travails of the past few weeks. Some would be drinking as though there was no tomorrow, and for some that's how it would be. The formula was always the same, hearty organised song and banter would gradually deteriorate into a drunken, befuddled Tower of Babel, everyone would be singing a different song, then the chairs and bottles would become airborne. Anyone with only one leg to stand on and a clear view of the exit, would be outside like a shot to escape before the ruthless patrols moved in. I reckon I was in the first few dozen to make Main Street. I was alone, separated from my drinking oppos. Soberly I made my way back to *Felixstowe*.

I should have left 'Sharkie' to his own devices, he was alone like me and practically legless, but with each step he was in imminent danger of ending up in the harbour. Thus it was that I decided to see him safely back aboard. Sharkie Ward was a stoker, with a reputation of being very aggressive under the influence of drink. We were making steady but erratic progress and I was having to support him under his armpits. He suddenly lurched forward and I went with him, unable to extricate my arms. I hit the curbstone with my face, my nose and mouth were in a fearful mess and two of my top set of teeth were knocked out as clean as a whistle. Sharkie, oblivious to what had happened, was unmarked. I was drenched in blood and looked like I had been hit by a train. The effect on the seamen's messdeck was dramatic, everyone came to the conclusion that Sharkie had, in Naval parlance, 'filled me in'. For the next ten minutes or so it was hard to distinguish between the seamen's mess and the fracas I had just left in the *Universal*. Retribution was being sought for the damage Sharkie was quite wrongly thought to have inflicted on me. Eventually I got my message through and peace once again prevailed. The sick bay Tiffy attended to my injuries and I was left to lick my wounds. The loss of my teeth was serious, but I was to be back home as a civvy before the damage was redressed. Conceivably I may have sustained less damage to my person had I not made my exit from the fracas in the *Universal*.

Chapter 41

The decision was suddenly made for *Felixstowe* to have a boiler clean and refit, just when we thought we were leaving Gib with a convoy.

The attention to our ailing engine room was a must, but there were many who thought the decision to do a nose job on *Felixstowe* was the start of our troubles. *Felixstowe*, you may remember, had been operating since the North African landings minus about four feet of its bows, due to its collision with *Clacton*. She was rusty, disfigured and the flat nose had quite conceivably robbed us of a couple of knots off our speed. Otherwise at this stage she was still intact and operational like the rest of the thirteenth flotilla. The thirteenth that had taken everything the enemy had thrown at them and survived - high level torpedo and divebombing, shore batteries, E Boats and of course the submarines. We had suffered six collisions between us, any one of which could have been fatal, and survived them all. Then, of course, there were the mines, all types, hundreds of them that we had swept and exploded. It had been hard, dangerous and tiring and like their ship, the crew's own batteries were in urgent need of recharging. There were places much less suitable to do this than Gibraltar.

Soon the ship became a shambles of welding machines, compressors, tubes, hoses, acetylene torches and dozens of dockyard mateys. It was a chance for Kenny Ferrier and I to renew our acquaintanceship and fondly relive some of the great times we had enjoyed together in the UK on leave and, of course, there was Durban. I talked at length with him about my romance with Mary, the ships' deserters in Durban and of the tragic death of the girl in which we were embroiled. It was to be more than two years before next we met.

The dockyard mateys departed having completed their cosmetic surgery in record time. *Felixstowe* was returned to the crew and we set about with enthusiasm to restore her to her former glory. Most matelots took a great deal of pride in the appearance of their ship. I was over the side on a stage putting the last brush strokes of black paint to *Felixstowe*, number J126. The stage was then hoisted inboard and that was it, we were on our way, looking as pristine as the first day of our launch. That number J126 was to be of some significance to me in the not too distant future, but no longer would *Felixstowe* be recognised by her noted flattened bow.

Many of the crew were convinced it would never have happened but for that refit and that she should have been left with the wound caused by the collision with *Clacton* as a battle scar of war. We left Gibraltar with a convoy bound for Bizerta.

The Med, as far as the Royal Navy was concerned, was now transformed, the Axis forces were gradually disappearing from most of its sandy shores and beyond. The sea, with the skies above it that had so recently been dominated by the enemy, was now a considerably safer place to be. The cost in ships, planes and men had been horrendous, the enemy planes were still much in evidence, but they now had opposition in plenty. There was one lethal menace that was still there in abundance - mines, mines that were becoming increasingly dangerous to deal with, mines with explosive charges on their mooring cables that destroyed the sweeping gear, mines with shallow settings and devices we were yet to encounter. There were, in addition, thousands of our own mines that had to be swept to make the waters safe for all shipping. The most extensive minefields were sown by both friend and foe off the Tunisian headland of Cape Bon and the narrow water between Sicily.

We entered Bizerta, that wonderful French Naval base in Tunisia, tied up and, as usual, got orders to store and oil ship, replenish sweeping gear and get back out there as soon as possible. That's how it always was, it seems we were never allowed to swing around the buoy.

Before we left harbour I was summoned to the Captain's office. I entered and stood before him feeling a little anxious.

"I've got some good news for you Cairns," he said with a smile, "your replacement will be arriving shortly in Bizerta." My eyes lit up and my heart skipped a beat, home, back to the UK, it was wonderful news. After a full eighteen months justice had been done and a relief torpedoman had been sent out from Chatham. I mumbled something like "Thank you Sir, that's great news, will I be going ashore now?" He said "I'm afraid I can't do that, you must wait until we return to Bizerta."

I turned as I was leaving and said: "Well I thought it was worth a try."

I had just completed my fourth continuous year of foreign service, that is apart from my one leave and very short respite in Chatham. I was still young, strong and healthy, but I would be lying if I didn't admit that I'd had enough. Only by the acquisition of the very revealing diary of the *Stornaway* was I made aware of what we were enduring at that time.

The euphoria of my good news very quickly resigned me to my fate, after all I had now got my return ticket and I had only to step aboard the ship bound for the UK.

To be truthful, it would have suited me fine to have been dumped ashore just as I had been on the *Kent*, I could have well done without this last trip and perhaps it would have been better not to know about the imminent arrival of my relief. It was therefore with some trepidation that I set out for pastures new in the relentless task of mine clearance together with *Rothesay*, *Stornaway* and *Brixham*. *Felixstowe* was heading for the Straits of Bonifacio, between Corsica and Sardinia.

We were now in the channel leading to La Meddelena in Sardinia, proceeding line ahead, *Rothesay* in the lead, when what happened next is recorded in detail in the *Stornaway* diary.

"9.12.43 (1310) - steaming at ten knots when we struck a submerged object, there was a bump and we listed heavily, first to starboard then to port, four times this happened before we slid off into free water. We carried on steaming, then Brixham close astern suffered the same fate."

Aboard *Felixstowe* we turned violently to port and avoided any damage. Stornaway and Brixham had been on the rocks. Both were exceedingly lucky to have escaped sinking, both were badly holed and Brixham, more seriously, had damaged her 'screws' badly enough to put her out of commission. It was a disastrous start to our attack on another minefield. Hasty temporary repairs were carried out on Stornaway in the harbour of La Maddelena and with Pulruan as a replacement for Brixham we set out on our first sweep.

Was the damage to Stornaway and Brixham an omen? The submerged rocks off the coast of Sardinia had nearly succeeded in sinking two of the flotilla, something that bomb, torpedo, mine or gunfire had so far failed to achieve. Once again I refer to the Stornaway diary of events as they happened.

"18.12.43 (0730) - left harbour with Rothesay, Polruan and Felixstowe for clearance sweep in west channels.

"(0845) - commenced sweeping line abreast.

"(0850) - two mines go up in Rothesay's sweeps.

"(0858) - Polruan picks up mine which explodes in her sweeps.

"(0905) - Felixstowe stern covered by explosion, looks as though her stern has been blown up. At the same time Stornaway catches a mine in her sweeping gear.

"Felixstowe requires immediate assistance as she is drifting onto swept mines.

"We heave in our sweeping gear, trying to shake off the trapped mine, mine is now twenty feet from our stern, we cut our sweeps and mine immediately explodes.

"(0910) - Stornaway detailed to assist Felixstowe who is now listing heavily to port.

"(0920) - now abreast of Felixstowe and taking her in tow, men not required are jumping into the sea from Felixstowe.

"(0930) - Felixstowe in tow but listing heavily to port, stern now awash.

(0940) - we see Felixstowe abandon ship as she lists still more.

"(0945) - we cut the tow and thus freed, she rolls over on her side.

"(1000) - Felixstowe rolls over bottom up.

(1005) - Felixstowe stands on end and goes down stern first, we had lost the first ship of the thirteenth mine sweeper flotilla."

We didn't know then that Felixstowe was the fifth sweeper to be sunk on this one minefield, from which one hundred and thirty four mines had been swept. Four of the flotilla had left harbour, but only three were returning.

Seven days later the second of the flotilla was sunk. HMS Clacton struck a mine amidships and sunk with the loss of half her ship's company. Polruan who rescued the survivors said many of them were burnt and hardly recognisable; my mind went swiftly back to the horror of the Sidi Bel Abbes.

It was inexplicable, Felixstowe had also struck a mine and sank, there was no loss of life, only minor injuries. The fortune of war, fate, the luck of the draw, any number of clichés would fit.

Suddenly it had all gone horribly wrong, two of the thirteenth were no more and Stornaway and Brixham were lucky to survive their grounding on the rocks - they could also quite easily have been lost.

When Felixstowe left Bizerta on what proved to be her last voyage, I spoke of my feeling of trepidation. I knew then that my return to the UK depended on my safe return to Bizerta, where I would bid farewell to my shipmates and, alone, I would set sail for home.

To the remainder of the ship's company it was just another minefield to tackle, but to me it was much more than a routine job, it had taken on a significance never in evidence before.

H.M.S. 'Felixstowe' *Some of the crew*

We left Maddelena to begin the sweep, the pipe "hands to sweeping stations" sounded for the last time. It was a line abreast sweep, always the most dangerous, the complicated quite technical routine was completed, the sweep wires were unclutched on the sweeping drum and they raced out to their respective positions, about five hundred yards astern on the port and starboard quarter, the Oropesa floats bobbed busily on the surface. Felixstowe was now operational as a mine sweeper. If the mines had been sown by the enemy the sweeps would sever them from their moorings. They would then bob to the surface where they would either explode or have to be sunk by gunfire. Jimmy the One, the officer in charge, would stand the sweeping party down, and out would come the 'ticklers'. It was now a time to relax, a good job done, that was the routine that had now been carried out hundreds of times, that's why we were good at it.

It soon became evident that this time it was different, there were a series of explosions, nothing unusual in that, it was common for mines to explode on being swept. One after another in the space of a few minutes mines exploded in the sweeps of Rothesay, Polruan and then Stornaway, then a rain squall sent the Felixstowe sweeping party scurrying off the quarterdeck for cover.

We scrambled through the after watertight door right to the heart of the exploding mine that sank us, it might have been the number of bodies crammed into a confined space that saved us, I don't know. I remember being lifted off my feet and crashing into a bulkhead, bodies were crashing into each other. Felixstowe had been mortally wounded, but the deck below us had held and that is the reason no-one in the sweeping party was seriously injured.

The damage was confined to below deck level and the officers' quarters below were mercifully completely empty of officers or crew.

Felixstowe was grievously wounded and officers and men feverishly set about the enormous task of saving her. Damage repair parties swung into action, discharge pumps were put in operation, collision mats specially made to stem the flow of incoming water were placed in position. Officers were assessing the damage and the precautionary order "stand to abandon ship" had been issued. There was still hope in spite of our list *Stornaway* was ordered to take us in tow. *Stornaway* who had just narrowly escaped having her own stern blown off when the mine caught in her sweep wires exploded, was now attempting to tow us into Maddelena, or at least beach us.

The tangled bodies of the sweeping party sorted themselves out and surprisingly everyone made it to their feet, albeit with minor injuries or bruises. I have no recollection of the events taking place around me, but I do remember having an irresistible urge to make it to my messdeck and rescue all my worldly possessions.

All my worldly possessions were ensconced in my 'ditty box'. They comprised my twenty first birthday watch, the ring from my mother, my prayer book, rosary, all my lifetime cash savings and a few letters, all from one source, Mary. All the other letters had long since been dispatched down the gash chute.

Events very rapidly made the rescue of my ditty box a non-starter and so my Naval issue, twelve inch by eight wooden safe deposit box, like *Felixstowe*, was destined for a watery grave.

I remember going in one direction, forward, when suddenly I turned and headed for the stern. I went back onto the deserted quarterdeck, which a short time ago was a hive of activity, as we prepared to get out sweeps. I had a job to do, and I remember hoping I had enough time to complete it. The depth charges circling the stern were all lethal time bombs once *Felixstowe* sank beneath the waves. Threaded into the centre of each depth charge was a brass assembly which held the primer and detonator, which would explode the depth charge at the selected depth setting. The list of *Felixstowe* didn't seem excessive at that time, but I purposely commenced my defusing of the depth charges at the lowest side. I must have completed most of the extractions when a voice made me turn. "What are you doing Cairns?" The voice was that of the young Temp Acting Sub Lieut McCloud. Was he asking me because he didn't know what I was doing? It was quite feasible. On the other hand he may have known what I was doing and was querying why I wasn't replacing the pistols into their purpose made, individual boxes, which would have been the practice in times of normality.

I was in the process of throwing the pistols as far as I could over the stern and for a good reason. The fuse, a glass cartridge filled with one of the most sensitive explosives known, fulminate of mercury, meant each pistol had to be withdrawn with the utmost care and once safely clear of the depth charge, because of its lethal sensitivity, the safest place for them in the present circumstances was over the side into the 'hoggin'.

My reply to the young 'Subby' was unprintable, suffice to say he departed and left me to my own devices. I hoped he had something more important to do other than help me, but I doubt it very much. Having completed the defusing I left the stern and proceeded forward. At this point the reader may be forgiven for thinking that the writer is indulging in a bout of self appraisal, so an explanation is called for.

Although aboard ship depth charges like the electrics were the province of the torpedomen, there was no order or routine for rendering depth charges safe while sweeping, it had never even been discussed. Whenever we came off escort duties to sweep mines they had always remained primed. What I had just done was impulsive and quite voluntary, it was not a duty, nor did I at the time consider that I was in any danger. I had performed the task many times and I knew the utmost care had to be taken during the operation. There were men in the water, all surplus crew had been ordered to abandon ship, I knew of the possible danger if *Felixstowe* reached the depth setting on the depth charges and if anyone else aboard knew they certainly took no action or yet issued any orders.

HMS Algerine, the first of this famous class of sweeper, was sunk on 17th November 1941 off North Africa, the survivors numbering about thirty were picked up by *HMS Alarm*, cleaned up and fed then place ashore, apparently in good health. Tragically twenty four of them died from the effects of exploding depth charges when she sunk. There were many more examples, crudely speaking the inner organs of their bodies had been fatally damaged by the compression of the explosion.

Since these sad events that at the time were felt to be of no consequence, I have acquired, apart from the evidence of the daily diary, copies from the archives of the Admiralty Board of Enquiry held aboard *HMS Mutine* into the sinking of *HMS Felixstowe*. There were three reports submitted, three officers were questioned in detail, Lieut Comm Powney, *Felixstowe* Skipper, was asked more than seventy questions. Not once was the question of depth charges and their condition even mentioned, no-one on the Board thought it of any consequence. It was a grave omission. Most of the questions, as the reader will see, were mundane in the extreme, compared to the possible grave results of exploding depth charges. I wish to stress that no charge could have been laid against either of the torpedomen if a major calamity had occurred, had I not voluntarily made them safe. Had I not taken up the pen I would not be aware of the facts as detailed, and I also would have found it of no consequence. There were other recorded incidents involving exploding depth charges but not all of them had time to carry out the make safe procedure owing to the speed of their demise.

At that time I had no knowledge of casualties, there were men in the water and a boat full of survivors was making for one of the flotilla. With the vision of the carnage below decks on the *Kent*, in my mind, I went over the side to be picked up by an American motor launch, sent in because of its shallow draft - remember we were on a minefield. From the deck of the 'Yank' I watched the death throes of *Felixstowe*, still wondering if any of my oppos had bought it. She appeared to turn right over exposing her naked bottom and then began disappearing below the waves, stern first, her number J126 that I had so recently repainted in Gibraltar gradually went below the surface and she was gone. It is my guess there would have been many tears shed for her among the watching survivors.

We all headed for La Maddelena, where we mustered on the waterside, familiar faces began to appear one by one, miraculously not one of the crew were lost. A view repeated by the Board of Enquiry into the sinking.

Now that I knew, by the grace of God, all the crew had been spared, my relieved mind turned to another consequence of the sinking. When I became a reluctant, disgruntled member of *Felixstowe's* crew, the one joy I was impatiently waiting for was my replacement to arrive, then having the satisfaction of saying farewell and walking alone down the gangway to begin my journey home to the UK.

Fate had now decided that was not to be, for we would all return together as survivors. Once again I had drawn a short straw and that wasn't the end of it, there was another waiting for me just across the water in Algiers.

No-one was sorry to leave Sardinia which had proved to be so disastrous to the flotilla and we made the crossing to Algiers in the *Brittany.* There we temporarily berthed aboard a liner that was in harbour. One of the most moving days in a matelot's life must be when the Captain has to say farewell to his crew after the loss of their ship. We were all mustered on the Algiers dockside to hear Lieut Comm Powney say his last sad farewell. Crews were always broken up in these circumstances and it would herald the end of many long friendships, unions that were cemented by the very nature of living so closely in a hard and dangerous environment. Of necessity his words were full of clichés, but we knew they were genuine and as a Captain he had served us well since his appointment at a moment's notice.

I was still feeling cheated at being denied my smug satisfaction of walking alone down the gangway and waving a fond farewell as I departed for the UK and home. My chagrin was somewhat tempered by the knowledge that not one man had perished in the sinking, I would now have company on the journey home. We were allowed to send a telegram home to our next of kin, which simply read "Safe and well, don't write." It didn't tell them much about the drama that we had endured, and they were to learn no more until we arrived safely home. It did, however, warn them of the impending news bulletin that again would briefly state "The Admiralty regrets to announce the loss of *HMS Felixstowe*, next of kin have been informed," and that would be that *Felixstowe* was now just a statistic.

The Cox'wain had instructed us to make our way in twos and threes to Naval 'slops' to draw our new kit and that meant everything, for our total worldly possessions were what we stood up in. Attired in only shirts and shorts, with an oppo Lofty Hemmings, I made my way in brilliant sunshine through the dockside to the Naval stores. The date was 22nd December 1943. Like most dockyards there was no pavement, just a wide expanse of stone and concrete.

The road traffic was sparse and mostly American and military, so the noise of the large American truck behind us was of no interest, that is until the last moment. It was a direct hit, the bombs and torpedoes had been close, but they had all missed. The truck didn't, we were both hit in the stern, the screeching brakes had been applied too late to be of any help to us. The last thing I remember was hurtling through the air and rolling over and over at speed.

THE CASUALTIES
(Up to and including "V.J." DAY)

MINESWEEPERS SUNK

(a) By Mines in Home Waters	84	
Other causes in Home Waters	103	187
(b) By Mines abroad	38	
Other causes abroad	44	82
		269

MINESWEEPERS SERIOUSLY DAMAGED

(a) By Mines in Home Waters	60
(b) By Mines abroad	15
	75

OTHER SHIPS SUNK BY MINES

(a) H.M.Ships in Home Waters (excluding M/S)	121	
Merchant Vessels (Home)	452	573
(b) H.M.Ships abroad (ex. M/S)	46	
Merchant Vessels abroad	48	94
		667

OTHER SHIPS SERIOUSLY DAMAGED BY MINES

(a) H.M.Ships in Home Waters (excluding M/S)	103	
Merchant Vessels (Home)	124	227
(b) H.M.Ships abroad (ex. M/S)	33	
Merchant Vessels abroad	38	71
		298

ANALYSIS OF SHIP CASUALTIES DUE TO ENEMY MINES

(Up to "V.E." DAY)

(Not including those in waters controlled or swept by the United States alone.)

ABROAD	SUNK	DAMAGED
Fleet Minesweepers	7	9
Allied Fleet Minesweepers	-	1
Auxiliary Minesweepers	27	5
Allied Aux. Minesweepers	4	15
TOTAL	**38**	**15**
Other H.M. Ships	12	14
Other Allied Warships	1	3
Other H.M. Auxiliaries	25	5
Other Allied Auxiliaries	3	1
TOTAL	**41**	**23**
TOTAL WARSHIPS	**79**	**38**

	SUNK		**DAMAGED**	
	Ground Mine	Moored Mine	Ground Mine	Moored Mine
Merchant Ships & Fishing Vessels				
Up to 2,000 Tons	10	9	1	5
2,000 to 5,0001	10	5	4	
5,000 to 10,000	4	12	3	16
over 10,000 tons	-	2	-	4
TOTAL	**15**	**33**	**9**	**29**
Landing Ships	-	-	-	4
Landing Craft	-	5	-	6
TOTAL	**-**	**5**	**-**	**10**

Mine statistics (Courtesy Maritime Museum)

Chapter 42

I opened my eyes next in a hospital somewhere in Algiers and the voice that welcomed me back to the living world was American, I later found out it was an American ambulance that tended to me and delivered me to hospital. It was also American (Snowdrops) MPs who immediately arrested the drunken American driver whose truck had hit us. He had begun his Christmas celebrations a bit early, there were still twenty four hours to go.

They still had to do more X rays on me, I had been unconscious, quite remarkably I had no broken bones, but God how I ached, and much of my skin had been left on the dockside, peeled off by the abrasive concrete. The X rays, thankfully, proved negative, but it was some time before I became convinced that I had no internal injuries, such was the pain. My companion Lofty Hemmings was also in a sorry state, but survived. As soon as the pain subsided enough my mind gave attention to other matters.

I had been in hospital for twenty four hours when I was hit once again by a bombshell, a verbal bombshell, and Lieut Willie, a *Felixstowe* officer, was the one who delivered it. He blandly told me the hospital were of the opinion that I was unfit to travel home on the ship that would be taking the remainder of the crew back home to the UK. The ship would be sailing that very night, the 24th December 1943, it was Christmas Eve. My physical pain was now exceeded by my mental anguish, the irony of it all was becoming too hard to bar. It was me that should have been returning alone, but fate had cruelly decided otherwise. The thought of lying alone in a hospital bed in North Africa on Christmas Eve, denied all the natural justice of returning home, was too much. I exploded. Lieut Willie bore the brunt of it, I don't recall the contents of my outburst, suffice to say he got the message. I was mad, exceedingly mad.

He took the can for everyone of the dodgy hands that fate continued to deal me, but this time my tantrum worked, it reached the ears of my Skipper, Lieut Comm Powney, and it was he who worked the miracle with the Yanks. Very late in the day an ambulance took me from the hospital to the ship taking my shipmates home, I was taken on a stretcher to the sick bay aboard.

To say I was overjoyed is an understatement, my mental anguish disappeared and I believe my physical pain subsided somewhat. I understand that I was the last person to climb the gangway before it was hoisted inboard and we sailed for the UK, it was that close a call.

My injuries, which were mostly multiple abrasions, largely healed by nature, but a few of the serious ones would these days have called for plastic surgery, then in its infancy. The worst one by far was a hole in the right hand side of my backside, the size of a golf ball. It was to cause me not only a good deal of pain, but considerable embarrassment.

The four days aboard ship passed without incident and for my second return voyage I safely entered the Mersey and berthed in the vibrant city of Liverpool.

There are few experiences to surpass the thrill of a serviceman's return to his homeland in times of war. Each and every one of them were in reality survivors, for they had been to war and returned. Sadly for many their return tickets would not be used and that observation put my present position into perspective, I was alive and my wounds and scars took on a superficiality.

By an unusual coincidence, for the second time, I was to return from foreign service in a ship's hospital bay and in both instances the sick berth staff worked like stink to get me walking. For the second time I was to spend my leave incapacitated and the fact that I was an innocent victim of a drunken driver was of no concern to the Royal Navy. Like all my shipmates I received about thirty days' leave, regardless of the number of days I was receiving medical treatment during my leave.

In almost every detail my second return to the UK was a carbon copy of the first, the Mersey, Liverpool, Lime Street Station, the grossly overcrowded train to London, Chatham Barracks, which looked even more foreboding. I gave a cursory glance towards the DMAA's office that had cynically dispatched me aboard Felixstowe, for a moment I thought about venting my spleen on them, but it was only a thought. I was on my way home, but first I had to acquire the ten or more rubber stamps of approval before I left for the final leg of my journey.

We left Chatham with what seemed like most of the ship's company and set out for the 'smoke'. Eventually we surfaced from the London Underground at Charing Cross. The many farewells at Euston Main Line Station had been tinged with sadness, some deep friendships had been cemented in the crowded, spartan messdecks of *Felixstowe* between men who had endured much hardship and danger together. Friendships that almost without exception would disappear in the sands of time. Very few of these men were destined to meet again, that was the way of it, a short leave with their loved ones then they would be off to join another crew, aboard another ship. It was a relentless merry-go-round.

There were two of us who would definitely meet again. We crossed the Embankment and nostalgically looked down on the murky water of the Thames, then on the reassuring face of Big Ben and Mother Parliament, a pleasure that had so nearly been denied to us - that had been denied to many of our oppos on the *Clacton, Kent* and many others besides. This is what we had been fighting to preserve, yet came so near to losing in the dark days following Dunkirk, London and her populace had suffered badly in the process.

Now the tide had begun to turn, but there were no tangible signs of it here in London. It had all happened a thousand miles away in North Africa, Panterlaria, Sicily and on the beaches of Salerno in Italy. *Felixstowe* and *Clacton* had paid the ultimate price for that victory and the remainder of the thirteenth were still at battle stations.

It was a typically crisp, sunny winter's day and Old Father Thames was bustling with traffic, it was a busy thriving waterway. Cargo ships, dirty rusting tramps, colliers specially designed to allow them passage under the low London bridges to deliver coal to the riverside power station. Tugs with orderly lines of barges under tow and the famous Thames sailing barges, tacking across the Thames in their brick coloured sails. They all told a story of the days when London was the greatest port in the world.

To our left the riverside cranes were raising and dipping their jibs, like giraffes at feeding time, a Royal Navy destroyer was 'swinging round the buoy'. "Jam strangling bastards," said my companion, "don't they know there's a war on?"

The last river we had looked down on was the Volturno in Italy, when we had swept deep into its mouth with the Allies on one bank and the Germans on the other. Much of the traffic rounding Parliament Square was still made up mostly of private cars and I admit to looking with suspicion at the many commuters in civilian clothes, still wondering how many of them were draft dodgers, spivs and black marketeers. I was sore with the thought of them inside, and still sore with my injuries outside.

We turned our backs on this most historic of scenes, Mother Parliament, Westminster Bridge and Big Ben. Now more than ever, it was the scene of hope for all the millions of people still held in the bondage of war. Now we were homeward bound, I felt a thrill of pleasure and it surmounted my dark thoughts about the dodgers. I had made it back to England, I was now in the great city of London and about to savour the greatest thrill of them all when I walked through the ever open door of my home, at two Lawrence Crescent, Dagenham, but first I had to be careful when I crossed the road, there were a lot of American drivers in England.

Chapter 43

With John, a townie and now my sole companion, I made my way up Villiers Street and into the warm confines of the *Griffin Arms*. This time we didn't tempt providence, we had but two celebration pints, over which I recounted to my companion the spirit of my last fateful journey home from London.

It had begun in this very pub. We left and boarded an Upminster-bound train at Charing Cross. There were plenty of seats but not one that would accommodate the hole in my stern, so we stood up all the way. I was still casting wistful eyes at the boys in civvies, what a contrast to the messdeck of a fleet sweeper. No doubt for many of them their turn would come, and my heart went out to them as I inwardly wished them well.

I gave a wry smile as we passed through Upney Station and at Dagenham John and I parted company, but only for a while, we were to meet with two more oppos every lunchtime for the thirty five days of my leave, in the saloon bar of the *Chequers Inn*, now sadly the site of a motor spares multiple store.

Within the next thirty minutes I would descend on my parents, who had been anxiously waiting, wondering and guessing just when that knock would sound on the door. The knock that would herald my return to the fold, after an absence of eighteen months, a year less than my last spell abroad, but to them still an eternity.

Entering Lawrence Crescent my feelings were a mixture of excitement and expectancy, instinctively I went down the side of the house to the back door, a door that in my memory had never been locked. The tiny kitchen was icy cold, the inevitable stock pot and coffee percolator were on the gas stove. Pushing open the living room door I found my parents in the usual winter situation, as close to the coal fire as possible. Mum's legs would be scorched by the heat, whilst her rear would be frozen.

"What are we on for dinner then?" I announced my arrival with the subject I knew was dearest to Mary Anne's heart - food. They both swung around and the joy on their faces was all that I would ever need as a reward, or an acknowledgement of my safe return. The excitement of our reunion over, I was totally unprepared for what followed.

"Whatever have they done to you?" asked Mary Anne, concern written all over her face. I had for the moment forgotten the parlous state of my frame, I was completely unable to perform the perfectly ordinary feat of sitting properly on a chair, the scars of my meeting with the American truck were still visible. There were two other things about my person that were not very edifying. Two of my front teeth were missing, and I had lost about a stone in weight. No wonder my mother was disturbed, only a mother would notice such things. In the eyes of the wartime Royal Navy if you could make it from your mess to your action station, then you were perfectly fit. I spent many hours of leave attending my local medical Royal Navy agent. My loss of weight was perhaps partly due to my bouts of malignant malaria, but mostly was brought about by the inhuman workload and sleep patterns of life aboard Felixstowe, plus the almost total lack of a sustaining diet, the latter entirely due to the lack of concern by our Naval masters. The American Navy had no such problems, then again, these conditions were being imposed on men who at the time, to put it in the vernacular, stood for the prick, a Naval term loosely meaning subservience.

The pattern of my leave was a carbon copy of my last return home, my family must have despaired of me for I was never at home, although I must admit the bed and food were always welcome, but at the time I was oblivious to any adverse reaction to my behaviour. A short seven days ago I had been pulled out of the Med, a short five days ago I was flaked out in hospital. Every day for the past eighteen months, along with every other matelot away on foreign service, all I had wanted was to return home safely to my family. What then was wrong with me? I always had that compelling urge to be back in the company of my Naval oppos. I have hinted at the possible reason earlier, now in hindsight I am convinced it was then our system of counselling each other.

Stress, no-one then knew what the word meant, you just picked yourself up, brushed yourself down and started all over again. It's now also obvious that it was not possible to switch off, your mind and body had been programmed to think and perform in a totally alien way, in a world where death was at your door almost every minute of every day.

Chapter 44

My leave was at an end. It was now back to the trials and tribulations of Chatham Barracks. The Chatham Mafia saw to it that I was to draw yet one more short straw. The ritual draft chit appeared on the mess table and I viewed with suspicion the news that it was a home posting, remember my last home posting had resulted in a spell of eighteen months in the Med.

The next day I was aboard a train taking me to the North Western port of Fleetwood, from where I was to make the crossing to the Isle of Man. Chatham had done its damnedest, it was one of the remotest home postings they could have meted out.

The crossing to the Isle of Man was rough, as were most voyages across this turbulent sea, but it wasn't the sea that was the reason for my subdued and contemplative mood. My thoughts were now being concentrated more and more on a lady.

The dance floor in Ilford Town Hall was occupied mostly by the invading Yanks who, it appeared, had commandeered most of the local female talent.

We almost collided whilst making for a door, I stopped and apologised, the effect was instant, she was beautiful, but right from the start it was that smile that sent my pulses racing. We dance, and from the start I knew I was going to pursue her, it was a hunt that became compulsive. I escorted her home from the dance and on the journey learned with some dismay that she was already promised to another, who at the time was abroad serving in the Army. Brushing her cheek on arrival with a thank you kiss, I left her, having come down quite sharply from the cloud nine I had so recently been on. Now in my pursuit of the lady I was armed with only my pen and her address. In addition the wide expanse of the Irish Sea was to make her completely inaccessible.

Once again I had drawn a short straw. It seemed to my troubled mind that the powers that be were intent on keeping me from home and my loved ones right to the bitter end.

I was oblivious to the roughness of the crossing as I lay on my bunk and dwelt on the sudden alteration that had taken place in my affairs - and I mean affairs of the heart. I kept seeing her face, laughing eyes above the classic high cheek bones and above all, that beautiful smile. It was all making what was in front of me doubly difficult to contemplate.

I was a castaway on that island for what seemed an eternity, a period of my Naval service that was instantly forgettable.

HMS Urley was another stone frigate, newly formed to pursue the development of a new revolutionary Fleet Air Arm planc, a plane that was to be the answer to the devilishly successful German and Italian dive and torpedo bombers. It was all too late, it should have been on the drawing board in the late thirties to replace the ancient 'stringbags' the Swordfish. They were all our brave intrepid FAA pilots had to launch against the might of the enemy. The 'Barracuda' never did work successfully, it had a nasty habit of failing to come out of a dive, which was very disconcerting for the crew. Add to that the fact that the ditched crew, if they were still alive, had the utmost difficulty in freeing themselves from the cockpits.

The ferry which now reeked of disgorged innards of a few hundred of its passengers, mercifully berthed in Douglas Harbour. I alighted with a heavy heart and boarded the inevitable truck to join my new ship the IOM Airport at Ronaldsway, now basking under the impressive name of *His Majesty's Ship Urley*. Unfortunately the name did nothing to alter its image. The truck pulled up at the end of an orderly row of nissen huts, I kicked open the door to be confronted with an orderly row of beds down each side of the hut. In the centre stood a slow burning coal stove, it was all so depressing.

There seemed to be hundreds of them, they raced from the tarmac whooping like Indians, these then were my new shipmates, they looked so young. Why were they wearing matelots' uniforms? I very ungraciously thought - FAA this is not the bloody Navy. The meeting with my fellow occupants of the hut cheered me a little, they were all torpedomen, real matelots, but this was how squaddies lived, not matelots, orderly rows of huts and beds in the middle of a field.

The Isle of Man was notable for a few things, like the Laxey Wheel, the TT races, cats with no tails, and a population who believed that if you didn't say good morning to the fairies you were doomed to plague and pestilence. Oh yes, and Manx kippers were probably the best in the world. It was a shame because these attributes never even warranted one brownie point from me. What did warrant a brownie point was the mail, which for the first time in years I was receiving with some regularity. It may seem odd, but as my sentence to the IOM progressed I began to hate the mail. At sea in the heat of battle it became relegated to the back of your mind, you became immune to its scarcity. Here, because of its almost certain availability it was as the forefront of your mind. My letters home were still few in number, but regular, but it was a letter with strange writing on the envelope that had begun to consume my thoughts. I had written mine almost on arrival on the Isle of Man.

"Dear Iris," it began. It was probably the worst letter I had ever written, it was introductory, how do you write that first letter? We had only met twice briefly and not one word of substance had passed 'tween us, why should I even expect her to take the trouble to answer? She was courting, he was away, but they had worked together, they were very serious about each other, I had been told that at the outset.

There was just a little more to my chores than servicing eighteen inch Tinfish torpedoes at *Urley*. Straight after breakfast we were hurrying to the harbour at Douglas where we split up into parties of four and boarded three waiting fishing boats, leaving harbour we dispersed into three allocated positions. The submarine off our port beam was not only friendly, it was also a dummy, ahead of us and just visible was a floating target, this I was familiar with. The Barracudas came in a formation of three. It was spectacular, a divebomb attack on the sub and by a future FAA plane. For five years this had been the sole province of the enemy, even if this new aero dynamic plane proved to be successful it was too late, three, even four years too late. We had entered a 1940 war with 1918 equipment and this seemed to be par for the course. One of the missiles was close enough to have caused damage to the genuine thing, the other two were definitely outers.

When it arrived I had already given up hope of ever receiving a reply, the strange writing on the envelope was always going to be the clue. I opened the letter with some excitement and a feeling of anticipation. The contents of the letter was something of a disappointment but nothing could detract from the satisfaction that she had felt the compunction to reply. She had fed my ego and I felt my opening gambit had been nothing but a great success. I was elated, why was it then that I was at odds with everyone and everything at *Urley*? My total disenchantment with my present set-up had origins in other things than affairs of the heart.

In truth I had had enough, my birthday would be celebrated with twenty six candles on my cake, six of the best years of my life had been swallowed up in the prosecution of a war. I had given them unstintingly and almost without question, but now I wanted out.

I thought the time of my first leave would never arrive and when I was eventually packing my bag my spirits were high, as I set out on the long wartime journey back to Dagenham to continue my quest for the lady's hand.

Chapter 45

The two days' wait for the date were hell, but I must be patient, things were going well for me. My whole instinct was to declare my love for her but this was a romance of the times and there were rules to play to. I knew that I must wait for the return of the soldier at war, this had been made clear to me. It was as well that I would return to my servitude on the Isle of Man in a few days' time, for it would have been doubly difficult for me had I remained in calling distance of her.

We went to the cinema, it was the only place to go, that is where everyone began their courting. The cinema was the cultural centre of community where you learned about life, it was the only place that was post. The lavish interior was the only escape from the monotonous drabness of your surroundings. Immediately you entered its portals you were transported to another world, even the commissionaire, the imposing title given to the doorman, was dressed like a third world general, his word was law.

There were always queues lined up in orderly fashion behind a board showing the price of the seat of your choice. There were, remember, no televisions, cars or telephones in our walk of life, and home entertainment was provided by a cheap, crackling bakelite radio that needed a periodic boost to the battery. It was no surprise then that the local cinema was full from opening up 'til closing time every day of the week.

During the walk home through the total blackout, I learned that Iris had been called up from her job as a cafeteria manageress and chose to train as a welder. On completion of her training she was making Naval guns in a local engineering firm, which meant of course that we were both working for the same firm. I had found the first thing that we had in common.

My leave seemed to be over almost before it began, nevertheless I was delighted with the turn of events, we had learned a lot about each other, there was nothing tangible about it but I had just sensed that I was winning her over. It was the day of my return from leave, Iris walked with me to the station and we sat in the waiting room to await the arrival of my train. I picked up the rhythm of the wheels as it neared the platform. It happened so quickly, it had to, one moment we were fumbling for words of goodbye, then she was in my arms and I kissed her tenderly. There was a fleeting moment of protest from her, then she melted and I felt her response. I just made it before the train doors slammed shut, a quick wave and she was gone from sight.

I made for my seat oblivious to everything that was happening around me and nearly failed to alight at Aldgate East for my connection to Euston. I was in dreamland. My euphoria rapidly melted on the realisation that I was travelling forever further away from the object of my love, for make no mistake about it this time it was real, I was in love. The passage of time only exacerbated my total disenchantment with everything Naval, and Cornelius Finbar Driscoll once more became the object of my wrath. My impatience was heightened by the thought of having to wait another three months before I could see her, I desperately wanted to confirm the tantalising hope that brief response to my first kiss had given me - now I must wait for the letter that would perhaps provide me with the answer. I was like a prisoner out on parole, returning to complete my sentence, ninety days, that's about what you'd get in chokey for 'filling in' the Chief Buffer.

Chapter 46

The war in Europe was rapidly coming to a successful conclusion for the Allies and in May 1945 the Germans capitulated. The celebrations on the Isle of Man and particularly at *HMS Urley* were about the equivalent of the 'all clear' after an air raid. I remember the young 'sprog' FAA ratings attempted to liven up proceedings by setting light to the contents of their huts in the square outside.

The armistice only served to heighten my sense of injustice at the thought of my enforced isolation. It seemed only my body was on the Isle of Man, my head was back home in Dagenham. My battle was still to be won, the letter, when it arrived, was encouraging but also inconclusive.

One thing that was conclusive was the ultimate weapon which brought about the cessation of hostilities in Japan. It was a new perspective on the horror of war and the consequences are still reverberating around the world. On 2nd September 1945 about four weeks after the dropping of the bomb, World War II was at an end, the Japs had called it a day. Thus ended a war that had brought death and destruction to countless millions from the frozen wastes of Russia, right through Europe and down to the steamy jungles of the Far East.

I could now be forgiven for thinking "that's it, the war's over, let me out, my 'contract' read 'Hostilities only'." This, however, was altered to read 'until the end of the period of the present emergency'. I failed to grasp the subtle difference between the two, but never doubted it was amended to ensure the Admiralty had me by the short and curlies until their lordships decided where and when I would be released. It was to mean that once again I was destined to draw the short straw.

The days now dragged on interminably but to my delight the wonderful news of my release arrived, at last I was on the road to freedom. Then shortly before my departure from the Isle of Man a letter arrived to further raise my spirits. In my mind I had rehearsed my next meeting with Iris many times, and the prospect of having to do battle with a rival for her affections was to me very daunting. However, the contents of the letter was to relieve my of all my fears. In my absence she had met my rival, and had made her choice, it was now up to me, I now had to prove to her that her decision was right.

The sea for the crossing to the mainland was relatively calm for a change, but the train to Euston was again packed beyond any limit of safety.

For the first time I took in the devastation and havoc wreaked by the Luftwaffe on the East End of London. A monumental task lay ahead for the returning servicemen in the transition from the destruction of war to the construction of peace. The total blackout had been relaxed to a much more acceptable dim-out, peace was breaking out and it was a good time to continue my quest for the lady's hand. I alighted from the Underground at Heathway and there was a song in my heart as I headed for my home. No longer would my family have to speculate on whether or not this would be the last leave from which I had safely returned.

It was difficult to grasp that it really was all over and the carnage was at an end. These sentiments would be shared in a million homes throughout the land. We had won, but what would victory hold for the victors? Perhaps no more or no less than it would for the vanquished.

There would be no tangible evidence of victory, but much evidence of the price we had paid in achieving it, what of the homes whose loved ones would be lying in some foreign field? Their grief would be compounded by the sight of the returning sons and fathers who had survived the conflict.

My fears about my forthcoming meeting with Iris proved to be groundless. I was expecting some sort of recriminations, a battle to be fought and won, but to my surprise the problem had been resolved in my absence. My rival for her hand had conceded and I was never to learn any of the details.

It was two long days before we met in the ornate gilt and white of the famous Lyons Cornerhouse in the Strand, like the cinema at the time it transported you to a fairy tale atmosphere away from the drabness of your own environment.

We were looking at each other and holding hands across the table. The orchestra was playing *These Foolish Things*, a song that would be indelibly recorded in our minds. She was beautiful and elegantly dressed from her wide brimmed hat, fitted costume, lovely legs in seamed stockings (courtesy of the Yanks) and the ever popular court shoes. I was dressed in the total contents of my wardrobe, namely my number one Navy uniform.

It was the beginning of a time of hope and optimism, we were looking to change the world, and the key to the change lay in the ballot box. There was a rising tide of resentment at what had gone on in pre-war Britain. Now there was an air of happiness about, you could feel it permeating from all the people gathered there. We were a part of that happiness, and we left Lyons to wend our way home hoping to fortify our new found love. My head was in the clouds, as arm in arm we strolled along the Strand to board the Underground at Charing Cross and my sense of contentment was complete when, snuggled up close to me, she linked her arm possessively in mine as we sat on the home-going train. Once again I said goodbye to her on the doorstep, but this time it was different, this time she was my girl, this time there was no restraint, she melted into my arms. This told me everything I needed to know, after all it was our very first date, we were still learning about each other. I was already in love, but Iris would still be needing reassurance that her instincts had been right when she made the decision to change the object of her affection.

The period of the transition from war to peace was probably the most frustrating period to cope with, we were in limbo, the driving force and adrenalin that had been ever present during the pursuit of victory was no longer there. It was like winning the World Cup then being asked to hang about in the arena long after the final whistle had blown, still wearing your football kit. The triumphant swell of the victorious spectators' voices were distant echoes, leaving only the debris of the contest to be cleared away. This then was to be my final contribution, clearing away the debris of war.

In spite of its unquestioned beauty, the deliciousness of its oak-soaked succulent kippers and the kindness of the locals, it was with no feelings of regret that I said farewell to the Isle of Man. The ferry 'slipped' and left the harbour at Douglas to once again face the Irish Sea at its worst.

The wait for my release had seemed endless, but at last I was setting out on the first stage of my journey to freedom, a journey filled with uncertainty. It was a new world I was returning to, nothing would ever be the same. I was about to complete the final act of my six years on loan to HM Royal Navy - the swapping of my 'tiddly suit' for a free issue outfit of civvies.

Never in the annuls of Naval history could there have been another slops issue to compare with it. The huge indoor arena of Olympia at Earls Court in London was set out like a mammoth Marks and Spencer store, with a selection of suits, shirts, shoes and even a choice of headgear. The completed outfit was then neatly boxed and tied with string. I made a handle for ease of carrying and strode purposefully towards the exit of Olympia and freedom. It was the last time I would be in the uniform of the Royal Navy, a moment tinged with sadness and some regret. For a fleeting moment I had toyed with the idea of entering the adjacent toilet as a Naval rating and emerging as a born again civilian, dressed in my new civvy gear, but the thought quickly passed. The transition needed a better stage than that of a public toilet, for I had worn my uniform with pride.

Today I would wear it as a final tribute to the bravery, fortitude and sacrifice of all the wonderful men it had been my privilege to serve with. To those who didn't make the passage back, my they rest in peace. To those who did, may the live in peace. For me it was the end of my Naval contract, which had simply read 'Hostilities Only'.

THE END

Bibliography

"HOSTILITIES ONLY"

ERRATA

Acknowledgements line 8 Lestor should read Lester

Prologue line 19 should read;...HMS Kent a County Class ei
inch gun Cruiser...

Text Page	Line	Written	Should read
24	7	'Cheefy	'Chiefy'
25	18	C3JX167723	C/JX167723
26	33	cruiser line	cruise liner
28	39	by	be
29	17	Chrisp Street	Crisp Street
38	39	imaging	imagine
42	5	hears	heard
45	32	..this had aside	..this hat aside
47	1	Marjon	Mahjong
50	11	bullon	button
60	6	'doze'	'dose'
61	18	lea	lee
61	36	Albertrosses	Albatrosses
62	35	chartologits	cartologists
65	5	'slippers'	'sippers'
66	24	gaitors	gaiters
70	3	Delwara	Dilwara
71	39	Ascic	ASDIC
72	20	Oman	Oran
86	27	De Gaul	De Gaulle
104	5	Ot PVs	Out PVs
104	36	suiffy	squiffy
108	5	relived	relieved
109	31	obnosious	obnoxious
109	32	hugh	huge
115	3	compliment	complement
116	36	thought	though
124	20	Caiquak	Caique
125	7	Green	Greek
128	4	Dodeconese	Dodecanese
140	1	Easter	Eastern
164	23/36	stantion	stanchion
166	7	soft	sort
166	11/12	tiddy hoddy	tiddy oggy
176	11	Larqs	Largs
178	1	Larqs	Largs
180	2	U Boat Rodney	U Boat. Rodney
180	17	last dog(6am to 8pm)	last dog (6pm to 8pm)
186	27	tot of into	tot into
188	17	oor	or
197	27	short	shore
202	7/35	Panterlaria	Pantelleria
212	27	Arnham	Arnhem
216	31	HMS Crombie	HMS Abercrombie
217	33	at 'Gus'.	at Devonport.
221	18	short	shore
238	13	Panterlaria	Pantelleria

IMMEDIATE:

Addressed:- ALL CONCERNED HOME AND ABROAD.

From:-ADMIRALTY.

SPLICE THE MAIN BRACE.

D.T.G.081500B.

107 K/cs (BN Broadcast) TOR 1511.

Operator. CRC.
Coder. EWP.

dated:- 8th.May 1945.

DISTRIBUTION:- Top Bridge.
All Messes.
Coding Office Perm Log.
General Interest.

BNs 609/610 - CBNs 619/620. Groups 99/70;

CONFIDENTIAL.

MOST IMMEDIATE.

Addressed:- ALL CONCERNED HOME AND ABROAD
716 A.

From:- ADMIRALTY.

The German High Command has surrendered unconditionally all German Land, Sea and Air Forces in Europe, effective from 0001B hours (R) 0001B hours on the 9th (R) 9th May from which hour all offensive operations are to CEASE.

(2) Due to difficulties of communication there may be some delay in these orders reaching the Enemy Forces. Accordingly, danger of attack by individual enemy surface craft, U/Boats and Aircraft may persist for some time to come. The Fleet in all waters is to remain on a War footing and in a state of constant vigilance for the moment.

(3) Surrender procedure for U/Boats will be promulgated separately.

(4) NO (R) NO release is to be made to the press pending an announcement by the Head of the Governmen

D.T.G.(1st part) 080001B May 1945.
FINAL 080002B May 1945.

107 K/cs(BN Broadcast) N/CODE(R)"J" TOR 0159.
TOR C/0334.

Operator:- TB.
Coder:- EWP.

Dated:8th. May 1945.

DISTRIBUTION:- Top Bridge.
Coding Office Perm.log.
"A" Log.